Wings of Mentridar

Clair Verway

xulon PRESS

Copyright © 2008 by Clair Verway

Wings of Mentridar
by Clair Verway

Printed in the United States of America

ISBN 978-1-60477-337-8

All rights reserved solely by the author. The author guarantees all contents are original and do not infringe upon the legal rights of any other person or work. No part of this book may be reproduced in any form without the permission of the author. The views expressed in this book are not necessarily those of the publisher.

www.xulonpress.com

ACKNOWLEDGEMENTS

As with any endeavor as grand as a novel, there are too many people who have had an influence or made a contribution to mention everyone, but one must make the effort, mustn't one. I should begin with the cadre of caring Sunday School teachers who made me believe the characters in those stories were really people. Some of the other real people who helped me once I started getting words on paper are Kathy Smith, Tim Fullmer and DeAnna Westerbeek. These three graciously offered their eyes and expertise to ferret out my multitudinous typographical and just plain dumb errors. (Despite their efforts, I bet you can still find one or two. Those nasty little beggars hide is the most conspicuous places.) I also wish to thank my wife, Karen, who also read and re-read for mechanical problems, but more importantly put up with my incessant blathering about any number of arcane topics and fantastical ideas which I wanted to weave into the narrative. From Mesopotamian history to quantum physics she listened and lead me patiently to the expression of my imagination which you now hold in your hands. Finally, if I have any talent whatsoever in telling what I think it may have been like to live what all those flannel graph characters portrayed, I have none to thank but my Father in heaven, from whom come all good gifts.

PROLOGUE

The ancient one sat at the mouth of his cave surveying the valley spread wide below him. To the south and west the lush vegetation flowed as far as his dimming eye could see. A shallow stream coursed quietly down the valley, supporting willows and beeches near its banks while taller, more substantial varieties grew on the slopes which rose from the north and east sides of the plain. At the head of the stream, where it bubbled sparkling clear from the ground, a clearing was surrounded by a dozen huts fashioned from the brush and small saplings in the immediate area. They were not cut, rather bent, trained into sizeable shelters which opened onto the clearing.

The sound of children playing drifted up with the rising air. Occasionally an adult could be seen moving about among the huts. Everything had been thus for eight hundred years. The ancient one had taken to spending more and more time in the solitude of his cave rather than in the company of the tribe. His thoughts disturbed him more each season; the behavior of his children's children's children disturbed him. He had witnessed the birth of seven generations, only to be successively more disappointed in them. Only one of his grandchildren had pleased the ancient one; and that one was taken from the Araq before his time.

A shout from the clearing drew the ancient one from his thoughts. The eighth generation had arrived. As he watched the activity center on the hut where the baby had been born, he saw the valley transformed before his eyes. The lush green carpet of foliage faded and turned brown, then was not foliage at all, but swirling dust. The stream bed was dry, packed hard by the passage of many hooves over countless seasons. Where the circle of huts had been a walled city rose from the swirling gray-brown cloud, not dozens, but a hundred or more dwellings made of cut wood and stone. And in the center of the city, a tower struck skyward, one of the hateful temples he had seen in other dreams.

Just as quickly as it had formed, the scene became engulfed in a swirling gray mass. Then a giant cypress tree appeared and began walking, shuffling through the roiling gray like an old man laboring toward the place where the city had been. The tree bowed down and scooped something out of the water with two of its limbs. As the objects were raised clear of the turbulence below, the vision faded and the ancient one was once again looking at a circle of huts in a leafy green clearing.

When the appointed time came to name the child, the people gathered reverently for the ceremony. The ancient one shuffled into the center of the group where the mother stood holding the newborn. "This is an important child," he began. Looking at the father he said, "He will live many years, but you will see him taken from the Araq before your length of days is over." The father nodded solemnly.

"This life is important beyond others because of a son he shall sire," he continued. "His son shall deliver his people from the evil one who has enslaved and cursed the Araq." Placing two fingers lightly on the brow of the infant he said, "You shall be called Lamaq.

CHAPTER ONE

The first of two dim orange spheres crept over the horizon shedding a little light and less warmth on the gray landscape. The beauty of this planet was in her view of the surrounding galaxies. The twin stars around which she raced were pale in contrast to the brightness of the starlight which washed her dusty surface day and night. Because she had no moons, and because her path took her so far from the suns which held her in orbit, Mentridar was a planet lit by starlight from eons away. In the blackness of her always night sky, uncounted millions of galaxies lent their radiance in a diamond-like sparkle.

Not that it mattered to her inhabitants. None of the indigenous life forms would have noticed either light or warmth in the way a human takes for granted. Mentridarian life was not carbon based — nor did any of her creatures have spectral receivers after the manner of eyes. This is not to say that energy waves were unimportant; on the contrary, they were the source and purpose of life on Mentridar.

On this particular morning, two alien beings were digging in the dusty surface, gouging something like channels or irrigation ditches. The larger of the two was apparently supervising the other in some sort of gardening exercise.

"No, no, no! Don't be lazy. You'll have to get deeper — through the layer of dust on the surface and into the soil beneath as I have shown you. The mintus won't move into anything that isn't at least three or four centimeters into the soil," he was saying, or rather telepathing, as speech was unnecessary.

"I don't get it Mistrea," the worker responded. "We've been doing this for weeks now. Couldn't the Great One just make canals in the surface for the mintus?"

"I suppose he could have, or could even now if he wanted to," answered Mistrea, the larger one. "It is the wisdom of the Great One to assign tasks to his chosen attenders so that they can keep busy and — and I don't know what else. That is why he is the Great One. If I knew everything, you'd call me The Omniscient One."

This puzzled the little one. "But you have been with him since the Beginning, before the Rebellion. Don't his ways become clear to you?

A loud, musical laugh echoed off the surrounding hills. "You have a great deal to learn, my worthy assistant. Not even those attenders who spend every moment in the presence of the Mighty One are fully aware of all the mystery of his ways. I am at his throne only for the large Gatherings, and then I stand very far from his radiance. It is thrilling, don't misunderstand, and I feel I could take on all the dark host of the universe single-handed when I am basking in his light; but to know how or why he does what he does — that is far from my station to know."

By this time the tiny planet had spun far enough to reveal a pair of orange balls in her black sky. The two attenders were gradually being swarmed by small creatures who were following the advance of the rising stars' rays. If the scene had been elsewhere, one might have thought the tiny buzzing spots of light would be bothersome. But this was Mentridar; nothing was bothersome there. Looking for all the world like glowing gnats, tiny cxings gathered about the two while they worked on the canals.

"Good morning, everybody," Mistrea greeted them. "You've a lovely clear day for flying. Soak it up and enjoy it." The cxings seemed to respond by creating a sort of formation, sailing around in a kaleidoscope of light and color.

"Do they really understand when you communicate with them?" the little one asked.

"Enough to be of invaluable service when necessary," Mistrea replied.

"Just what can they do for us? They are so small."

"Don't let size fool you, young one. These will be able to save your light when the time comes. You'll see quite soon enough, I am afraid."

The change in Mistrea's mood was obvious. This much of the Master plan was evident: these cheery little spots of light would have gone through eternity in blissful ignorance had it not been for the Rebellion. The Rebellion — even to think it would bring an attender instinctively to his guard. Experiencing the utter tranquility of Mentridar, knowing that every creature there existed in perfect harmony with every other made Mistrea wonder how the Rebellion had ever happened.

He was interrupted by an excited thought from his young apprentice: "Here they come." The canal they had been working on was slowly being filled with sluggish, milky white fluid. The interesting thing about the fluid was that it had a look of blue-green iridescence, and somehow appeared to be almost alive. "Here come the mintus, Master."

"Yes," sighed Mistrea, bringing himself back to the job at hand, "they've come with the rising of the twin stars just as the cxings have. They take what little energy boost those red suns give and turn it into life and happiness."

"Do they know what they've been called here for?" asked the small attender as he continued pushing the canal further through the topsoil.

"I don't think so — at least not exactly. They will come and do what is natural to them at our command, or rather at the Great One's command; but I don't think they have the intelligence to fathom much beyond their pretty blue channels."

The view from a hundred meters above the two attenders would have been pretty indeed. What had been light gray tracings in the darker gray dust were coming alive with the same radiant blue-green brilliance that was in the new canal they were digging. The vast extent of their work was obvious when seen from above the surface. Geometrically perfect tracings of blue covering several hundred hectares told of long labor in a highly organized fashion.

Not far from where the two stood working, the canals were bordered by small wisps of what appeared to be plants. Without leaves or flowers, the growths were not fully opaque, looking almost like frozen wisps of smoke from some smoldering wick. Yet as the reddish daylight became more intense, they began to take on an orange cast near their tips, while at the base, each appeared to be absorbing the iridescent blue of the feeder canals.

A few kilometers away the same color scheme was repeated in a larger scale, for there stood the giant parents of the tiny wisps nearer the attenders. What they were actually doing was creating a nursery for the propagation of zensak. A small sea of the blue-green fluid lay beyond the forest, with canals spreading outward in a quilt work from its edge.

After finishing the section of the canal system they were working on, the two aliens moved to the forest of giant zensak. Nearing the tall creatures, the attenders could see millions of the tiny cxings flitting among their branches and lighting momentarily, much as a swarm of bees might do in an apple orchard. But there were no blossoms, and these were not apple trees. Towering hundreds of meters into the blackness which was sky, the mature zensak dwarfed the two gardeners. The multi-colored array of cxings gave a festival atmosphere to the forest as it swept the sky.

The tall one stopped when he reached the edge of the forest, and the little one halted behind him. With his arms outstretched above his head, Mistrea began looking into the tall branches swaying slightly over him. No sound came from him, but the stately creatures seemed to be responding to a command. They slowly bent their uppermost branches down until they formed a canopy around the two attenders. Mistrea then lowered his arms before him, palms upward, and began gathering small twigs from the tips which hovered about him. The zensak were actually offering their twigs to him, separating them from the branches of their own free will.

The little one took the twigs from Mistrea as his hands became full and placed them in a flat tray which had a thin coating of the fluid from the sea canals. There was an almost ceremonial air about the whole proceeding, as if the zensak were making an offering of their tiny branches.

When they had filled the tray and moved back to the freshly dug canals, the little one asked his teacher, "They enjoy giving, don't they?"

Mistrea slid his hand under one of the twigs in the tray and lifted it in front of him. "They are under orders to give, but I am certain the Mighty One would have only to ask, or express a need without asking, and they would offer their whole selves. This is how much they wish to please him."

He set the twig in the soil near the edge of the new canal. Almost immediately the mintus in the fluid could be seen gathering near the newly planted zensak. A trail of iridescent blue wormed its way through the soil between the canal and the twig, soon reaching its base. When they connected, the fine gray wisp began to turn blue near the bottom and slightly orange at the top. It wasn't long before cxings would be buzzing about the tips, acting almost like miniature caretakers, stroking them and seemingly massaging life into them.

"It's a beautiful relationship, isn't it, Mistrea, my master?" The little one was starting to feel the harmony of Mentridar. "Each one does his part, taking what he needs and giving what he must to the other; the mintus take their sustenance from the fluid and pass the by-product into the zensak who in turn thrive and respire exactly what the cxings need."

But a question began to form in his mind; something he had been curious about since the beginning of his apprenticeship. His teacher caught the thought. "You are wondering why we must speed the propagation of the zensak, aren't you?"

"I have figured that it has something to do with the Rebellion," he responded, "but I still don't see what these creatures can do on this far away peaceful planet."

"Perhaps you are ready for the next stage of your training. Help me set these last twigs, and I will show you something," Mistrea said with a purpose.

When they had placed the last of the tiny branches in the soil near the canal, the larger one signaled the pupil and they rose into the sky above the zensak field. At an altitude of two kilometers they halted their ascent as Mistrea directed the gaze of his disciple back down to the planet below them. The sight was indescribably beautiful. The iridescent blue-green sea was surrounded almost completely by large channels which radiated from its rim. Each channel separated into a perfect matrix of smaller canals like the one they had just been working on. At the back of the sea and the channels were stands of majestic zensak, blue, gray-white and orange as they rose into the atmosphere. Each smaller canal had a faint tracing of zensak color along its back where the twig-offerings had been set.

Completing the scene below them were waves of color, the cxings being undetectable as individuals, but obvious as masses of moving multi-colored light. And there was something more. The little one had begun to feel something while on the surface, but it overwhelmed him from this vantage point. There was a feeling, or rather a sound emanating from the planet. It was a chorus of life being sung by the creatures who dwelt below. It was as if one had walked past a building where a string quartet was rehearsing and the sound wafted through the windows into the passerby's ears.

Mistrea could see the wonder on the face of his pupil. "It is inspiring, isn't it?"

I feel as if I could lie back on the sound and rest in it forever," the little one sang. "It is so peaceful, so beautiful in its perfect harmony. But he began to be puzzled again, "Yet this does not answer my question—-?

"—-about the Rebellion," the teacher completed his thought. "Perhaps you are ready to know more about the larger purpose of our work here.

"Long, long ago, before the Rebellion there was an attender who worked on a planet as a service to the Mighty One. He became the master of that planet as I am master of Mentridar. Everything there was just as beautiful as what you see here — more beautiful, I am told. The music of that planet joined the music of all the spheres in a grand symphony. It pleased the Mighty One more than all the planets in all the galaxies to hear the music of that one globe.

"This made the master attender proud of what he had accomplished — rightly so I imagine, but the pride took an awful turn in his mind. He began to take pride in the work for its own sake, and not as service to his Master. Eventually, he demanded complete autonomy to deal with the planet as he wished, reasoning that he had earned the right to own it for himself. He began to see the restrictions of the Great One as interference in his world."

"Ultimately it came to a showdown. The haughty attender wanted complete dominion — ownership. The Mighty One patiently tried to make him understand that what he was asking was not in his best interest, nor in the best interest of his beautiful planet. But the roots of pride were too deep to be plucked out; the damage had been done.

"The Mighty One warned him that if he was given his desire it would mean banishment from his presence. No creature can thwart the purpose of the Mighty One and remain in fellowship with him. This incensed the rebellious one so much that he dared to challenge the right of his Master to make such a threat. He called on the attenders who were with him in the work on the planet to rise up against the Mighty One to overthrow him.

"What a foolish thought that was — and what terrible consequences it brought." Mistrea looked into the face of his rapt pupil and asked, "You know that the Mighty One has more power than a million of the strongest attenders, don't you?"

"You have taught me that the Mighty One has power that is without limit, "he said as if reciting a lesson well taught.

"And so he does," the teacher continued. "It would have been possible for the Mighty One to crush the Rebellion right at its beginning, yet something held him back. He banished the rebel and all those who sided with him to the planet they took such pride in. He gave them dominion, but swore he would not stop his efforts to bring the whole system back into his control despite the rule of the rebels."

The pupil thought for a moment then asked, "Are there creatures on the planet like our cxings and mintus? Does the dark one control them too?"

"Not entirely. They are of a different form than Mentridarian life, but they all have much the same choices. The simpler life forms, like the mintus, respond almost entirely to the natural order of things, whatever system they are created in. The higher forms, such as cxings and zensak, are given varying degrees of latitude in their actions. The highest forms, like attenders, are given complete freedom of what they will do and whom they will serve."

"So these higher creatures can choose to leave the planet if they don't wish to be ruled by the rebels?" the curious one asked.

"No, as I said, they are not like you and I or the cxings. They are more closely bound to their own planet, due to their physical forms."

"But they are beings of light, are they not? You said the Father of lights created them so..."

Yes, little one, but the Father has created many life forms not exactly like himself or us," Mistrea corrected.

For a moment the pupil tried to imagine a totally different form of life, then asked, "If they are not like us, what are they like?"

Now Mistrea thought for a moment, struggling to find a way to explain. "Imagine this," he began after a pause. "Imagine we were to form a jar of the clay on Mentridar and then fill it with fluid containing mintus and cxings. If the clay jar could borrow energy from the creatures inside — if it could move about and live this way, this would be a poor picture, but something similar to the creatures on the dark planet."

He made an effort to imagine moving clay jars, but in the process, another thought occurred to him. "But Mistrea," the pupil interrupted, "if an attender is unable to gather in the presence of the Mighty One to feel his radiance, he will expire, won't he?"

"That is partly correct, my young friend; you or I would cease to be who we are if we did not partake of the radiance of our King. As Creatures of light we must share in his light to be who we are. That is why we call our Master the Father of Light; he is the source, the well-spring of life and power for all creatures.

"When the rebels were driven from the presence of the Father of Light, they began to detest anything that reminded them of his radiance. Eventually, they could barely stand the pure energy of any source of light at close range; it had become detestable to them, so much did it remind them of the Master. This made the planet to which they had been banished almost untenable, as it moves in a close orbit around a medium bright star. They were forced to keep to the dark side of the surface, or stay in caves or deep forests.

"For this reason, the leader of the Rebellion has become known as the Prince of Darkness — for this and for the terrible weapon he fashioned."

At this Mistrea stopped short. "But that is enough lesson in history for now. We have more work to do on Mentridar."

"But master, this leaves so much unsaid," the young one protested. "You have answered nothing about how Mentridar fits into the Rebellion. I want to join the fight against this Prince of Darkness. If he is against the Father of Light, then I am against him. Oh how I wish I were not stuck on this forgotten planet, but could engage in battle right now."

The huge attender stiffened to his full height, towering over the suddenly silent little one. "May the Wings of Mentridar never take you into such folly!" The rebuke stung the once eager pupil, yet he sensed in it a word of protection as well. "There are powers in this universe you know nothing of which would cause you to slither into hiding for the dread of your very light."

"Besides," Mistrea continued in a softer tone, "The Mighty One has no need of half-trained attenders; what he does need are thousands who will learn obedience and grow strong in his light. These will take wing to do battle for him against the dark ones."

"Forgive me, master; I forgot my place," the young one repented.

"For your rashness, you are forgiven; for your zeal you are commended," Mistrea said to him with kindness again.

Taking advantage of the softer mood the little one dared to ask "What are the Wings of Mentridar? I heard you speak of them once before when we were at the last Gathering. I sensed that your listeners held them in high esteem, yet I see nothing here on Mentridar that would interest a warrior unless he needed a peaceful rest."

"If we can work while we talk, I will tell you." At a nod from his pupil they returned to the surface and he continued, "Can you believe that the mighty Wings of Mentridar are even now all about us?"

The pupil tried to sense all that was around him at that moment, and although it was very pleasant, as before, there were no weapons or war machines that he could detect. "I know that there are things that do not appear even to our keen senses, my master, but I sense nothing that would seem to be an instrument of war here in this blissful harmony."

"Your senses serve you well, for nothing in its present form ministers any such evil as war. Yet, behold." With these words the teacher gracefully stood to his full height and turned his back to his pupil. He stretched his arms downward, slightly away from his sides, and a sudden confluence of cxings formed on his back. They melded together and became perfectly symmetrical wings of seven colors vibrating together. In an instant, Mistrea was gone.

The startled little one moved immediately in the direction his master had gone and soon discovered him standing on a ridge several kilometers distant. "They are beautiful," he exclaimed, "but what is their purpose? We can move just as well without them."

"Is that so?" The teacher pointed towards the distant forest, "Do you see where the two nearest channels part?"

his pupil nodded. "I will take wing to the channel on the right and you will move to the channel on the left. We will race; if you beat me, look back to watch my approach."

"I can not beat—"

"Watch my approach from where you land," Mistrea interrupted. With this his wings erupted into a transparent vee-shaped rainbow of color and he was gone again.

The obedient pupil moved to the appointed position and turned to see his master gliding to stop at the other channel. "What do you see behind you?" Mistrea asked.

He saw nothing unusual at first, but suddenly realized that his path was marked briefly by a faint trail of light. The path Mistrea had taken was invisible. His teacher glided over beside him and asked, "Do you see any strategic advantage in my method of arrival here?

"If an enemy were close enough, he could track me easily," the young one reasoned.

"Well done," congratulated the teacher. "And further more, anyone within sensing distance of this horizon could find your trail of light and know you were about."

"I am beginning to see why the Wings of Mentridar are so highly valued," said the pupil.

"Yes, and what you can't know is that in atmospheres more dense than this your trail would be even more apparent. In the sky over the Prince of Darkness, you would look like a shooting star or a small comet. All his minions would be aware of your presence and position in an instant."

"So how do the cxings move you without leaving a trail?" the inquirer wanted to know.

"They ride the invisible waves of energy which are all around us and they carry me along with them," was the response. "The waves are rivers of life to them; they are sustained and carried by them. At my request, a colony of seven cxings which has been assigned to me forms the wings — the Wings of Mentridar."

"The seven — are they each a different color?" asked the pupil. "I noticed many colors in your wings."

"Yes; the seven cxings, each of a different color, comprise a colony. They bond for life and in fact become one life when they colonize. Each color represents a different type or gender, and each is necessary for fullness of life — and for reproduction for that matter."

This fascinated the young one. "Reproduction? You mean cxings are self-propagating?"

"Oh, definitely. In fact it is one of the most beautiful things I have seen, apart from the Father of Lights himself. Someday perhaps you will be on Mentridar at the season of color."

"When is that?" interrupted the little one.

"When the planet courses nearest the suns on its elliptical orbit, the energy from the waves is at its peak. That is when the cxings form their colonies and reproduce. It is called the season of color because for a few weeks this gray world bursts with rainbows of explosive color.

"When the cxings create their seven-fold union, the energy they generate emits dozens of sparks. Each spark is a newly formed cxing. You just witnessed the color of one colony on my back; imagine hundreds of thousands of colonies each exploding in multi-colored rays."

"That must be glorious to see."

"Not only to see, but to hear as well," the teacher continued, "for in the act of union of the seven each sings a special song of ecstasy. The harmonies of those days are something, once heard, one never forgets."

"Is it more grand than the music we heard in the sky this morning?" asked the pupil.

"Immeasurably more!" was the response.

The two worked on in silence while the younger tried to imagine such music. In a few minutes a question occurred to him. "So it is for the cxings we plant zensak, I see; but I don't understand why we are speeding the process. Is there some rush?"

"First, to answer your question, we must increase the rate at which zensak propagate. We want a huge forest here for the next season of color. Our Father has requested this, presumably to foster greater fertility in the cxings.

"Secondly, you are only partly correct in assuming that it is just for the cxings that we plant zensak. Zensak also has strategic value in certain circumstances."

Now the little one's curiosity was truly piqued. He looked at the forest of zensak in the distance and tried to imagine something battle-worthy in those wisps of mist.

Catching his thought, Mistrea continued, "Things are not always what they seem, are they?" he paused only briefly. "On other worlds, these creatures take on greater significance just as the cxings do."

Remembering his recent flying lesson, he stopped working and looked up at his teacher.

"No," Mistrea chuckled, "I can't demonstrate their abilities as I did the cxings'. I can only describe it to you.

"When we are in a different atmosphere, we can spread the zensak about ourselves and be disguised to some extent. They are beings of energy, as you know." The young one nodded. "This energy field disperses our light so that our true nature is less obvious. It also has something of a confusing effect on the followers of the Prince of Darkness. Zensak can be used as a force field around an area we wish to protect from the enemy's prying, although more powerful agents will soon discern the presence of the zensak and become suspicious.

"When we enter other worlds, it is sometimes necessary to take on forms which will be less intrusive than our true light nature even though cloaked in the lower life form. For this reason, we clothe ourselves with zensak as a precaution."

"Then there is deception in our ways!" exclaimed the astonished pupil. "How can we fight the darkness if we use darkness ourselves?"

"You are to be praised for your depth of insight, my son," said the teacher with pride in his voice. "You are learning very quickly the ways of our Master. However, it is a mystery even to me how things are done in the realms of darkness. The Father's ways are always true, and yet sometimes pass through clouds in our feeble minds."

Suddenly, both attenders stood erect and faced the same direction. Out of the sky they both sensed and then saw an approaching light. In an instant there was a being before them who stood even taller than Mistrea. There was a presence about him that bespoke authority and raw power. All attenders radiated light, for that was their nature, but this one glowed like a sun, lighting a large area of the surface of Mentridar. When he spoke, it was a combination of rumbling and music which made even the beautiful sounds of the planet seem small.

"Greetings, Mistrea, from the Father of Lights. I trust all it well with you and your charge."

"All power to him who sends you, Damon; I am pleased to say that Multar is growing strong in the light, and we are progressing well in our work." Mistrea had given a slight bow as he began to speak; the little one, Multar, swelled a bit as his master used his name in praise.

"It is good that your work proceeds, but you must leave it for a season," Damon continued. "There is a call for you elsewhere, and a need for wings and shadows."

The little one could hardly contain his excitement. This meant that something was happening that might give him escape from Mentridar.

"Excuse my pupil's thoughts," Mistrea interrupted apologetically. "He is anxious to join the battle. Only this morning we were talking of the Rebellion and the use to which we put these forms." With this he gestured toward the towering zensak, alight with cxings in the orange glow of the risen suns.

"Perhaps he should accompany you on this mission," the visitor suggested. "There should be little outright warfare; nothing more than skirmishes at most. It might be good training for him."

"If this is the will of our Master, so be it." Mistrea turned to his young pupil and asked, "What do you say; are you ready for a look at another world?"

Multar tried to look as tall and formal and powerful as his meager light allowed. "To any world with you and for our Master," he replied.

"Then collect what is necessary, and be off," commanded Damon, and with a flash he was gone as quickly as he had come, leaving two attenders standing under the two suns.

What had started as a day with a purpose ended as a day with a mission.

CHAPTER TWO

Could there be life in anything as dead looking as this? The thought of burying something to make it live was strange logic anyway; how could life come from dirt? These were the ruminations of the young man as he knelt in the warm soil following his father's instructions. Measure the rows; measure the space between settings; place each root carefully to the correct depth. Hours of labor in the growing heat had produced a graveyard of stumps to mock his efforts.

To stretch his knees he turned and sat looking at his morning's work. Although there might have been a sense of pride in the accomplishment before him, he was still enough of a boy that the present held more interest than the future. He was at the awkward age when young men long for the responsibilities of adulthood, yet youth still beckons them to the freedom of childhood. Once it had been fun to help his father in the vineyard, knowing that when he tired, his father would graciously allow him to run off and play. Now if he was caught in idleness, he was dealt a lecture on the benefits of industry and perseverance.

His father reveled in the life-giving soil, it seemed. "If you reverence life," he would say, "you must reverence the soil which gives life to all things." As the boy looked at his soiled hands, dirt packed under the nails and clinging to the skin, he saw not life but dirt. His father would hold a handful of soil and relish the very feel of it. Somehow it made him feel closer to the Giver of life. The boy had witnessed the mystery, but felt no awe for it. He was not yet enough of a man.

With age one came to realize that there is great strength in being rooted to the earth. There is stability and calming sameness to be learned from plants. They grow slowly but steadily, reaching toward the light. They take nourishment and find security with their roots in the soil while exploring the region of vapors with their stems and leaves. In due season they entertain all who can see with colorful displays of petal and foliage; best of all they make offerings of fruit and grain, leaf and stalk to nourish the ones who dwell in the vapors.

There was a time, his father had told him, when all this took place without the sweat of man's brow. When the Araq was young, she gave her gifts to men willingly. But something happened to turn her against those who dwelt upon her, and it became necessary to coax her into bearing gifts. At times, according to his father, roots were especially important: they reached deep down for hidden water beneath the surface; when the howling wind tried to tear man's tents off the ground, the plants remained rooted firmly.

All of this his father shared with him year by year waiting for the day when the boy became enough man to understand the wisdom of roots. Today the young man was too much boy to appreciate this. As he toiled through the afternoon sun putting set after set in its place, covering the roots with soil row after row, he only thought of the many other things he might be doing which gave more immediate pleasure.

When the sun had finally traced its arc to the prescribed point above the western hills he stood to leave the vineyard.

Gazing toward the orange light he saw a caravan coming through the pass in the western hills. They were still too far away to be sure, but he thought he recognized them. He stood long enough to count the camels as they slowly lumbered around the canyon wall; the number and the colors of their drapes were right — yes, it was the one.

He picked up his things and ran to tell his father that they would be having company for the night. The only good thing that ever happened in his estimation was the visit of a caravan. His boyish curiosity was piqued by the tales of distant lands and strange cities. The merchants often tried to sell his father the treats and trinkets they carried, but seldom with any success. "We have everything we need," he would always say. "Fine cloth and fancy metal does us no good here in the desert."

His father was afraid that the presence of things from the city would cause his sons to be lured there. He knew that if they developed a taste for things they couldn't get from the land, they would leave. He was not inhospitable, but he regretted being exactly three days journey from the nearest city; it meant that most caravans stopped at his water for the night. It meant his boys were constantly being reminded that there was a world beyond the vineyards he had carefully established apart from it.

The boy had always enjoyed the visits of the caravans, but one in particular held a special delight for him. Since childhood he had marked the passage of the seasons by the coming of one caravan, not for the merchandise it carried, but for the friend he made of the merchant's daughter. They were nearly the same age and had grown up playing together in the hills around the vineyard.

When the boy was very young, the merchant's wife had been ill when they passed by. His father insisted that she stay with them until she was well enough to travel. The merchant agreed, leaving his young daughter to help care for his wife.

The two children became inseparable. Several weeks later when the merchant returned to find his wife well, he also found that leaving was going to be painful for his daughter. The tears of the two children were only somewhat stayed by the promise that on the next passage, they would stay for several days to renew the acquaintance.

Thus had begun a long relationship in segments. The caravan would stop for a few days on each passage, for which the merchant left generous gifts with his hosts, both for the kind hospitality, and for lingering thanks for helping his wife recover. Some years later when his wife died, it became a way to offer some solace to his growing daughter. The men enjoyed talking of things in the world, and the two children ran and played as if it were a festival.

"Father!" the young man shouted as he entered the compound. "Father, a caravan is coming in!" A grey bearded head appeared at a window; "I think it is Sharaq's, Father."

"It would be about time, wouldn't it?" the old man reasoned. "They will be on their way back to the eastern lands soon."

"May we go onto the ridge and watch the sunset?" the young man asked. "If I take something to eat and meet them we can just make it in time."

"You may," was the reply, "as long as you are back before the third star appears."

"Very well; but I think I am old enough to remain out of the compound a little after dusk," came the near indignant response.

"The danger I fear for you has nothing to do with your youth, my son. Some things, in fact, become more dangerous as you age."

Thinking his father referred to robbers the boy shot back an ill-thought retort: "I'll match my staff against anyone who thinks to harm me or my friends."

"You would, would you?" his father chuckled. "Well then I see I was wrong to worry about the most pressing dangers after all. Your staff is surely a match for any unfortunate who would challenge you, I'm sure. But if only for the peace of Sharaq's father, be back before the third star."

"Yes sir," came the bewildered reply as the boy picked up a skin, some cheese and a flat loaf of bread.

As he turned out of the compound toward the approaching group of camels, his mother moved into view at the window. "He is still very much a boy in some things, isn't he?" she mused, watching him trot down the dusty road. "He is as big as a man, but in heart yet a youth."

"Would that he could stay as such, woman. Many things there are which will not be pleasant in his maturing. When we were young, one seldom heard of robbers; now they are everywhere. At that time, worship of the Giver of life was universal in all but the distant clans of Kahn; now men in every city debauch themselves with other gods. Cities," the old man spat the word out in disgust, "are everywhere. I feel myself torn between an urgency to bring him into complete manhood and a reluctance to make him suffer the pangs of the passage."

"All things come in their time," the woman softly replied, almost to herself. "All things come from the Source of life."

"You need not rehearse the old lines to me," the man sighed without rebuke. "I yet believe them; only I grow curious over the years as I see things become so distasteful to me. Surely these city dwellers must be as a mouthful of sand to the good Giver of all life. Must he not take their lives as he gave them when they turn against him so wickedly?"

"Remember your own wickedness and speak softly, my husband," was the kindly reply.

"You are bold with me, woman. It is well your are so wise, for I would not take kindly to rebuke from less than yourself. Your insight is exceeded only by the gentle beauty of your countenance. You must train our sons' wives so that they too may be wise; only hide from them the lessons on boldness so that our sons may not suffer from impudence."

A coy smile hinted at the corners of the woman's lips as she said, "To what purpose will our daughters put such wisdom if they can not speak openly to their husbands?"

The man reached out an took her face gently in his strong hands. "They can teach it to their daughters." To preclude further discussion he pressed his lips against hers, lingering just long enough to intimate volumes of adoration, respect and desire. Then he released her and spun out the door to prepare for the arrival of visitors.

The girl who walked beside the first camel was in that innocent first blush of womanhood that is so attractive. Her forward motion and the gentle evening breeze caused her lightweight summer dress to caress the gentle curves of her body. Soft brown hair cascaded about her face, spilling around the edges of the hood she had been wearing for protection from the harsh sun. Her face, tanned from days spent on the roadways, appeared as though it had been carved by some skilled artist of rich olive wood and polished to a silken smoothness. Her nose, chin and cheek bones seemed chiseled into sharp, beautiful perfection. Her lips were drawn in a full bow which could pout and bring rain or smile and light up a room.

But it was the eyes which captivated. They were rich brown pools which seemed to have the depth of a clear night sky with all the sparkle of the stars. Among the twinkles of the stars were small golden flecks, minute, yet nearly glowing with a light of their own. These wonders were set in her face at a barely perceptible angle so that they were at once laughing and tantalizing with a suggestion of mystery within.

As she walked, she searched the distant settlement for signs that their approach had been noted. Of all the wonderful places they visited, this one held special meaning for her. Not only did she have a friend here with whom she had spent many hours of youthful play, there was also a serene peacefulness that always engulfed her when she was here. There were other places where she felt welcome, but in recent years she had begun to sense something in the stares of the men at those other places, something that made her excited yet uncomfortable at the same time. She was not unaware of her own beauty, but she was not fully aware of its effect on men. Here at this place she knew her presence was appreciated, and she felt the relaxed comfort of being at home with no awkwardness.

"Sharaq," her father spoke from astride his camel, pulling her out of her reverie, "I see a young man on the road ahead. Could this be the boy Sha'ym?"

She had seen him at the same instant. "My father's eyes do him good service still," was her teasing response. This was a game they played often. He would challenge her to be first to sight a familiar landmark or encampment. It helped to pass the time and to create anticipation for the pleasures of shade, rest or water in the hot desert paths they measured step by step.

"Surely this cannot be Nuwach's vineyard already; that must be some other man's son who runs down the road to meet us."

"I can see him well enough and I can see through you," she gently poked his leg with her walking stick. "May I leave the lumbering pace of these camels and go ahead to greet my friend?"

"Go on, my lovely one; leave your poor father with the animals while you enjoy renewing friendship." He pouted dramatically as he looked into her upturned face.

"You take such pride in these animals that I am sure you prefer them to me anyway," she taunted.

"Not so, not so!" he retorted. "Though these be symbol of my wealth, take them all, but never say my Sharaq will leave me. There was a serious tone in his remark that made his daughter sting just a little.

She reached up to put her hand gently on his leg, "I'm sorry father; I don't doubt your love for me." She turned toward the young man still trotting down the road. "Look, he is almost here; I will not even be out of hearing." With this she slid lightly away from the side of the camel her father was riding and floated over the road toward her friend.

As her father watched, he thought of the conversation he had shared two nights before with a different young man. Her beauty had recently entranced the son of the city magistrate. Throughout their travels there were more and more men interested in his daughter. It was not so convincing anymore to plead that she was too young for marriage. She looked every inch ready for marriage and there was no hiding it. He wondered how much longer he could delay the inevitable.

That night in Armoun he had been close to saying yes to the request, but something held him back. This would be a good marriage for him as well as her. It would be the young man's first wife, and he had excellent prospects. He was strong and good looking — at least to an old man, but that was really unimportant. He knew down deep that what he wanted most for his daughter was her happiness. What he didn't know was how to insure it. To be the wife of an important city official would be secure and afford many pleasures not available to common people. Yet he couldn't bring himself to say yes that night. He had promised to consider the offer seriously.

As he watched Sharaq reach the approaching Sha'ym, they grasped one another's hands and danced around in childlike, happy innocence. Like a wedding dance, he thought;

then it struck him: why not Sha'ym? He would be ready for a wife soon enough. Perhaps he would talk to Nuwach about it tonight.

The two young people swung each other around and laughed their breathless greetings. After a moment Sharaq noticed the dirt still clinging to his unwashed hands. "Have you been playing badger and digging dens, Sha'ym?"

Following her gaze to his earth-stained fingers he replied, "Oh Father has had me planting a new vineyard on the rise. I hurried to meet you so fast that I forgot to wash.

"You remembered to bring a skin and a bag," she said, indicating the bundle slung carelessly over his shoulder. "Did you have something planned?"

"I thought we could climb the ridge and watch the sun set... if you wanted to. I knew you would be thirsty and hungry after traveling all day, so I brought bread and wine."

At this point her father had nearly caught up to them, so she turned and shouted to him, "Father, Sha'ym has brought provisions for a journey and wishes to take me over the mountains to far away lands; may I go?"

"You may go," he answered, provided you are back in camp before the third star."

"Yes, father," was the reply thrown back over her shoulder as she took off up the hill. "I bet I can beat you to the top, slowpoke," she challenged the boy behind her.

She did.

The sun was descending over a vast plain that stretched westward to the sea and north to the city she had left three days ago. The horizon had begun to glow in anticipation of the flaming arrival of the orange ball. Slivers of feathery clouds traced pink and orange lines randomly across the sky. "This will be a good one," she said as he gained the top, panting.

"Do you ever travel to where the sun sets?" he asked her wonderingly.

"I have been to the sea into which it sinks. That is a wondrous thing, to sit on the shore and hear the waves bubble and rush at the sand." She described the vast beauty of unending water and told of seeing ships come into the quay from distant countries. She described the babble of the wharf market and the smells and sounds of the docks. He sat in rapt attention, as he always did when she told of her life as a merchant's daughter. Then she returned to her thoughts of the setting sun. After a moment of quiet she continued, "I imagine it is like dropping a glowing coal into a puddle — the sizzle it makes."

"My father says there is more to the wonder of sunset and sunrise than we can imagine." They were silent for a moment, then he went on, "I only know that I wish I could travel to the horizon. I get so tired of seeing the same hills every day."

"Strange, isn't it? I often envy the peace of these hills as I travel to and from the horizon." They were in their own thoughts for a few minutes when she interrupted, "I met someone special in the city."

"Who?" the boy asked absently.

"His name is Lamaq; his father is the chief of the town." She was picturing the tall, strong form and the handsome face. "He took me to some places I have never seen before, to the hall of judges and the temple. He said that one day he will be the chief magistrate in his father's place."

"I wish my father would let me go to the city," moaned the boy. "I don't know what he is afraid of; you go there all the time and nothing has ever happened to you, has it?"

Sharaq thought for a moment before answering, "we have been robbed a couple times, and...." she hesitated with a look of puzzlement on her pretty face.

He noticed her furrowed brow and asked, "And what?"

"I'm not sure exactly. Lately my father has been very protective of me — almost to the point were I am getting tired of it. He treats me more like a baby now than when I was a baby."

"This is really odd!" the boy exclaimed, turning toward her. "My parents were talking to me as if I were a little boy just this afternoon when I wanted to go meet you. They said the same thing as you father about getting in before the third star...."

At this both of them spun toward the eastern sky. The first star was twinkling a merry greeting at them. They scrambled to their feet and started down the rocky slope without another word. The concentrated effort to find sure footing and make good speed precluded conversation for the next few minutes.

They angled down the ridge so that they intersected the road into the settlement a few hundred meters from the gate. When they were trotting easily along the path, Sharaq said, "I think I know what is going on, don't you?"

"I haven't the least idea, Shar. I thought maybe they were worried about robbers, but my father said I could match staffs with anyone I might meet."

"Think about it," she paused in the dusty road.

He stopped a few paces farther. "I don't know what to think," he said, looking into her eyes for an answer.

"How old are you, Sha'ym?"

"What kind of question is that; you know we are nearly the same age. Old enough to handle myself is what I think."

"You have no sister, so you haven't had men coming to ask your father for them in marriage...."

"What in the world does that have to do with being out after the sun sets?" he asked in exasperation.

She laughed in a kind, knowing way; he realized that he had missed something. Not understanding what, he stood still, looking into those deep knowing eyes, smiling only because her laughter told him something was funny.

"What?" he pleaded, "what is going on?"

"My sweet Sha'ym," she said as they began walking again, "I think I love these hills even more than I knew."

Frustration was building now as his mind raced to make a connection. "I know how to make you tell me," he said, stepping in front of her and taking her by the waist, "I'll tickle you until you tell." With this he began to wriggle his fingers in the slender hollow between her ribs and hips. As a child this always dropped her helplessly to her knees, writhing and giggling uncontrollably.

Tonight she began to laugh, but much more in control of herself, she placed her hands on his chest and pushed, breaking away from his slight grasp of her midsection.

In response he lunged for her, thinking she would dart away, but caught her closer than anticipated so that instead of regaining his hold around her waist, he had his hands behind her lower back. "I won't let you go until you tell me," he said pulling her close to his body. It had been a long time since they had wrestled, so he was surprised at the soft fullness of her body next to his; this was not the skinny girl he had tumbled with in years past.

As she looked up into his face, now only inches away, the full effect of her eyes sent shock waves rumbling through his awakening hormone system. Slightly out of breath from running and tousling, they stared at one another for a second which took years.

"Sharaq?"

She reached up to his face and pushed a lock of hair aside which had fallen in the ruckus. Her hand hesitated for the briefest instant at his temple, then she drew a circle with her finger across his forehead to the tip of his nose. "There are more than two stars in the sky," she said softly.

Torn between the thrill of exploring his new feelings and the dread of his father's discipline if he tarried, he repeated the question, "Sharaq?"

"Either my son does not remember how to count, or he is seeking the vengeance of a righteous Father!" came the thundering interruption from the compound.

Feeling as if he had been caught at something, yet not quite knowing what, Sha'ym released his warm captive and bolted toward the compound. "I bet I beat you this time!" he shouted over his shoulder. He stopped running after a few strides when he realized that the other contestant was only ambling in his direction as if lost in thought.

Two men with gray beards stood shoulder to shoulder near the well where servants were drawing water for thirsty camels. They watched through the deepening twilight as youth fell away from their children and fullness of life crept upon them. They watched as their children ran and played in the hills on sunny days; they watched them build cities of clay and people them with stick figures; they watched them exchange gifts hand made or brought from foreign trade; they watched them cry together and share the comfort when a mother died. They saw all this as the stars multiplied in the eastern sky on that night when the two children who went for a walk on the ridge returned as more than children.

"Have you seen what I have seen?" asked Nuwach.

"I have hidden my eyes from seeing such as this for some time, my old friend," came the sigh from the traveler. "Just today I have been considering the latest offer to take my lovely Benim-sharaqa'ym from me."

"The 'latest' offer?"

"For two...no three seasons returning I have had approaches from worthy suitors. But no, it is polite to call them 'worthy'; not the king of the finest city could worthily take this jewel from its place in my heart. I have easily convinced myself, if not them, that she was too young before now. Yet I realize that I am a fool to think that my love for her will prevent the river of life from taking its course.

"But you asked of the latest offer," he continued. "I spoke with the chief magistrate in the city of Armoun three days ago. He asked concerning Sharaq for his son. This is a high family, you know. The young man is popular and strong; he will no doubt follow his father or exceed him if the stories of him are true.

"All reason suggests that this is a good position for my Sharaq, yet I found no words to accept the proposal; I begged for time to consider. I fear I greatly displeased his honor — more still his son as I heard angry words between them when I left the courtyard. The young man has a reputation for getting those things he desires either by strength of arm or by his right as son of the chief magistrate."

Nuwach stroked his beard thoughtfully. He knew the lugal and his impetuous son better than he would say, and after a moment suggested, "This sounds to me like cause for you to hesitate; a violent, selfish man would not make the best husband."

A servant stood respectfully at a distance; Nuwach turned to give him orders for the care of the camels in preparation for the night. His gaze turned upward to the ridge, now silhouetted in deep purple with faint tracings of lighter shades where clouds intersected the black line of its tip. The sun had set on youth, he thought. Then, still facing the ridge, he said to his guest, "There is much to be said for the friendship between your daughter and my eldest son."

"They are like a brother and a sister," came the reply.

"That was true before sunset." He paused briefly before continuing, "Many things came out with the stars tonight."

"In the city they would have the stars credit for this, no doubt," the traveler responded. "You have never sought the stars' direction, have you my friend?"

"If the stars tell us anything, it is because one greater than they has whispered it to them. In the old religion, there is he who casts the stars into their places. This same one shaped us from this dirt we stand upon; we are closer to dust than to stars in likeness; therefore, from Araq I seek wisdom. Though we have risen from the ground and walk about, we are still bound to it in many ways. There is no life apart from the soil; he who understands this can learn much about how to live in harmony."

"When I spend time with you, my old friend, I see the wisdom of that, at least. In the city there is no harmony — in spite of all their priests and judges preaching about it day and night."

"For this reason you will consider Sha'ym as the most worthy suitor for Benim-sharaqa'ym will you not?" The old man turned with his question to face his visitor once again.

"We will speak of it again before I leave."

CHAPTER THREE

His voice resounded in the courtyard and throughout the neighboring streets. In the light of the full moon which fell into the central courtyard, the young man's tall, muscular frame was positioned rigidly before the elder, feet spread, arms flexed stiffly downward at his sides. The veins in his neck bulged as color rushed to his face in crimson waves; and the words with heated vehemence were spat from his tight lips.

"How could you let them get away! All I asked was that you do the formalities, and you didn't even get that right!"

"They will be back..." the elder man began.

"I had her right here," the younger one continued, oblivious to the other's words. "I had her in my arms, in the temple; then..." he hesitated, groping for an explanation, "then I don't know what happened. But I do know I wouldn't have lost her if you had done your part."

"She is just one of many women..." the elder began again, only to be interrupted again.

"No! She is not just one of many; she is one of a kind; the beauty of that face, the perfection of that body, the silky softness of that hair..." with these words his voice had trailed off into gentle caresses of each word as her cool memory stole back into his fiery thoughts. His arms were circled in front of his body now as if holding her then. When he realized his arms were empty, the steam began to rise again, "And you just let them walk out of here!"

"Not even the city magistrate can hold a freeman without charges. Would you have me imprison them for you?"

"You have let this business of laws go to your head, old man. These laws must work for us or we must change the laws. What good is it to be the chief if you can't have what you want?"

"Sometimes the good of many outweighs the happiness of even the chief," the elder began to explain. "There are times when..."

"I don't believe I am hearing this from my own father," the young man growled in disgust. "I know how you came to be the chief magistrate. Oh, I was a boy then, but I heard the talk. It seems to me that the blood of others was not too dear then to be spilled if the new chief found it expedient."

This time it was the elder who interrupted, rising suddenly from his chair and grasping the young man by both shoulders. "You will not speak of that again, or I will find ways to make you regret it. You are my son, but I am still the chief; I hold the power in this city."

Their eyes met for an instant, fire darting from the young one's as he threw both arms upward, breaking his father's grip on his shoulders. "But for how long?" he hissed as he turned and strode out of the courtyard.

"Lamaq!" the father shouted, "Come back here; I am not finished with you."

The young man ignored his father's command as he stormed through the room facing the street, grabbing his cloak as he passed it. He bashed open the front door which revealed a small garden porch, overhung with vines from the exposed rafters which ran several meters from the house to the wall at the street. When he reached the gate, a servant attempted to open it for him, but the unfortunate youngster was tossed aside like a discarded towel as the fuming young man nearly tore the thick wooden structure from its hinges and burst into the street beyond.

A block away he could hear the sound of pipes and strings and many loud, happy voices. "Good," he thought to himself, "there will be drinking and women to make me forget my father's ineptitude."

The building he was heading for was the nightly meeting place for revelers. It was actually one of several anterooms of the central temple. The gods honored at this temple were part of a pantheon of deities worshiped by the people of Armoun. The patron of Armoun was Inanna, goddess of the moon and stars. Her husband Dumuzi was the favorite of the younger people, pictured as he was by the image of a warlike, conquering ram. The simple shepherding nomads recognized Dumuzi as the god of procreation responsible for the increase of their flocks, but the growing city population focused more on the pleasurable aspects of procreation.

It was a very religious society; hardly a day passed or a duty was completed without paying homage to some deity. If one cut wood for a fire, for example, the tree god Meslantaea demanded a sacrifice. When drawing water from a well or stream, Ninazu was paid homage for clear water. The grain harvest involved paying homage to Ezen. The men were anxious to pay homage to Inanna since it meant a visit to one of the many temple priestesses to play out the conjugal rights of Dumuzi.

There was said to be a grand struggle for power going on among the gods, not that the common people usually noticed. This was the arena of the priests; it was their job to keep track of who was dominant at any given moment.

Outside of Armoun there was said to be a battle forming between the tree-god Meslantaea in his dual role as god of the underworld, and Sababba, a newcomer represented by the ever increasing presence of thunderclouds. The priests told stories of giant cedars walking human-like through the ground, sweeping their branches skyward in defiance of the upstart sky-god.

In Armoun, Inanna had held sway since her marriage to Dumuzi, which overturned his reign and ended several years of conflict between them. This unlikely union was precipitated by an invasion from Kamaresh and their patron, Ningirsu, god of the foothills. Meslantaea had joined forces with Ningirsu hoping to defeat Inanna. The priests explained that neither Dumuzi nor Inanna wished to face the combined forces of Meslantaea and Ningirsu alone, so they wed to join powers and save themselves from disaster.

None of this meant much to the younger men of the city; they went to the temple for entertainment. They were served wine and stronger drinks, and the temple prostitutes made themselves available to anyone who wished to worship at their public altars.

As evenings wore on, the music generally increased in volume and tempo, the drinks got stronger and the activities more bizarre. This was where Lamaq held court, and the later it got, the better he liked it.

Tonight as he entered the door, cheers went up for him from the already half-drunk crowd. "Hail Dumuzi! Welcome the conquering ram," someone shouted from near the door.

Lamaq's eyes sought the speaker as silence fell in the wake of his burning gaze. "Who speaks of conquering rams?"

A young man of Lamaq's approximate age swallowed hard as he said, "We have all heard of your conquest, Prince. We have paid homage to Dumuzi. We have already toasted your new wife."

By the end of this sentence Lamaq had reached the pitiable speaker and stood towering over him. "I will conquer you, at least." With this his right fist exploded into the surprised man's face. The terrible force of the blow lifted the man off his stool slightly and sent him sailing backward into the people seated behind him. When he landed on the floor at their feet, blood was already flowing generously from his nose and upper lip. He lay there in stunned semi-consciousness while his attacker addressed the crowd.

"Would anyone else mock Lamaq?" he thundered as he swept the cowering mass. When no one moved, he ordered a drink and walked through the subdued crowd to a table near the back where several men sat with girls from the temple. He snatched one of the men by the neck of his tunic and lifted him aside. Taking his place beside a particularly beautiful young girl, he put his hand behind her neck and kissed her lustily. "You've just been waiting for me, haven't you, Dahlya?"

The girl smiled devilishly and returned his kiss, leaning heavily toward him so that she could press her breast against his, running her fingers through his dark, wavy hair. "Does Inanna lust for Dumuzi?" When their lips had parted he downed the remains of his drink and roared, "What's the matter with everybody? Music! Dancing! Now!" As he shoved his cup at the one now entangled in his arms and legs he ordered, "And get me more drink, woman."

"Anything you want from me is yours. I am Inanna, the Evening Star risen to meet Dumuzi, the conquering ram." As she stood she purposely rose so that her body passed along his in a slow, tantalizing stroke.

Before an hour had passed the other two men at the table left and the three girls were vying for positions closest to the young prince. At one point he disappeared into the temple with two of them, returning within a few minutes to take a place at another table, displacing the men who had been there.

The liquor continued to flow and the tempo and volume of the music grew. Wild dances were being improvised by men and women progressively clad in less and less clothing. In various places around the dimly lit room, couples were writhing in the shadows, dancing to their own version of the music. Men and women were constantly flowing in and out of the doorway leading to the temple chambers.

It was a typical night, but Lamaq found it unsatisfying on this night. Sometime after the moon had set he conjured up a new entertainment. To those heartier revelers who had not yet succumbed to the power of sleep and drink he posed a question: "I am the conquering ram, am I not?"

The slurred response was a unanimous chorus of approval. The admiring, misty eyes looked for him to continue.

"I am the conquering ram; follow me." With this he stood and led the mob into the street and along the side of the temple to a fenced corral in the rear where the sheep and other sacrificial animals were kept. The bleating of the startled animals could be heard as the group pushed into the pen.

Watching from the street one would have witnessed some unusual things that night. First was the bleating of a ewe and a man shouting, "I am the conquering ram!" Amid sounds of hooves and bleating there was the repeated chant, "Behold the conquering ram!" and laughter and more bleating. Soon there were women on their hands and knees imitating the bleating of the ewe. Men and women behaved like animals and there was such confusion that it became difficult to tell which was which.

It was an unusual night, but not beyond the imagination of certain persons who took a great interest in the young Lamaq and his friends. Nor did it go unnoticed by dark eyes watching from the temple. Had one been watching from the empty street, a sound might have been detected coming from those dark inner rooms, a sound that began almost like distant thunder or the roar of hundreds of animals galloping across a savanna at sunset. It had a pulsing rhythm, rising and falling like laughter in slow motion. After it began, other sounds joined in, higher in pitch, yet still barely distinguishable as sounds. These too might have been laughter had they not so resembled some horrific growling at the same time they sounded like chortling.

Then, at the height of the detestable debauchery going on in the animal pen, one might have seen forms hardly more visible than smoke drifting out of the upper windows of the temple. As the vapors neared the creatures below, they assumed human-like shapes, though they remained semi-opaque black presences. The vapor-forms moved selectively to the women in the corral, sometimes overshadowing those who were still on their hands and knees, mounting them as a large dog will take a smaller bitch. With this the imitation of bleating stopped and stranger sounds came from their human throats.

Some of the dark figures moved into knots of entangled men and women and swept the men aside with strokes from barely perceptible limbs. The men seemed to be struck unconscious, but the women sensed the dark creatures now upon them and began to gasp in horror and pain; pleasure and agony both were translated from the unearthly moans they made as the dark creatures climaxed the midnight activities.

Soon the women were silent too. The forms of human men, almost opaque in crusty blackness, gradually faded into vapor and rose into the warm, fetid air above the corral. The dark cloud passed back through the windows in the upper wall of the temple, and the night was left silent.

The first gray light of morning found Lamaq lying in a pen at the back of the temple, wondering how he got there. As his eyes began to focus on the scene around him, he recognized many of his friends, awakening in similar states of confusion and undress. Two young girls were moving about, their tunics loosely draped over themselves, attempting to rouse their friends, covering them with cloaks or robes as they resumed consciousness.

The sheep were huddled in a far corner of the pen, acting strangely afraid of the human residents of their temporary home. Lamaq looked at the animals and began to remember some of what had taken place in the dark hours of the night. Something told him that his memory of the night was incomplete, but he had no inkling of what was missing.

His next impression was of the taste in his mouth, which to him could only be likened to dung. He raised himself to his feet, using the rail of the fence against which he had been sleeping. He pulled his cloak around his otherwise naked body and belted it at the waist. Running his hand through his hair he dislodged several pieces of straw; for that matter, his hair felt to his coarse hands like straw, matted and dirty from sleeping on the ground.

He stumbled around to the front of the building, entering the room they had come from hours before. There were a few people still sleeping in corners, but many of those who had not made the trip to the corral had awakened and groped their way home through the dark streets. There were still cups of wine and other drinks scattered here and there; from one of these Lamaq took a long draught to wash the taste from his mouth. As he tossed his head back to drain the cup, he nearly lost his balance, his head not yet being clear of the night's drugs.

He fell onto a nearby stool, and his elbow crashed into cups and other vessels strewn on the adjacent table sending them flying onto the floor. The clatter alerted a young man outside that he was there. Coming through the door, he found Lamaq seated with his head in his hands.

"That was quite a party last night," he remarked as he slid onto a stool opposite the moaning young man.

"Speak softly, Donar my friend, or I shall have to silence you with a beating," came the reply from between the large hands covering the face.

"You need not beat me into silence; I suspect that my head is already beaten just as yours — from the inside out."

Were we attacked last night...in the...street or behind the temple? Do you recall a fight?"

"I remember the way you belted our poor friend Gardic when he attempted to congratulate you on your betrothal. But that was no fight; you laid him out with one punch. What did happen yesterday, anyway?" Here the young man reached out and gently laid his hand on those still covering Lamaq's face before he continued, "Please don't answer me as you did Gardic."

"No, I..." he dropped his hands to the table as he tried to put the events of yesterday into perspective. "I was showing Sharaq the temple — you know what I had in mind to show her — when I heard a scuffle outside the window of the chamber where I had led her." He rubbed his brow and temples as if to stimulate the recollection of what took place. "I glanced briefly outside to see what was happening and then took the woman into my arms to show her what the temple is really all about.

"At that moment...I really can't explain it, Donar...it was as if someone grabbed me from behind — from through the window or something. I reached up to take the arm from my throat and was thrown to the floor face down. With my head toward the wall, all I heard was the running of the woman's feet down the hall. I struggled to get up, but there was a foot on my neck and a knee in my back; both my hands were being held behind my back." The description halted here because of the look on Donar's face.

"I know what you are thinking; no one has ever bettered me in a fight. There had to be three or four of them at least... I..."

"Didn't you get a look at them?" came the incredulous interruption.

"No, and that's what's so strange. They threw me against the wall by the bed; I wheeled around to return the attack and they were gone — back out the window I assume.

"I ran straight to my house, thinking that the girl and her father would be there, but they weren't, nor was my father. I then went to the hall of judgment, then the inn, but they were nowhere in the city. And here is the really strange thing: I suddenly realized that it was nearly sunset. I had taken Sharaq into the temple long before noon, yet without the passage of time, the sun was setting." "You must have passed out or been knocked unconscious by the men who attacked you," was the explanation offered by the other man. "Perhaps when they threw you against the wall you struck your head."

"Perhaps. I only know that when I made my way back home my father informed me that he had let them leave. The girl's father had promised to consider my offer. Consider my offer! Can you imagine what he would have been considering if I hadn't been interrupted? Or if my weakling of a father had not found this notion of laws that can not be broken."

The volume was rising, as was the color in the young man's face. Anger began to drive the drug-cloud from his brain. "How could he ignore my wishes and let them go?" he bellowed. But this was too much for his still sensitive head, and he took it into his hands again, groaning.

On a hill overlooking the city a conversation was taking place as the sun cleared the horizon and began to warm the rocks there. The town below was still in the last shadows of morning twilight; from the vantage point of the hill, rays of light could be seen racing down the trees, approaching the top floors of the temple. As the tallest building in the town, it received the first light. The inhabitants of the temple were working their way to the chambers below ground level to avoid exposure to the light.

"We'll be safe now, Hamayn;" one was saying, "the light is sure to have driven most of them away from the windows by now."

"After last night, I imagine they are celebrating too hard to be looking for us anyway. You almost got us caught yesterday morning though."

"I had no choice; Lamaq's intentions were severely harmful to the plan. You don't think he was in the chamber on a simple tour, do you?"

"Oh no! He definitely had a demonstration in mind. We are fortunate that only one of them was superintending his actions, that's all. Imagine the ruckus we would have created if a host of them had been spectating — that's just the kind of thing they enjoy, as you well know."

"Yes, I know," came the response as the taller one stood up. Looking down into the city he continued, "The fact that more weren't involved leads me to believe that we are still safe. They apparently have no idea who Sharaq is yet." He turned back to his partner and said, "And you, Hamayn, that was some move you put on Lamaq. He is still wondering what hit him."

"You are to be congratulated for the way you handled the dark one too. Imagine! Dispatching one of them in their own temple. Do you think he had time to put out any sort of alarm?"

"No, almost certainly not. Think how close we were to ones of great darkness. A mere thought would have called them crashing into that chamber instantly. No, I think he thought we were human at first, then when he learned differently, it was too late."

"Do you think we will be needed in the city today, Talizar?" the seated one asked.

"I don't think so; with Sharaq and her father safely on the road we should be able to keep watch from here. I just hope a band of innocents doesn't wander in. I lost most of my cloaking in the scuffle yesterday. There are too many places where the watchers in the temple could discover me if we had to guard anyone or intercede again."

At this moment the speaker suddenly crouched beside his smaller partner, who, sensing the same thing, lowered himself closer to the rocks. An imperceptible darkness moved through the sky toward the town. It might have been a shadow, except that there were no clouds to cause shadows. To the ones on the hill it had more material substance than a cloud, for a cloud is only vapor whereas this darkness was caused by a palpable absence of light itself.

The aura moved over the city, then centered above the temple, engulfing it in living darkness before it gradually seeped through the walls and roof, finally disappearing as does a drying watermark on cloth.

"Did they notice us?" the smaller one asked.

"I don't think so, but we must move immediately. Seldom will that much darkness move anywhere without setting out sentries. We will be discovered before long; if only I hadn't lost my cloaking. Come!" On the command he rose, raised his arms slightly above is shoulders and as his partner did likewise they were gone in a motion faster than can be perceived by a human eye.

They halted their ascent when just high enough in the eastern sky so that the sun was directly behind them relative to the city below. Had anyone or anything looked, they would have been blinded by the light before detecting any kind of form.

"Take wing directly to Moriah, Hamayn. Tell them of the events of yesterday and this morning," the tall one continued. "There must be something in the works — something more serious than the discovery of yesterday's loss. Neither the loss of one innocent nor the insignificant minion they are missing would demand a council of that much darkness. I sense that Dumuzi himself may be in the city.

"I will remain here to watch further developments." Suddenly he held out his arm in front of his partner. "Look, here come the sentries."

As he spoke, dark vapor-like shapes drifted out of the windows of the temple in every direction. They halted at the perimeter of the city, taking positions equidistant around the wall on all sides.

"They are not staking out anything beyond the city; perhaps this is only a short conference. Let us hope so." He dropped his arm and turned toward his smaller partner. "Do not go directly as I said. Take a path straight into the sun to the outer atmosphere; then circle over and down to Moriah. We must take no chances." Almost as an afterthought he added, "Give me your cloak. I know it will be stretched quite thin on me, but it will be of some help. You will not need it to travel as I have instructed. You can requisition more zensak before you return to me." He clasped the smaller hand and said, "May the Wings of Mentridar take you safely, Hamayn."

"And may the Father of Lights protect you, Talizar."

When their hands separated, the smaller one raised his arms and disappeared into the sun. Talizar, the guard of this city, now returned alone to his vigil. It might turn out to be a long day.

CHAPTER FOUR

𝒮

The process of readying zensak and cxings for transfer to another world was not lengthy, but it did involve some preparation and caution. While the creatures were a lower form of life, their cooperation was still voluntary, and they were enlisted, not coerced. In addition, packaging was important, due to the methods by which inter-galactic travel was accomplished, and the strategic positioning necessary upon arrival near enemy territory.

Zensak served as containers, both encapsulating and cloaking the masses of glowing cxings. To move to the point of transfer, cxings were deployed around the outside of the zensak to ride the energy waves and tow the container.

Mistrea stood at the edge of the forest with his arms raised, making a combined song/thought plea to the giants before him. Multar was fascinated by the language and the reaction; the forest seemed to suddenly converge in front of the tall attender, lining up in a majestic, orderly throng. It amazed the younger one to see these towering creatures glide along and through the soil, slowly yet purposefully arranging themselves to register their willingness to their master.

As Mistrea bowed to the being at the head of the line, it gracefully lowered its branches from the sky and laid them along its massive trunk. Thus in the form of a cylinder, it apparently poured itself onto the dusty surface of the planet. As succeeding zensak followed the first, they lay in formation like a mammoth cylinder, itself made up of giant cylinders.

The cxings which had been playfully cavorting among the zensak branches were now within the huge cylinder, having stayed with the limbs as they folded onto the trunk. Mistrea turned to the newly formed shipping container and with a wave of his arms, brought more cxings about himself. More music/thought dispersed these glowing colonies along the surface of the cylinder in rhythm to the sweep of the tall one's arms, as if he were both a conductor and painter of some living symphony.

When seven of these transport modules were ready, Mistrea turned to his rapt pupil. "Now for your preparation," he said with some formality.

The young one hadn't thought for a moment of his own readiness, being willing to go in any state, so naive was he. "My preparation!" he blurted wonderingly.

The master laughed out loud for the second time that day. "Yes, my willing helper; you have need of some wings."

Again the tall one stretched out his arms and cxings gathered around him. Multar nearly shivered with excitement, now that he knew the purpose of the creatures and the meaning of the preparation.

"Turn your back to me and drop onto one knee," Mistrea commanded. This done, he sang/thought a moment and continued, "Raise your arms just above your shoulders as you have seen me do." When Multar had done as directed, Mistrea swept his arms in a wide, slow arc above his head, ending with his hands pointing to a spot in the center of Multar's back. Immediately a colony of cxings separated from the glow above him and collected on the spot he was indicating, forming the same multi-colored array the little one had witnessed on Mistrea earlier that day.

"Think of them as your friends, allies and fellow warriors against the darkness, for so they are," Mistrea instructed. "They can read the simplest of your thoughts; all that is necessary is to direct your needs to them and they will give their all to help you."

At that moment Multar was experiencing a new sensation. There was a tingling, buzzing feeling, yet it was not altogether inanimate; he felt as though a word was trying to form in his consciousness by means of the buzz. Suddenly he realized the cxings were saying hello; they were introducing themselves.

About the time he discovered this message, Mistrea interrupted. "Rise, attender," he was continuing, "and know the Wings of Mentridar."

A rush of pride filled the young one as he stood. That phrase had always been uttered with such reverence, such dignity that he was overawed to think that he was now partaking in its full meaning. When he turned to face his master, he was again infused with a sense of his new status, as the look on Mistrea's face spoke of the pride a teacher feels when a student reaches a new plateau.

"We haven't time to properly train you here; hopefully there will be opportunity when we arrive in the Lechan galaxy. For now take a practice flight to the ridge and back. I'll wait here."

"But how...I don't..." Multar stammered.

"Just think of your need to be on the ridge, then direct your thoughts to your new friends. Raise your arms and you're off," came the instruction.

The pupil turned hesitatingly toward the distant hill, thought, gestured, and was gone. In a moment he was back, bubbling, "There's nothing to it, but it is different from thought travel, isn't it?"

"Oh! Immeasurably different," agreed Mistrea. "And you haven't experienced passage through matter."

"Through matter!" exclaimed Multar.

"Of course," came the reply. "Have you considered that we regularly pass through material substances when we travel by thought?"

"Yes," answered the pupil, "but we are in immaterial form when we travel by thought. Can that be accomplished with the cxings as well?"

"When you dematerialize the cxings will stay with your essence unless you disengage them. They can transport you anywhere they can travel. This includes passing through certain material substances. Of course, this would be impossible if you remained in a material form, so the cxings are sensitive to your need for clear flying when you are in a corporeal state."

"I am anxious to try all these things, Master," the young one effused. "There is such a feeling of exhilaration when I fly; there is a sense of time and space passing which is absent when we travel by thought. Can't I try a few more flights?"

"In time there will be opportunity, I am sure. At this moment, there is a more pressing issue; we must acquire your weapon."

"My weapon!"

"Yes, we must go to the regions of light so that you may be granted a weapon befitting your new status." Leaving the material universe to enter the regions of light was attraction enough to make Multar forget his new wings momentarily, and to be granted a weapon was the greatest honor he could imagine. Just then a thought occurred to him; "But will I stand in the presence of Mekayel?" He froze instantly.

"Do not be afraid, little one," calmed the Master. "He is truly a gentle person; his concern for you is surpassed only by that of the Father of Lights. And you know he is the only one who can grant an attender his sword of light."

"But he stands next to the Great One," the pupil gasped. "There is no one brighter than he."

"This is true; his light will pierce completely through your being, as it will mine." Mistrea put a hand on his assistant's shoulder and continued softly, "Does this frighten you?"

"Yes...I mean no...I know it shouldn't, and I have nothing to hide...at least I don't think so." The little one's mind raced to discover anything that might shame him in the presence of the second greatest light in all existence.

"It is good that you do this searching. I sense that your motives are true, but you might be able to hide something from me. It would be almost impossible to deceive Mekayel, however. The teacher squeezed his pupil's shoulder gently and added, "Even if there is a spot of darkness, it can only be to your good to have it removed."

"Yes, I understand that, my Master, but wouldn't it bring you shame?" he asked, looking into the tall one's eyes.

Mistrea smiled. "If that is your only worry, then there will be no shame." He released his grip on the younger one's shoulder and turned to the waiting zensak. "We will set these off to the transfer point, and go to Mekayel with a good heart." Saying this he stepped toward the giant parcels which rippled with the light of the cxings on their surface. He communicated a few simple directions to them, and they began to rise slowly into the air. When they hung suspended just above the surface, they formed two groups of three, connected at their ends, with the seventh centered in front of the others.

Just as Mistrea pointed to a spot in the vast empty sky, the whole train seemed to disappear, streaking into nothing in the direction of his outstretched arm.

Turning again to his pupil he said, "Come, stand beside me." When Multar was at his side he continued, "Place your hand on my shoulder and join with my thoughts. We are going deeper into the regions of light than you have been before; I must take you there."

Excitement rushed through the young attender, but he felt assurance when he placed his hand on the confident one beside him. Then, in the twinkling of an eye, they were gone.

The dark, cool, dusty surface of Mentridar had been exchanged for the most brilliant light Multar had ever experienced. There was music permeating the atmosphere as if a thousand symphonies were playing in concert with each other. But it was more than music, for it had substance to it which seemed palpable. One was suspended by it, buoyed in its liquid tones as if floating within it.

As he was experiencing the wonder of the music, Multar realized that the light was the music. He couldn't have said how he knew this; he just sensed it completely. On the heels of this revelation he discovered that the light/music was the great Mekayel, or rather that the greatest attender was so much a part of the music that he became indistinguishable from it.

At that moment there was a swelling in the music, a punctuation, a rhythmic pulsing which both rumbled and sang in the mind of the young attender. At the instant he felt this sensation, he understood that he and Mistrea had been told to materialize for the ceremony. Without a thought they appeared, on one knee with heads bowed in honor to the one before them.

"Rise, Mistrea of Mentridar," came a voice so deep, so melodious that it seemed to roll through their very beings. "Greetings in the name of our Father, who reigns in majesty and light over all creation."

Mistrea stood but kept his eyes lowered, not looking directly at the brilliant one before him. "I am your fellow-servant and the Father's slave for all eternity." The timbre of his voice, the richness of which Multar had always admired, was thin in contrast to the music that surrounded them.

"Our Master is pleased to send you on a mission of great import to the Lechan galaxy and to us all," the music rolled on. "It is good that your pupil has advanced in his training; this too pleases our Master."

This nearly overwhelmed the still kneeling attender: the thought that he was involved in something that pleased the Great One. Then he heard his name spoken in a way that made it sound as if he were the ruler of some galaxy.

"Rise, Multar of Mentridar."

He stood, following the example of his teacher, keeping his eyes averted.

"Right hand or left, Mistrea?" came the musical question.

"May it please my Master, he may compliment me well if he takes the sword in his left hand," he respectfully requested.

"Yes that may well be an advantage in the battles you will face. So be it." With this Mekayel again addressed the younger one, "Extend your left hand to me, Multar." The small hand was dwarfed in the larger, as would a toddler's in his father's. A band of brilliant silver was placed on the middle finger of the smaller hand. It hummed with the music which was in the air; it warmed and stimulated the hand which wore it. Multar could sense that it was infinitely more than a ring, but he was not sure what it meant. Then the voice went on.

"Close your hand and raise your arm, Multar of Mentridar."

He obeyed.

"Center your thoughts on the Father of Lights and on his glorious brilliance." The great attender paused a moment before continuing, "Now, call for your sword."

There was a flash of question as to what that meant, then a surge of confidence emanated from the ring itself into his whole being. He centered on the Light of lights and thought, "A sword!"

Instantly a shaft of light extended from his hand and sang in striking harmony with the fluid music that still surrounded them all. He could feel power flowing in his arm in a way he had never experienced before. At that moment he felt he could take on the dark host of the universe single-handed, so strong did he feel standing behind this sword. Nothing could go unvanquished when he wielded this mighty weapon.

All this went through his mind in an instant, yet it seemed he stood there reveling in the feeling for hours. His reverie was interrupted by the music of Mekayel again, "Give honor to the Father."

Instinctively he lowered his arm, sank to one knee and extended the sword in his hand so that its point rested at the feet of Mekayel. He noticed that Mistrea too had bowed again and likewise extended a sword before him.

"All glory, honor and brilliance of light belong to the Creator of light who reigns forever, amen." Saying this, Mekayel raised his massive arm and extended a sword so bright and so loud that it sounded as if a thousand voices were singing in glorious harmony to the symphony around them. Then he turned and bowed in the same direction Mistrea and Multar were facing.

It was at this point that Multar realized there was a being before them all; in a sense, he had been there all along, unseen, yet fully noticeable in the light and the music if one cared to notice. The instant he perceived this, he fell completely on his face with both arms outstretched. He was only a twinkling later than Mistrea and Mekayel in doing this.

Then something happened to the young attender which was virtually indescribable. It seemed for a split second that the music and the light were both centered on him, as if some mystical funnel had been placed above his head and the mixture poured over him. The ecstasy and rapture he felt swelled beyond the power of words to describe. He thought briefly of the music he had felt emanating from Mentridar. As marvelous as that was, it was as the plucking of one lone string compared with ten thousand orchestras playing in concert.

In the midst of this, Multar sensed a message. It would be inaccurate to say he heard a voice. Rather he felt meaning in the flood of music washing over and through his being. If it could be translated into words, which it can not, it would be something like this: "Be well, my son. Take your light into the darkness and face the enemy. You will be victorious; we are always victorious together.

The music didn't really stop, just as it had never really started, but Multar and his companions stood in a different state than they had fallen, though nothing had changed. Nothing had changed except that Multar now felt the power of the sword of light contained in the ring on his left hand. This and the recollection of the Wings of Mentridar at his back. Nothing had changed indeed.

When they arrived at the receiving point of the matter transfer conduit in Lechan, Multar was surprised at the volume of activity. The zensak containers had arrived and were waiting for Mistrea's orders. They had been separated from their transfer formation and were scattered across a wide expanse of space.

Seeing the confused look on his pupil's face, Mistrea began to explain. "You remember that on Mentridar I spoke of the transfer point?"

"Yes, but I assumed we would do the transferring. Did you not enlist the cxings to move the zensak containers?"

"Only as far as the conduit. You see, we are now half way across the universe from Mentridar. It would take the cxings hundreds of thousands of years to ride the energy waves that far. For this reason the Great One has created channels through which it is possible to move matter and energy at nearly the speed of thought."

"Why could we not think them along with us when we travel? The cxings on my back went with me to the regions of light and now here without a thought on my part."

"So they will go wherever you think. Remember, that is a seven fold union on your back. The colony, once mated thinks as one, and now they think with you as they have chosen to bond with you in the battle.

"It is possible to take sentient creatures which are not purely material with us when we think only if they are in perfect union with our thoughts. I do not have the thought energy to bring about such unity of thought in the thousands of cxings involved in our transfer today. Perhaps Daman could; surely Mekayel would have no trouble. This may be how the Great One moves them through the conduit, for surely he has the power...I don't know exactly how it works, I only know that it does."

"And that is enough for me, my master...but why are the zensak spread so far apart in this region of space?" the pupil was still wondering.

"This is a precaution against spying by the dark ones," Mistrea replied, his face suddenly more serious as he looked into the star-studded blackness. They are not great enough in number to patrol the whole galaxy, or even this star system, but if a lone scout stumbled upon a collection of alien beings this close to his base, it would doubtless be reported.

"We will set up strategic delivery points which can be protected long enough to send in what we need without raising the enemy's curiosity. The cxings can take material into a landing zone on the planet's surface with relative obscurity. Gebarour orders us to take no unnecessary chances."

"Gebarour!" Multar exclaimed. "Gebarour who fought at Mekayel's side in the Rebellion? Gebarour who won the battle of Sqotianus against thousands of the dark host? He is here?"

"Yes, the Warrior of Light spoken of in our legends is in charge of the Araq operation," Mistrea answered. "His presence should suggest something to you."

The little one's mouth gaped as he considered. "My Master, so much has happened today: my wings, my sword, a mission..." Again he stared in wonder into space. "But to be going into battle with Gebarour in command..." He paused again to soak up the import. Finally he said, "I am honored that the Great One thinks me worthy to be of service in this matter. It must be of tremendous importance to him, no?"

"You are correct in that, although I think that you are overstating this to say we will soon be going into battle. Some skirmishes, no doubt, but we do not have the numbers presently to wage major warfare.

"Our present assignment is to make preparations for such, however, and to that assignment we must go. Let us speak with the officers in charge here to learn when we will go to the planet for reconnaissance." He placed his hand on Multar's shoulder and said, "Come with me; an adventure awaits."

"Hail, Daman of Araq," Mistrea thought/spoke as they approached a large attender, whom Multar recognized as the one who had met them on Mentridar.

"All glory to the Father of Lights, Mistrea of Mentridar," came the reply.

"We have arrived with the supplies you requested and await your instructions," Mistrea said formally.

"Well done; the planet is nearly in position now for a transfer window." He looked at Multar and added, "How is our newest warrior feeling, now that he has arrived near the front lines?"

"I am ever ready to serve the Father, but..." he hesitated.

"Go ahead, little one," Daman said reassuringly. "A little curiosity is a healthy thing for a pupil."

"Thank you," Multar tried to organize his thoughts. "I was just trying again to imagine the clay creatures Mistrea told me about."

Daman shot an inquisitive look at Mistrea who explained, "I told him the creatures of the Araq were something like clay jars that gained their life from the light within."

"Oh-ho," Daman laughed. "I see; not a bad analogy, really." Looking back to Multar, "Shall we go take a look while we wait for the window?"

Multar could not contain his excitement, and Daman laughed again at his thoughts before the little one could even speak them. "Follow me," he said as he flew a short distance parallel to the surface, then dove down for a closer look.

The vista that lay before the young attender was not entirely unlike Mentridar. The surface of the planet was partially covered with a grayish-blue fluid and the remaining dry area was mottled with brown, grey and various shades of green. The colors were richer than on Mentridar due primarily to the greatly increased light provided by the nearest star. Indeed, except for the waves of color provided by the cxings, Mentridar was mostly shades of grey.

Mistrea and Multar followed Daman closer to the surface as he dropped toward a large patch of green. At first, Multar thought he was looking at an immense moss-covered plain, but by the time they stopped to hover just above it, he could see that the green was foliage suspended many meters above the surface by large stalks. Although he couldn't see any other life forms, he sensed that there was much more before him than the foliage.

"There, to the left," Daman signaled, "Do you sense that?"

Multar reached out with his senses, only to be assailed by numerous conflicting impressions. Everything seemed to be peaceful, but there were too many inputs for him to sort out anything individual.

Sensing his difficulty, Daman suggested, "Try picking up just the atmospheric compressions. These are the most common signals produced by the creatures of the Araq."

"Oh my," the young one exclaimed as he began to hear the singing of birds, chatting of squirrels and a slight rustling undertone caused by the wind in the trees.

Sensing another creature nearby, Daman signaled the two visitors to follow him into the treetops. As they descended toward the forest floor, he motioned to a spot where the trees parted, forming a small open glade. Multar first sensed, then realized he was seeing a small brown creature standing in the shadows. It was covered by light brown fur which blended into the similarly colored fallen leaves beneath it. As they moved closer, Multar could see it had four long slender legs supporting a small body with an arching neck and head with big ears and a pointed snout.

"The Araqans call it a deer," Daman announced. "They are quite beautiful when they run," he continued. "Watch."

Saying this he suddenly became very thick and solid, right before Multar's gaze. The effect on the young attender was to cause him to realize suddenly that the three of them were not as solidly visible as the rest of the scene around them. The effect on the deer was to make it jump and run away as if startled.

As the question about both of these effects was forming in Multar's mind, Daman answered, "The deer had only a vague sense of our presence at first. When I materialized fully, my sudden appearance startled him. If we approach carefully and materialize gradually, they are not afraid of us."

"They do not look at all like us," Multar began. "They are so much..." he searched for the right word "...thicker."

"Yes, that's not a bad way to say it," Daman agreed. "They carry their light in a more restrictive vessel than we do — remember Mistrea's clay jar analogy." Multar nodded as Daman continued, "It is far more complicated than that, having to do with their slower motion through time. When we materialize as you just watched me do, we are simply bringing our outer selves in synchronized time with them. That's why I appeared more substantial, more visible they might say, and that visual sensation frightened the deer momentarily."

Daman moved a few meters away and continued, "Come here and look at something." So saying he reached out with his arm to a nearby tree trunk and Multar sensed that he was calling something. Almost immediately a small furry brown creature scampered down the trunk and leaped onto Daman's hand.

Stroking the little creature gently, Daman turned to Multar and said, "Look deeply into this little one's eyes."

Multar obeyed and found himself looking at a creature far more familiar to him than the furry brown one. Though dim, he could sense the life energy within the creature and it resembled the ones he was used to on Mentridar. Simple, peaceful, hungry and slightly anxious, as if it had better things to do than be this attender's lesson for the day.

"It's like a large mintu wearing a fur coat!" Multar exclaimed at last.

Mistrea and Daman both chuckled. "Very much like," Mistrea agreed.

Daman placed the tiny animal back on the tree, and it climbed quickly back out of sight, only to stop and poke its head around a branch part way up the tree and chatter noisily at the three strange creatures it had just left.

"I think he just said, 'Nice to meet you; good bye,'" Daman laughed.

"Can you show me how to materialize?" the young student begged.

"I am afraid that will have to wait until another time," Daman answered. "We should return to the outer atmosphere as the window is now upon us."

Mistrea added, "Don't worry, my friend; there will be an opportunity to practice embodiment, I am sure."

Though disappointed, Multar thought the prospect of continuing their mission also presented many exciting possibilities. As the three sailed back into the sky, he was ready for whatever might come with the rest of this day.

CHAPTER FIVE

A yellow-orange ball was slowly descending onto a distant ridge as the camel caravan plodded westward. The last breath of the gentle sea breeze which soothed the valley ahead swirled tantalizing coolness and moisture around the backside of the hills. The travelers could just begin to sense this, knowing it meant the refreshment of water and respite from heat lay only a few hours away. So many times had they passed this way that they could almost predict when the pleasant zephyr would reach them.

Imanaq had traveled this route for many years with his daughter Sharaq after his wife died. He had loved his wife deeply, thinking of her more highly than most men of his day would their wife. This came in part from his good heart, and also from his association with Nuwach. There was a man who was different from others, he thought to himself; his women were treated almost as equals. Nuwach said this was the way in the old religion. Wherever it came from, it had its effect on Imanaq over the years. Every few months his circuit purposely led to Nuwach's compound. Of course, the city of Armoun was always a profitable stop, but the subsequent visit to Nuwach's had become the true destination.

He adjusted his position in the saddle to rest his aching bones and looked down at his daughter riding beside him. When his wife died, Sharaq had slowly crept into the empty place in his heart. He was now more thoughtful and protective of her than any father of a mere daughter. Girls were to be used to barter advances in one's social or economic position. They were typically betrothed before puberty and married off as soon as they became capable of bearing children. As wives they were chattel, used for pleasure and procreation.

But Imanaq the merchant would never treat his Benim-Sharaqa'ym that way. Even her name had been chosen to honor her: "mother of choice sons" she was called. As he thought of the day he and his wife had given her that name, his eyes became misty. They had talked of choice grandchildren sitting on their knees when they grew old.

Now the days of grandchildren had arrived, and the father was not ready. This is what caused him to struggle over the two proposals he now entertained on his daughter's behalf. On one hand was the long friendship with Nuwach and Sha'ym; this almost assured Sharaq's happiness, and he knew she would not be more loved or better treated anywhere. And yet, Nuwach was at odds with the entire world. It seemed that the world was progressing into new and wondrous stages while Nuwach kept his compound locked in an earlier age.

His old religion affected everything he did. He constantly spoke of his god as if he were someone with whom he communed daily. In fact, he had said that he heard things from this god. Nowhere else did simple farmers presume to take the functions of the priests. The whole world had realized the necessity of building shrines and temples to please the gods, and they had found it imperative that only chosen ones communicated with those gods. There were horrible stories of people in the old days trying to make their own peace with the gods.

In the face of this now ancient tradition, Nuwach held his own meetings with his god. It was as if he walked with him every day, holding his own private councils. And there was no temple or even a shrine. Nuwach held that his god dwelt in all the world, in each thing he created. For this reason he felt especially close to the Araq, drawing many analogies from her life-giving soil and the plants and animals she succored.

"Father," Sharaq interrupted his thoughts, "is the city not just beyond the next ridge?" From his seat on the swaying camel he strained his eyes into the mid-afternoon sun. "Yes, lovely one; you have good eyes and a better memory for the land."

"So often have we come this way to Armoun its landmarks are familiar friends to me," she remarked. "And who could miss the change in temperature and the moisture?"

Imanaq gave a little harumph of agreement, and they continued in silence for a few moments. His thoughts went back to weighing his daughter's future. If Sha'ym represented peace and quiet, stability and tradition, Lamaq meant excitement and adventure, wealth and position. It also meant a better position for the bride's father. The gates of the city and its markets would doubtless swing wide open for the father-in-law of the city magistrate. He might even settle down and send others to do his trading in foreign cities. Nuwach had even said this was understandable.

And what would he lose? Nuwach's friendship would still be there. It seemed unlikely that he would take personal offense if the offer by his son were refused. After all, was not Nuwach's the second proposal, he reasoned to himself.

On the other hand, he stood to lose a great deal if Lamaq were rebuffed. The market in Armoun would most likely close to him; this would make his route very awkward. Even now his camels were laden with fine woolen weavings and the latest metal trinkets from the mountain cities of Kamaresh. The next closest city with enough wealth to buy these luxuries was all the way down the valley at the sea coast. He had grown accustomed to his current route, and he resisted the thought of change.

Then a frightening thought struck him: what if Lamaq decided to take Sharaq anyway? His temper was renowned. Imanaq might be treated very badly indeed, even killed. With this thought he turned to look at his daughter, who had fallen back and was riding her donkey behind him. She was so beautiful, so regal looking riding along on her little beast. He knew he mustn't do anything to jeopardize their relationship.

"What is it Father?" she asked, noticing the worried look in his face. She gently coaxed her beast alongside his.

"I have something very important to talk with you about before we reach the city, my beautiful one. I have been thinking a great deal about your marriage." He broke off and looked at her for her reaction.

"I know Father; Sha'ym told me that you spoke to his father about us."

This was a shock to Imanaq; he had not counted on her knowing about that discussion. He should have guessed, considering the closeness she and Sha'ym shared. "That discussion was private and not final. You had no right to that knowledge," he said defensively.

"Father," she said sweetly, "now you are sounding like other men who do not share everything with their daughters. On our last visit, I discovered that I could be quite happy living there with Sha'ym."

The camel and the donkey kept pace side by side for a moment, raising small explosions of dust with each footfall. The gentle breeze carried the miniature clouds off the road to the north and east, settling them on the grass and leaves of the sparse vegetation. When the eddies stirred the leaves more briskly, they shook off the larger particles of dirt as if cleaning themselves to get a better dose of the life-giving sun.

The old man let the silence dwell for some time, listening to the rhythmic breathing of the animals and their hooves clopping on the hardened surface of the road. He was beginning to feel ashamed that he hadn't told her about Lamaq's proposal; he didn't even know why he hadn't.

"Nuwach's was not the first proposal I have heard," he began, testing her reception of the idea. "Do you remember the young man who spent the afternoon with you when we last visited Armoun?"

"Remember him?" she exclaimed. "Father, Lamaq took me on a tour of all the important places in the city. We had a very..." Here she paused, remembering that she had not told her father everything that had occurred. "...a very pleasant afternoon."

He looked closely at her, trying to read her eyes, trying to understand the hesitancy he detected. He decided to dig a little deeper. "So you enjoyed his company?"

"Yes. He's...I..." Now she was caught. She didn't even know exactly what she was feeling. Lamaq was attractive and intelligent, if a little egotistical. But there was something uncomfortable lurking in the shadows of her memory. She had felt it then and not known what it was; it still remained. Perhaps she was feeling guilty that she had not told him of the fight. She ventured, "Father, there is something I haven't told you about that afternoon."

"What!" he exploded, "Did he do something to you? If he laid a hand on you I'll..."

"No, Father, nothing like that. He was very kind to me. He even arranged to have one of the priestesses put on a little show for me. She looked at my hand and gazed into my eyes and made some sugary sounding prophecy about me being the queen of nations and a mother of chosen sons. I know what my name means; anyone could have figured that out.

"What I didn't tell you was the real reason why I came back alone. There was no important business as I said. There was a fight, and I ran away. I was afraid that if I told you, your protective nature would prevent me from ever leaving your sight again."

"How did this fight happen? What was it about?"

"I don't really know," she answered, a little mystified. "Lamaq had taken me into one of the inner rooms of the temple..."

"What!" He sat bolt upright and stared at her, his eyes wide with horror.

In her guilt, she was looking down the road, so she missed the eyes of her father as she continued, "...and he said he was going to show me something, when suddenly there was a noise in the street, and...I don't know; it all happened so fast. I guess someone jumped in through the window and grabbed him...No, two men came in the window and I was afraid the other one might grab me, but he seemed to fly right past me, so I just ran down the hall out of the temple. When I got to the street I didn't know what to do, so I went back to the house and...and lied to you about what happened."

"My daughter hears a prophecy from a priestess, nearly gets kidnapped or killed and doesn't tell me about it for three months." Suddenly another thought occurred to him. "What do you suppose became of Lamaq? What if they think we had something to do with it? Daughter, you may have created a tangled web for us in Armoun."

The pass was now in sight which led to the short descent to the city. The sun was still four fingers above the horizon, meaning they would have time to reach the city before the gates were closed for the night. The question was whether they would be welcome. The silence which now accompanied them was deeper because of the thoughts racing though both minds. She was wondering if the prophecy really did have any meaning and wondering if Lamaq was all right; he was wondering if they were riding into captivity or worse.

Then Imanaq struck upon a plan. "We will camp on this side of the ridge tonight. In the morning I well send a servant into the city to find out what our reputation is. If we are not welcome, perhaps we can slip away and get back to Kamaresh. If we are still in the good graces of Armoun, we will ride into the city as if nothing happened."

"But what if someone rides this way before we know. Or what if they set a watch? They have in the past."

There hasn't been a raid here in years. They will not be watching. As for a rider, we will have to take that chance. Come. There is an outcropping to the north that will shield our fires from the road. If we keep them small the smoke will not be visible.

"Ride back and tell Meltsar what we are doing. I will lead the way."

As the caravan left the road, there was a struggle going on above them out of the realm of their sight. Two creatures struck at one another with weapons of incredible power. The large dark one wielded a black rod fully three meters long and as thick as a young sapling. The other, a bright one, held a glowing sword, not as long as his opponent's staff, but equal to its strength. Each swipe of the sword was blocked by the staff, and return swings of the staff were warded away skillfully by the sword.

The dark one had an advantage. Rising above his massive shoulders were huge wings, spanning four meters. On the tip of each was a set of three long claws, sharp as razors. Each time the light one thrust in to strike a blow, a wing would lash at his back. Thrusting and dodging, swinging and lashing they tumbled and shot through the air above the caravan.

"These are innocents, you foul creature," the light one was saying. "Stick to your demented worshipers in Armoun." He drove upward, taking a swing at the dark one's head as he catapulted past him, barely missing entanglement with the deadly claws that reached for him.

The dark one spun around to face him again. "They are not innocents; they are ours. Listen to how she has lied to her father already."

The light one was studying his opponent's tactics. If he could count on a pattern, he might have a chance to better him. He lunged once more at the mid-section of the dark warrior, again ducking below just in time to avoid the wingtip razors.

"You might as well admit defeat, small one. Your light is no match for me. As for these, they will be welcomed into our city and be out of your reach by tomorrow." He did a complete somersault, coming down at full strength at the head of his opponent. To his surprise, no one was there to meet the blow of his rod. As he stretched out his wings to arrest his fall, the sword of his enemy sliced a large portion off his right wing. He roared partly in pain, but mostly in self-disappointment at having been outwitted.

He barely missed losing both feet as the arc of his opponent's sword continued after passing though the wing. Now slightly off balance, he looked for some solid ground to stand on and regain an advantage. But the light one was not giving advantages. With the claw gone from the right wing, the attender now battered with his full force toward the right side of his dark opponent's body, keeping him off balance.

The dark warrior took one last swipe with his good claw This is what the attender had been waiting for. He put his sword above his own head and did a back flip just as the wing was closing on his body. His sword arced through the air and came full circle under the black wing and severed it at the mid-point.

Seeing his opportunity to finish the dark creature, he drove at his head, as if to take a swing at it. Just as the black one raised his rod to block the blow, the light one spun longitudinally and his sword passed completely through the dark one at his waist.

The last thing the dark one heard was the dreaded curse, "Be gone, in the name of Light!" as his essence was banished to the realms of Qavah Khoshek.

At daybreak, Meltsar was sent into the city. Following his master's instructions he sought out a merchant in the market whom he hoped could be trusted. He mingled with the early morning throng, people going about their business at the start of another day.

From the windows of the temple tower, dark eyes were watching, waiting for a stranger to enter the gates. They expected someone, having received a report from an outer sentry on the Kamaresh road. They were especially watchful for two reasons: they had specific orders concerning a young girl in this particular caravan, and they had lost contact with the sentry. A scout sent to investigate reported no sign of the sentry other than a foul stench hanging in the air, signifying the loss of the warrior's life.

Meltsar was spotted before he found the stall he was searching for. In moments two large men appeared at his side and conducted him to the home of the chief magistrate. Just as he was cursing his ineffectiveness, sure he had cost his master his life, Lamaq walked into the back room where he was being held.

"I understand you are a servant of Imanaq, the father of Sharaq; is this true?" he asked, using all the formal legal bearing he had learned from his father.

The servant stared at the muscular young man in front of him. He was dressed in a light robe, apparently hastily thrown on, with hair having the look of sleep tousled disorder. Were it not for his size, he might have been mistaken for a little boy in sleeping clothes playing magistrate.

"I used to be in his service, yes," Meltsar replied, hoping to convince him that Imanaq was nowhere nearby.

"Used to be...Oh, that is too bad. I was hoping that your presence here meant that my good friend Imanaq was in the caravan just outside the city. I was going to send you to him with my welcome invitation to my home," he intoned sweetly, pasting a significantly large smile on his handsome face.

He was trapped. Meltsar's mind sped through a hundred explanations he might offer, but none seemed plausible. He finally decided that truth was the only way out, since Lamaq already seemed to know more than he expected. "Worthy Lamaq," he bowed low as he began, "Forgive my awkward deception. My master has sent me here to learn of your feelings toward him. It was under..." he paused to find the best word, "...there were unusual circumstances when he left your fair city after his last visit. He feared you might have taken offense at his failure to beg leave of your gracious company."

"Offense?" Lamaq faked surprise. "How can true friends cause offense. No, no, I was only disappointed that Sharaq... that is Imanaq and Sharaq could not stay longer. I have looked forward to their return with fondest anticipation." Again he was smiling fully about his mouth, but something in the rest of his face was not in agreement. He stooped to touch Meltsar on his shoulder and continued, "Good servant, go tell your master that he is a welcome guest in my home tonight. I will send two of my men with you to aid in his preparations to come."

When Lamaq next appeared, he had dressed for the occasion as if he were greeting royalty. His linen tunic was covered by a sleeveless cloak of finely woven wool striped in red, brown and white. He wore a small turban of red, with a dyed leather band woven through it and sandals that laced up his calves and disappeared under the linen below his knee. On each of his hands he wore the latest in jeweled adornments, newly fashioned rings of gold which Imanaq had only recently discovered in Kamaresh.

"Imanaq, my friend," he gushed as he entered the center courtyard where they were waiting, "I have looked forward to seeing you again with great longing." He strode toward them with his arms outstretched. He placed his right hand on the older man's left shoulder and placed his own left hand on his chest in the typical greeting.

When he looked past Imanaq his glance discovered Sharaq standing in a corner of the courtyard. His hand dropped from the father's shoulder as he brushed past him toward the daughter. "Is it possible?" his voice filled with affected wonder. "Could this vision of beauty be real? Sharaq, you are even more lovely than I remembered; and believe me when I say that I have thought of nothing but you ever since you left." The words dripped from his tongue like liquid music.

He took her hand and placed it against his breast, a gesture of deepest affection which shocked the young girl and thrilled her at the same time. Such a posture was normally reserved for closest friends, kinsmen or betrothed lovers. There was only one interpretation here. Looking into her eyes he became captivated as he had before.

"Surely you have returned to tell me that you accept my offer for your daughter's hand," he said to her father, never removing his gaze from her eyes.

"We have come to...discuss it," came Imanaq's measured reply.

Sharaq and her father had talked long into the night as they sat encamped above the city. No decision had been reached, waiting for the report of their current status with the headstrong magistrate's son. Now that his intentions were plain, a decision would be required. There would be no slipping away this time without severe offense.

"Good!" Lamaq burst out as he turned toward Imanaq, still holding the girl's hand. She was compelled to follow him into the center of the courtyard. "We will discuss it," he placed careful emphasis on the word discuss, "at a feast in your honor tonight. I have already begun preparations.

"Your camels and merchandise are being taken care of even now. I am sure you will have no trouble selling all you have brought; you always bring items of such good taste and unique value." With a sweep of his hand toward the city he continued, "I have instructed certain merchants to come here to bid on your quality wares. You may spend the afternoon in comfort while you count your profit. This is the life you deserve, Imanaq. Send others down the dusty roads while you enjoy the profit here with us."

Imanaq was slightly overwhelmed, whereas his daughter was completely awash. She was still held by the hand at Lamaq's side, feeling for all the world that the discussions of the evening were anti-climatic.

That day and the next day and the next weeks whirled by as in a dream. Soon she was waking in her soft bed to the realization that it was her wedding day. As she went through the events of that day, the details stood out with crystal clarity against a backdrop of scurrying servants and murmuring watchers.

First there was the ritual cleansing done by the temple priestesses. To begin, a turtle dove was sacrificed and the entrails read for signs of ill. Then a she-goat was led into the altar room and slit across the throat. The blood was caught in a bowl and brought to the waiting bride. With loud prayers and incantations, the priestesses opened the ceremonial gown Sharaq was wearing to reveal her abdomen. They then took an elaborately carved, sharpened ram's horn and scribed elaborate figures on her pale flesh as insurance of fruitful womb and loyal servitude.

The marriage ceremony itself was a solemn affair, with the priests in their elegant robes chanting about the blessing of the gods and fruitful wombs and other ritualistic enchantments, all burned into the memory of her dreamlike state. The giant feast which followed lasted for days and blurred into one vision of throngs of happy people wishing them well and eating and drinking and dancing.

Then she was lying in the bridal chamber, waiting for her new husband to come to her. The room was lit by dozens of scented candles, making it glow with warm anticipation. She was floating on a huge feather mattress, her body covered only in the sheerest linen. She tingled with excitement as she thought of her lover. She had been bathed in milk and perfumed with soft powders by smiling young attendants who were now her servants. As she lay pillowed in the softness of the down she imagined the pleasure she would offer to her deserving husband.

Then he stepped into the room. He had on only a light tunic belted at the waist. His muscular torso showed in the loose opening down to the belt. As he glided across the room the bulging strength of his thighs appeared briefly as the tunic parted with each step. When he reached the bed he loosened the belt and the tunic fell away as he slid beside the soft body of his waiting bride.

His strong hands gently brushed the rich brown curls away from her face as he leaned to kiss her luscious red lips. One hand began to slide down the opening in the top of her gown as he kissed her neck and then each of her collarbones in turn. As the other hand parted the lower half of her gown he slid his leg over hers. Her body was reeling with excitement; her breath was beginning to come in short gasping sighs. With her eyes closed she was imagining him finding the greatest pleasure in her soft willing body.

Just as he was about to move completely on top of her, a shout came from somewhere. She opened her eyes to find a dark semi-opaque form being lifted off her uncovered body in a flash of brilliant light. Her heart was beating crazily from the excitement of the dream and the shock in the waking. As she pulled her gown back around her now shivering body she tried to find the place where dream and reality separated.

It had definitely been Lamaq in the beginning of the dream, but when she awoke.... Her sleep clouded mind tried to make sense of what she thought she had seen. The flash of light seemed real, yet there was no light in the room save one candle. She felt as if the shout was still ringing in her ears, yet there was no one in the room with her. Worst of all was the face that had hovered above hers for one brief instant when her eyes opened before the vision disappeared. It was unspeakably ugly. She struggled to recapture it in her mind. The eyes were yellow, and the mouth...no it was almost a snout, human but not quite human. There were no lips, only long brownish-yellow teeth with foam between them.

At this point she shuddered violently. Surely this was all a dream. But what could it possibly mean? Without really thinking, she reached down and scooped up a small cat which had been snuggling against her thigh since she sat up. As she nestled the warm furry creature next to her breast, it purred contentedly as she stroked its head. The cat's eyes, half closed with delight, showed only a sliver of yellow between the lids.

A few blocks away in a room deep under the temple a black form poured itself discreetly through a masonry wall into the adjoining chamber. Once inside it was apparent that a meeting was in progress and that its entrance had not gone unnoticed.

"So Glaxxin, do you hope to impress me by being late when you are called?" a gravelly voice hissed menacingly.

The creature drew himself fully through the wall and assumed his full height — just short of the one who had addressed him. "No imperious one; if I were trying to impress you I would not have come at all," came the indignant reply.

Those dark forms who had been near his entrance slid slightly back as the largest one in the room drifted quickly toward him at his retort. When they were face to face he placed a wing-claw on each side of the impudent one's neck and forced him to stand just a little taller than he was able to do comfortably.

"What is this I am reading in your light dazzled mind? Are you contemplating a Rhuyh Klaxxin? Can you imagine that you can subvert my power, you son of the morning light?"

With this the claws pressed slightly into the substance of the underling's neck. He was madly trying to fill his mind with thoughts other than what he had just been attempting. It would be fatal to be discovered in a failed Rhuyh Klaxxin; success could bring the kind of honors that gave the dark one's their station. It was a perilous undertaking. As he tried to focus his mind on the pain in his neck he realized that there was also pain in his back. He pondered momentarily what had caused this searing stripe on his dorsal side. This was enough to throw his present antagonist off the track.

"I doubt you are capable of any such treachery; you are too much in love with the light," the controlling one mocked. "I should not consider anything if I were you, Glaxxin. Your fate would be to find yourself sunning on a lily pad bound to the life of a frog. How would you like to hunt flies in the sun all day?" he sneered.

"I am your servant," he lied convincingly. "I do your bidding unhesitatingly." The larger one pulled the claws away from his neck skillfully so that they sliced shallow reminders in the surface. The pain increased for a moment, but as soon as he was standing freely, he felt anew the pain in his back.

As soon as his tormentor had resumed his position at the front of the gathering, Glaxxin tried to reconstruct what had happened to his failed attempt to penetrate the human girl. Something had sent him screaming from the room...something on his back. His yellow eyes searched the room for signs of any creature recently entered. Then he catalogued those present; it seemed that all but a few peons on sentry duty were there. Surely no one strong enough to wound him was missing.

He was puzzled. Never had he carried pain from an embodiment into his dark essence. Only another of his type could inflict such a wound. Yet it felt as if he had been clawed the full length of his back. Again he searched the yellow eyes around the chamber, looking for any sign that one there had bettered him. Perhaps they slipped in while he was in the claws of the master.

Everyone appeared to be ignoring him, listening intently to the leader's directions concerning the entanglement of the innocents who had recently come to Armoun. Entanglement was precisely what Glaxxin had been attempting; not within the master plan, to be sure. This was the essence of a good Rhuyh Klaxxin: thwart the master plan with a better one of your own. His had been working precisely. The girl's sentinel had been lured away on a false scent; his embodiment had been skillfully accomplished, and the approach to the sleeping girl was entirely unnoticed — or so he had thought until his back caught fire with searing agony.

He could only imagine that some other dark one had been plotting the same treachery and had interrupted his attempt. He was twice miserable now, licking his wounded pride and feeling the result of two insults to his body. He pulled the darkness of the chamber around himself and sulked as his master droned on endlessly. This was not the end of anything.

CHAPTER SIX

A young man sat on a ridge that rose steeply above the western limits of his family compound. The sun was making its descent into the distant horizon, but would disappear sooner tonight than usual; a bank of menacing gray clouds was racing to capture the sun in its arc. The silent watcher could already detect a slight hint of moisture on the breeze which had shifted from his back to his face.

He had been timing the approach of a small band of travelers, counting their number and waiting for them to get close enough to identify. The clouds, he reckoned, would be overhead just about the same time the caravan rounded the pass at the northern reach of the ridge on which he sat. They might just make it into the compound before it became dark.

When the sun and clouds met, the light dropped enough that it was impossible to distinguish colors in the traveler's drapes. The young man was still uncertain of their identity and so anxious to know that he ignored caution and headed down the western face of the hill to meet them. He chose a path that would intersect theirs at the road and keep himself invisible to them. He did not want to be mistaken for a robber, sneaking up on them from a position of ambush, but he wanted to have the choice of the time and place of his revelation or seclusion in case they turned out to be unfriendly.

By the time he reached the level of the road near the pass, it became clear that this was not the group he had hoped. They appeared to be men of position, although they were not traders, a fact that was obvious by the small number of beasts of burden in their entourage. They had only enough pack animals to sustain them through an occasional night on the road. A large tent was laid over the back of one donkey and two others had what appeared to be water bottles and the typical utensils of travelers.

There were three men in the train: two masters and one servant, judging by the latter's position at the rear with the donkeys. The two led the way seated regally on fine looking horses, walking side by side. Their demeanor suggested military training, yet they carried only minimal weapons as far as the young spy could see. Besides, they seemed to be riding into the pass without a thought for their safety; men of war would know better than to act so carelessly. In his boyhood he had always imagined this was the perfect place for an ambush. He had pretended as much with his brothers from behind the very rock which now concealed him from the approaching group.

They were close enough to be heard faintly now. They were apparently having a friendly debate over something. The one on the right, slightly taller and broader than his companion, sported a sharply trimmed curly black beard and animated bushy eyebrows that danced as he talked. His skin was dark, even by the standards of those who spent their lives working in the sun. He was gesturing dramatically as he argued his points. The one on the left obviously disagreed with his partner, shaking his head now and then in defense against the lively arguments. He was plump in the face and of ruddy complexion, obviously not accustomed to being out in the sun regularly. His voice had a sharp whining sound, making it unpleasant to listen to.

The sounds just became words in the ears behind the rock as the black beard was saying, "I tell you, he is just a harmless crazy man — an eccentric to be pitied. What harm can one religious outcast do? You are not so religious that you care what others think, are you?"

"I am religious enough to know that the gods can make or break a man in this world of theirs," came the reply. "Who is to say that the cloud which has covered the sun will not send fire from the sky and leave you smoldering on the ground? In the time of our fathers, there never were such things. It is a great evil which blots out the sun and pours down its light only in burning streaks. More and more these clouds are gathering. Can you tell me it is not because of the self-righteousness of such crazy men as you call him?"

"I think you listen to the priests too much," black beard replied. "They want to protect their station. It would not do for every man to find his own peace with the gods — that would undermine their ability to exact tribute and offerings."

"Do not underestimate the power of these priests, Delzar. Don't forget that they are responsible for the rising water in our city wells. Soon we will be able to reach the water without a rope. This kind of power you must not fight. I have seen stronger men than you groveling before them, begging to give tribute. Dark and mysterious things have happened to those who have openly crossed them. You know they are not happy with your decision to leave them."

A few meters above them and to the south a young man crouched behind his protective rock and listened.

"But look at this one: he defies them openly and seems to live on in prosperity," Delzar responded. "Be reasonable Donar; could one crazy old man bring about changes in the earth and sky. My father told the ancient stories before they were banned; there were others like this crazy one. Perhaps he is just the last of a dying race."

The riders had passed beyond the hidden one and their voices became lost in the distance, muffled by treading hooves and the fact that they faced away from him now. Their conversation tantalized the young man's curiosity; he could not imagine who they were talking about, but yearned to find out. His interest in their debate had caused him to forget his disappointment that they were not the people he had been waiting for.

After the train was well past, he moved out from his hiding place and headed over the rise toward home. He kept to the hill with its brush and small trees as cover as he paralleled their course. The road curved around several small rock outcroppings, making it a longer path to the compound than his beeline through the trees. Besides, he was trotting at a pace slightly faster than their horses' walk. This would bring him to his home several minutes before the travelers arrived there.

As the young man broke from the trees near the outskirts of the family enclave, he tossed a quick glance over his shoulder. Less than two hundred meters down the road the party he had been pacing was steadily approaching the front entrance. Obviously they meant to seek water and shelter for the night; there was apparently no cause for concern. In fact, Sha'ym was glad they were stopping; it would give him a chance to listen in on more of their discussions about the climatic changes which were such a curiosity. Then too, there would undoubtedly be news from the cities, maybe they had even crossed paths with Imanaq recently.

"Father," he shouted, somewhat out of breath from his run, "we have visitors coming." He surveyed the compound for signs of his father's whereabouts. The main house in the center had smoke curling out of the vent in the roof. His mother, he reasoned would be cooking supper at this time, but it was too early for his father to be inside yet. He scanned the other structures and noticed one of his younger brothers standing near a pen on the south side of the grounds. He appeared to be talking with someone near the compound wall behind the lean-to shed which served to house a few goats.

He cupped his hands and shouted in that direction, "Yefeth! Is Father with you?"

His youngest brother turned toward him and replied, "Yes, one of the goats has twisted a leg, and he's trying to save it."

Sha'ym trotted over to the corral. "Father, there are travelers approaching..."

"Is it Imanaq?" he interrupted.

"No, it is an unusual group of men — there are two men and a servant. They are not merchants."

"Do they appear to be military scouts?" his father asked as he finished wrapping a strip of cloth tightly around a stick-splint on the goat's leg.

"No," came the reply, "At least I was unable to see the typical weapons of soldiers."

"How far off are they?" the father asked as he stood and looked past his eldest son toward the entrance.

"Nearly to the gate, I imagine." As he spoke, he turned to see the black bearded one striding into the opening.

As soon as the stranger noticed the three of them standing facing him, he extended his right hand forward in salute and said, "Delzar of Tyriea bids you greetings in the names of all the gods. Peace and prosperity to the master of this city."

It was a standard bit of protocol, although the designation of Nuwach's compound as a city was unarguably false flattery to say the least. Had the stranger known anything of the master's disdain for cities, he would have withheld that ploy altogether.

"It is Nuwach who welcomes you in the name of the god who has made Araq and the skies. By his providence I can offer you rest in my humble camp," Nuwach returned as he started walking toward the stranger. "If you come in peace you would honor me with your presence at our table this night?"

"It would be my honor to sit with you, noble sir," the black beard replied, again elevating Nuwach to a complimentary status.

"Then you are welcome — your companion and servant also. My servants will see to your beasts." By this time, Nuwach had reached the entrance and stopped where he could see past the speaker to his caravan beyond. As he looked over the entourage, he agreed with his son: it was hard to determine the nature of the business these men held. He too would be anxious for conversation around the fire later.

A short time later, after the donkeys had been relieved of their burdens and watered, Nuwach and two of his three sons were joined at table by the strangers, Delzar and Donar. The interior of the main house was simple. Nuwach and his sons were as much carpenters as farmers. The table, the benches on which they sat, indeed, every piece of furniture had been fashioned from timbers taken from the plentiful stands nearby. The work was not as ornate as some found in the cities, but it was precise and highly functional.

The outer walls of the building were formed of roughly shaped cedar logs which were notched at the corners and pilasters which framed each of the doors front and rear. A compound of pitch and vegetable fibers was laid between each layer of logs to keep out the wind. Inner walls were of rudely woven cloth stretched across frames made from split cedar. A fire burned in a stone-circled pit in the center of the main room. The table and benches stood a couple meters from the fire.

After a satisfying meal of seasoned, baked gourds and an assortment of fresh vegetables and bread, the men took up positions around the gently flickering fire, now the main source of light in the room. Conversation at the table had been limited to courtesies and compliments on the food. The three boys were pleased that their father thought them old enough to join the circle. All those around the fire, each with his own reasons, were now interested in turning to more serious topics.

Donar began his agenda: "How long have you been here, Nuwach?"

"I have seen more harvests from this vineyard than I can count," the elder one replied, his gaze remaining on the fire.

"In that time, has the sun often been veiled?" Donar continued to probe.

"We see the sun much more often than the clouds," came the short reply.

"Yes," Donar replied, somewhat liturgically, "the sun god makes his power felt in spite of the darkness."

"The god who made the sun has also made the clouds which veil it," Nuwach countered.

Donar bristled. Delzar broke in before his companion's heated thoughts could escape, "You are obviously a man of great wisdom, Nuwach. Time must have taught you a great many things concerning the gods. Before you came to this beautiful spot, were you also engaged in farming?"

Sha'ym was impatient to change the subject from his father and the gods to more contemporary topics, particularly concerning the whereabouts of Imanaq and Sharaq. But, it would be improper for him to change the subject chosen by his elders, so he chafed under the present discussion.

"I have always been what you call a farmer," Nuwach responded as he raised his eyes to meet the stranger's. "I think man is most fulfilled when he remains close to the Araq."

"This may be true," conceded Delzar, "for I have seen more fighting and disagreements in cities than on farms. Farmers continue to till the soil and herdsman to follow their flocks no matter who is king in the city; isn't that so?"

Nuwach continued to look into the stranger's eyes while he nodded slowly in agreement. He wondered what the well-spoken flattery of the black-bearded one presaged.

"You were not here when this place bloomed altogether, were you? I am sure you know there was a time when grasses covered this plain. Now the only thing growing is dust raised by the winds which chase the clouds."

The old man could see that this stranger had serious questions, but could not imagine why he was being asked for answers. Perhaps it was just the opportunist taking advantage of an elder's knowledge.

"When you were younger, before my time, did the fire fall from the sky?" Delzar asked.

Nuwach looked up, as if searching for a window into time past, then began, "In the days of my fathers, the sun walked across the sky with no company. There were no days of veiling, no shadows. At night, the moon was a soft glow when its time was full. When my father was a boy, men began to count stars in the sky as they multiplied like mice over time.

"As the stars increased, so men increased their fascination with them. The sun grew hotter by day, and the moon and stars brighter by night. Before I took a wife, I saw the first wisps of clouds. They were like feathers from a giant bird floating across the sky.

"Men began to see this as the war of the sky gods. They lost faith in the god who made Araq, the god of my fathers, my god." With this he looked back into the eyes of the stranger.

When their eyes met, Delzar felt slightly uncomfortable, as if he were being gently challenged. "But you have not lost faith," he said.

Nuwach picked up a hefty stick which had been lying near his feet and poked at the logs on the waning fire. By repositioning them he caused a fresh blaze of light to leap from between their glowing surfaces.

Nuwach looked deeply into Delzar's eyes. "There is great disharmony with the Araq. Men in the cities follow after the gods of every tree and bird and beast; this is not right. This brings about much confusion and distress in the Araq and the skies. Man must stay in harmony with the Araq or he will die. The only way to live is in harmony with the Araq; this can only be achieved by remaining in harmony with the god who made the Araq."

Donar interrupted, "This is the old religion; we have progressed beyond these old myths."

Nuwach's ancient eyes bored into the puffy-faced man's arrogance. "Yes, it is old; my father taught it to me; his father to him, and his father was there when the Araq was formed. It is old because it is true."

The visitors around the fire squirmed a little; partly because of the ring of truth in the old man's words. Then he continued, "The god who made the Araq and the skies will not allow this disruption to continue forever. The disorder will destroy the whole creation if it is not stopped." Looking at Delzar he added, "Surely you can see this in the skies even now."

Delzar found himself nodding his head involuntarily. He reached up and stroked his beard as if to stop the assenting motion, but could not help seeing the wisdom in the words of his host.

"There is a special relationship between the Araq and the sky. The plants show us this; we bury their seeds in the ground, and they reach up toward the sky. Men look into the dark sky of night searching for meaning in the lights there; they build temples to the sun, moon and stars; they exact tribute for the maintenance of these temples." The old man put down the stick and returned his gaze to the stranger. "Why is this?"

Donar had been listening in silence too long, so he blurted out his answer, "To please the gods, of course."

Delzar closed his eyes and sighed slightly, as if he had lost something.

Nuwach shifted his gaze to the puffy red face of the impatient one and said, "And are they pleased?"

"Sometimes...most of the time, yes," he responded. "We are very prosperous in Armoun, and the gods have protected us from invasions for many years. Yes, I would say they are pleased with us."

At the mention of Armoun, Sha'ym was especially alert. Perhaps he could bend the conversation more to his interests with this. "There must be many merchants who trade in Armoun, is this not so?"

"Yes," Donar answered, turning to the younger man with pride in his voice, "We have a market that surpasses any in Tyriea. Even the coastal cities are jealous of the merchants in Armoun." This kind of talk was of great interest to Chamah, Sha'ym's middle brother. He talked endlessly of the bright glitter that the mysterious cities held. Sha'ym had other interests.

"Do you know of a caravaner named Imanaq?" the young man asked. "He is known to trade in Armoun."

"A multitude of caravans trade with our merchants; I am not familiar with all of them..."

"This man has a daughter named Sharaq who travels with him; she is..." At this point he paused briefly, for he felt himself strangely at a loss for the right word. He had never tried to describe Sharaq before. "She is very beautiful," he concluded.

"There are so many beautiful women in Armoun. In fact, the temple at Armoun is known to have the most beautiful women in all the land. And they are more than just a pleasure to look at, if a young man such as yourself can understand what I mean." With this he cast a look as Sha'ym that made the young man uncomfortable.

Delzar saved him from the embarrassment of replying by asking Nuwach a question more to his own purpose again. "Did the clouds begin to veil the sun at the time men began to turn from the ancient god?"

"There is wisdom in your question," Nuwach began. "The words of the fathers speak of a time when men began to seek to please themselves instead of the god who made them. This happened when Araq was very young. The clouds did not come until many sons later, but I think that they are part of the same relationship. Men must try to live in harmony with Araq. All the beasts and plants know this; only men fight with their maker."

Sha'ym had heard this before: live in harmony with the soil, the plants, the animals. The god who made us formed us from dirt and when we die we go back to it. Araq is the mother of men and god is their father. This was all in the words of the fathers which Nuwach had begun to teach his son. Only now did Sha'ym begin to see any connection with what happened on a larger scale.

"I believe the strong one who made Araq would have all men cease striving and live in harmony," Nuwach continued. "The changes in the sky will be understood by those who seek to walk with the ancient one."

"Those who seek to walk with him," Donar broke in, "must be careful that they don't fall into disfavor with those who now rule the Araq."

Nuwach stiffened and stared at the puffy-faced one with searing eyes. "At this time, the requirements of honor and the duties of courtesy war within me. You are welcome to stay the night here. In the morning you will be on your way."

Delzar again interceded, "Forgive my companion, noble sir. His zeal for his gods overtakes his manners at times. Accept my apology for his affront. We respect your devotion to the ancient god you worship." Saying this he too gave Donar a look that clearly was meant to silence him. Looking across the fire at his host he continued, "If we have not fallen from your graces completely, I would be interested to hear how the harmony you speak of can be achieved."

"It has been the same from the beginning; honor the god who made us, care for your family, care for the Araq," came the simple reply. Even Sha'ym could have said as much; it was in the words of the fathers.

Delzar was quiet for a few moments, looking into the fire, obviously thinking. Then he said, "Men everywhere take wives and raise families; not everyone is closely tied to the Araq, but each one reveres her in his own way, for she is the source of all food. It must be in the matter of honoring the ancient god that we fall short of the ancient words." He looked again at Nuwach, "Is this true?"

Nuwach sensed a sincerity in the stranger's questions, yet he was troubled by his responsibility not to insult his guests. To truly answer the question would condemn the travelers' worship and probably their very lives. Instead of answering, he exercised the host's prerogative and said, "The night is getting on. Morning will find us tired if we linger. I will speak more in the morning." With this he rose, and courtesy compelled his guests and sons to rise with him. "Good rest to you."

It was some time before Sha'ym went to sleep. He was disappointed that he had not learned anything about Sharaq; he was also sorry his father had cut off the discussion just as it seemed to become interesting. The youth in him did not discern the strangeness in these strangers as did the wisdom of his father. That his father was very old was not unknown to him, but he had never deeply considered what it meant to have lived for several hundred years. If the Araq was changing as people observed, then his father could chronicle those changes better than most.

As these thoughts swirled through his sleepless mind, another suddenly surfaced: what had his father done prior to settling here — prior to starting this family. Surely he had not been unmarried and childless all those years. It startled Sha'ym to realize that he might have brothers and sisters somewhere that he had never met. It then startled him to realize that this had been true for his entire life, and he had not thought of it before. He suddenly felt blind and very small-minded.

This must be what it means to grow up, he thought. To make discoveries that reveal how little you know. The world of the compound, the vineyard and the surrounding hills had seemed whole and complete for all those years. Even his longing to see other places was somehow an extension of this place; this was the center of the Araq. Expeditions might be made into other regions, but always with the thought that this place would be home — that one would always return.

During all the years of listening to caravaners tell of foreign lands, he had seen them only as entertainment or a diversion. They were to him as vistas seen through the window of his house — pleasing, even fascinating, but somehow not quite real. Now, with the thought that his father had spent three, four, even five hundred years out there, they took on a new reality.

This was growing up: to see oneself grow smaller.

In the morning, after the men had broken bread and drank the vegetable juice prepared by Nuwach's wife, they led their reloaded animals to the gate. Sha'ym having fallen asleep shortly before the rising of the sun almost missed their departure; the rustling of the animals in the yard woke him so that he ran up just as his father was preparing to send them off.

There appeared an odd solemnity about his father's manner. True, a host properly gave his guests a blessing as they left his gate, but these strangers would not typically have merited more than the most perfunctory courtesy. Nuwach seemed to be investing great seriousness in his speech as Sha'ym came into hearing.

"If it is indeed the truth you are seeking," Nuwach was saying, "then, I am prepared to reveal it to you." The old man paused to read the eyes of the black beard. Satisfied with what he discerned, he continued, "There are many things in the city that displease the ancient one who made the Araq and the sky. The temples to those who are not gods are the most distasteful, but there is much more. In the city, people are more concerned with prosperity than propriety. This is selfishness. To do what is right must be first; to do what succeeds is incidental.

"Moreover, the ways of pleasure are vastly perverted. There is a place for women; there is a place for wine; there is a place for song. The ancient one has given all these to men for good purpose; men have turned them to their own purpose. Thus enters greed and lustful thoughts into the heart. Men no longer care for family when they cease to care for the honor of the god who made them. Men no longer care for the Araq when their only thought is how to advance their fortunes.

"I did not tell you this last night because I did not wish to insult you as my guests. Now you are travelers on the road away; forgive my boldness if it has affronted you, but you have asked for the truth — I have spoken it as I know it."

Delzar had not yet mounted his horse and stood looking at Nuwach in silence. His eyes strayed to the hills beyond the compound, his thoughts to the distant city he called home.

Something rang true in the old man's words, yet he was not ready to accept the totality of his pronouncements.

"Come!" Delzar's thoughts were interrupted by the impatient growl of his companion. "We must be getting on the road," Donar urged. "Let this old man die in his old ways."

Sha'ym's attention was drawn sharply to the source of this outburst. There on his horse, with the sun behind his shoulders, there was a darkness about the rider that made the young man shiver unaccountably. His puffy face had seemed merely discontented before; now it fairly glowed with malice. Being uncomfortable looking at him, Sha'ym returned his eyes to his father. Squinting slightly from the bright morning sun, he was looking at the mounted curser.

"May it be so, and gladly," he said smoothly. "But pity the man who dies in the new ways."

Donar let out a breath in such disgust that it almost sounded like a growl; as he did so, he wheeled his horse around and headed back down the road which had brought him there yesterday. Delzar mounted, looked once again at Nuwach without his partner's malice, and followed.

"I wonder if they got what they came for," Nuwach said after a moment of silence. Sha'ym hadn't considered that they were returning from whence they came, implying that this had been their destination. His father's words struck this thought like a hammer on an anvil.

"What did they come for, father?"

"I suspect they came to see an old fool." The words shocked the youth, but before he could think to say anything his father continued, "Perhaps it will be best if they found one."

CHAPTER SEVEN

With the sun at their backs, four creatures hovered, watching as the caravan started down the road toward Armoun. Mistrea and his apprentice were accompanied by two of the region's overseers. They were both nearly the size of Mistrea, so Multar was dwarfed by his companions, though he felt very large in purpose.

"This is the fortress which is of immediate concern, Mistrea," one of the overseers was saying. "As you can see, its presence is not unknown to the enemy." By this he referred to the dark shape traveling with one of the riders. The dark one's size, hardly bigger than the human he attended, indicated that he was no more than a peon, a scout perhaps.

"Have any forces of significance been here?" Mistrea asked his guide.

"Nothing more than the personal hosts that attend the frequent travelers who stop here," came the reply. "They are easily confused by the zensak screen at the wall of the compound. It is enough to befuddle them without alerting them to its presence. They attribute the confusion they feel to the lingering essence of the old religion which Nuwach still practices. They typically stay outside the enclave and occasionally joust with the local demis in the hills and trees.

"The battle we foresee will take place somewhere between here and Armoun, if we can arrange it thus. We are not anxious to be found protecting the fortress of Nuwach this early in the game if we can avoid it. The activities of his family outside of the compound, particularly in Armoun, pose the immediate challenge. One of the chosen ones is entangled there; we had a close call with her yesterday. Talizar can tell you more about that later."

Mistrea noticed traces of the demis his guide had referred to in the trees lining the road just ahead of where the caravan was currently moving. "How has Nuwach escaped the influence of the locals for all these years? They appear to be as entrenched here as anywhere," he asked.

"There has been protection ever since he came here years ago. The Father of Lights has had a special relationship with him for centuries. The old man's guardian will tell you more when you see him."

"Yes, I was thinking," Mistrea interrupted, "where is the family guardian?"

"He is surveying Nuwach's servants' activities in the North. Nuwach had a few men busy there harvesting trees to be used in the construction of the compound. Iadrea will return soon with an estimate of our needs there."

"Iadrea?" Mistrea exclaimed. "He who aided Gebarour?"

"The same; they fought side by side in the Rebellion. he has earned a great deal of power."

Multar joined his master in the magnitude of this thought. They momentarily reminisced about stories that teacher had shared with pupil. Stroke by stroke Gebarour and Iadrea had cut their way through scores of dark minions to save a besieged company of attenders. It was said that Gebarour's sword grew more powerful with each stroke as he slashed his way into enemy ranks. From stories such as these, hopeful attenders drew strength and courage that they too could be tested and found worthy in battle.

"Master," Multar finally spoke out loud, "if Gebarour has assigned Iadrea to this fortress, is it not then of some great importance to the plan?"

"Your young companion shows some wisdom, Mistrea," the second guide now spoke. "Does he understand also the importance of discretion in using names and discussing strength?"

"This is his first foray into a battle zone," Mistrea replied. "I will make discretion our first lesson today."

"That would be well. We must not place this fortress at risk because of a novice's ignorance."

"Chantar," the first guide broke in, "I am going to follow the travelers for a while. Last night it seemed that the black bearded one might be truly interested in the ideas of Nuwach. Perhaps I can do something to help convince him."

"Very well, Doulas. Things appear calm here for now. Remain in close communication, however; we may need you back here at a moment's notice," his companion replied. "We will see you at the gathering tonight if not before."

"As you wish. If I feel an embodiment is called for, I will check with you." With this he raised large colorful wings in the morning sun and sailed off in the direction of the small caravan now threading its way into the pass northwest of the compound. Passing a great distance over their heads, he dropped quickly toward the plain beyond the ridge and circled back. He positioned himself behind the same rocks Sha'ym had chosen for his observation the day before. Soon the travelers were within earshot.

"I am certain that is the name I have heard, Delzar," the puffy face was insisting.

"Even if it is, my friend, aren't the purification rights sufficient for any virgin? Why would it matter if this one knows of a rival god?"

"Don't you see," Donar whined, "That if Imanaq is of some concern to Nuwach.... How many traders must pass this way? The interest in this one tells me there is some connection worth investigating."

As Delzar remained in silent thought for a few moments, Doulas carefully inspected the invisible member of the caravan who hovered closely over Donar's head. Their earlier estimate had been correct: He was nothing of consequence, at least, not for a warrior of Doulas' skill, especially when cloaked adequately in zensak as he was now.

He drifted along a course parallel to the road, invisible to men and spirit alike, listening to the conversation.

"Think this through, Donar," the black beard reasoned. "If this trader were of the same religious persuasion as Nuwach, would he allow his daughter to be betrothed to the son of the lugal? He must recognize that she would be subjected to rituals and ceremonies at the temple. For a full year she will be pledging her allegiance to Inanna and Dumuzi. Long before the ram's horn scribes her womb she will have given herself totally to him and in turn to the Evening Star herself."

Now it was Donar who rode in silence, unusual for him. What Delzar said was true; it seemed clear enough, yet something plagued him as if a voice were whispering caution in his ear. Indeed, from Doulas' position, this was precisely the case, for drifting directly in front of his charge, a small demon was staring at the human and desperately trying to put thoughts into his head.

Doulas began projecting a few thoughts of his own into Delzar's receptive mind. Nuwach's perspective was valuable if only because of his great age. If there were some connection between the changes in the skies and the actions of men, this man might have the objectivity necessary to see it. The conflicting explanations of the priests Donar so respected certainly weren't convincing.

"Donar," Delzar began to speak, "if all these changes were related to Nuwach's god, why all the fuss about Sababba spreading wings of war against Meslantaea. Nuwach cares nothing about the great god of the mighty cedars or the wings of Sababba."

While Donar thought briefly, Doulas marveled at the casual mention of these mighty powers. Sababba and Meslantaea were well-known to him; no attender would long take wing over Araq without facing their forces at some time. Not that Doulas would likely meet either one directly; they were world-rulers more on the level of Iadrea — or perhaps closer to the power of Gebarour himself.

"I am not a priest, Delzar, that I can explain what the gods do," Donar parried, unable to come up with a reasonable answer for his companion. "I only know that Gishnan, the servant of Dumuzi, the god of your master Lamaq, sent us to question this Nuwach. Priests seldom reveal the reasons behind their requests. You should know that better than I; you were apprenticed to the priesthood."

Doulas pierced Delzar's mind with the thought that the priests themselves seldom knew the reasons for what they did, much less why things happened in the sky. Nuwach's simple view of a god pleased or displeased with the actions of men was good common sense.

"If Inanna were the supreme power," Delzar countered, "would she not have control over the gods of the sky and the Araq?" This very question was at the core of Delzar's reason for leaving the priesthood.

Unwilling to give in on this point, Donar side-stepped by saying, "What is your point?"

"It is obvious that neither the ever-spreading wings of Sababba, nor the towering strength of Meslantaea's cedars, nor even the Evening Star herself has complete rule. Our stories are full of battles between these and other gods who each claim to be the master of all. We now claim Dumuzi as our deliverer from the powers in Kamaresh, yes?"

Donar gave a tentative harumph.

"Why do we constantly worry that Kamaresh will again attack and overcome us?" Delzar gave his companion a moment to think. "Is it simply because Hursag has pledged allegiance to Ningirsu. He looked at his companion for a moment. "It is because," he continued, "there is no guarantee they won't attack. No thinking man believes that Dumuzi can keep Ningirsu out of Armoun forever."

Donar's dark partner was wildly flapping his wings and foaming at the mouth trying to get a counter-thought into his charge's befuddled brain. Finally the fleshy-mouthed rider shifted on his saddle to face his companion, "This is nothing but blasphemy, Delzar. You had better hope that En-lil has no listeners on the wind here to carry your words back to Dumuzi."

The black-bearded one threw his head back in a hearty laugh. "My friend," he said, still chuckling, "the way you talk, one would think that even now invisible beings were hovering about us waiting to catch us in a trap. I do not think myself so significant that the gods would bother with me."

Donar began to wonder if his carefree companion were right. As the thought crossed his mind, the dark one he carried rose up and grasped the fleshy head with his clawed feet. Pain developed immediately in the human's skull, slowly increasing in intensity. "No!" he said out loud, "Give honor to Dumuzi; give honor to the Conquering Ram." At this expression of allegiance, the claws slowly withdrew, and the pain subsided gradually.

Doulas decided he had done all he could do for now to cast doubt in Delzar's mind, but he didn't want to leave without pestering the dark one directly. He didn't dare send him to Qavah Khoshek, though it would have been a simple one-stroke job. If the dark pest didn't report to his master, the trip to Nuwach's would take on too much importance to the host at Armoun. No, a tease is all he could afford.

The attender, still cloaked and invisible to the travelers, took a position just above them as they rode and hovered along the road. Reaching down, he grabbed two clawed wingtips and immediately shot upward and backward as fast as the wings of Mentridar would take him. When he had nearly completed a full backward circle and neared the road surface, he let go of the helpless gargoyle. The momentum carried the dark one gasping several meters under the road. Before he could worm his way through the sand and packed earth back to the surface, the laughing attender was long gone. The black creep never knew what hit him.

A great distance above the dusty country of Tyriea a group of attenders was gathering. In the center of a nearly spherical formation was a glow of light roughly shaped like those around it. Immediately around this shape were several similar beings, smaller and dimmer, yet still awesome to behold. Next in order was another ring and so on like the layers of an onion. If one could have seen the creatures clearly, they would have looked like a bright glow surrounded by concentric rings of lesser brilliance, each revolving slowly around the center. However, the entire formation was veiled in a seven layer envelope of zensak, giving it the appearance of a large fluffy cloud.

Gebarour was holding court.

By nature of his master's position, Multar was far closer to the center of things than he would have been on his own. Mistrea, as god of a lesser planet, merited a position in the second circle, although he was not as luminous nor as large as others in that sphere. Multar was a mere speck, in his own eyes, next to the attenders gathered near him. He was awed.

The gathering came to order with songs, incredible harmonies transmitted by thought among the beings assembled there and presented as an offering to the ultimate Master of them all. The pulsing, fluid sound shot upward toward the source of light dispersing like the waters of a cosmic fountain throughout the entire galaxy and beyond.

After the harmony flowed on for a few minutes, a thought from the center said, "Peace and light to all those who gather in the name of him who is light."

The response, still in glorious harmony, welled out from the whole assembly, "Strength, honor and dominion to the one who is before all things. May we attend him with the full brilliance of our beings."

The mutual edification of joining minds, hearts and strength in this fashion always rejuvenated the feeblest light among them. Multar was completely enraptured by the whole situation, so it was nearly overwhelming when the central being welcomed Mistrea by name and alluded to his young aide as well.

"It is always a pleasure to welcome those from other galaxies, but this visit is especially timely; Mistrea and his apprentice have brought us reserves of Zensak and a wealth of cxings for the reinforcements soon to arrive." Then indicating one in the inner circle, the thought from the center continued, "Iadrea, bring us your report on the situation at the fortress of Nuwach."

One of the tremendous beings who had been orbiting just outside the center of the formation moved slightly toward the center and began, "Mighty Gebarour, may the light preserve you. Things are progressing nearly as expected at the fortress; the materials required for the next phase of the construction are being transported even now. Chantar and Doulas report that some interest is developing among the dark ones at the temple of Armoun, but no scouts have yet been dispatched, so we think they are only curious. This is inevitable given the concentration of power. The additional zensak delivered by the honorable Mistrea will no doubt help us maintain secrecy.

"I have reports that some impediments to the whole scheme may be imminent at Armoun. Talizar, the guardian of the city will give details of the situation there."

At this point Iadrea slipped back into formation in the inner circle and there was an almost imperceptible shift of focus in the orb to a place several layers out where Talizar waited. "Worthy master," he began, "one of the chosen was targeted for an attack by one of the dark lieutenants. I do not think it is of great significance, but is only their typical lusting after flesh, especially innocent flesh.

"I had been keeping a close eye on the girl and her father ever since they were lured into staying with the lugal. His son has romantic interests in this one whom the Master has chosen for his purposes. Since I dared not enter the city openly, I chose to materialize as a small cat, hoping to thus gain close access to our people.

"The dark host there evidently also has plans for this girl, as there was a sentry posted near her. Fortunately, he was unable to discover me in my embodied form. (I cloaked myself just to be certain.) However, last night after the girl had fallen asleep, one of the host, Glaxxin, I believe he is called, intentionally drew the sentry away. This accomplished, he took on a semi-human form and began to initiate intercourse with the sleeping maiden.

"I am ashamed to say that I too had been tricked by his luring of the sentry, and by the time I discovered the ruse and returned to my post, he was just about to conquer the girl. I summoned all my light to the claws of the creature I had become and threw myself on the back of the demon as he lay on his prize.

"Fortunately, the surprise was sufficient to send him screaming out of the building; indeed, he was so frightened that he left my range of sensing completely. For this I am grateful, as I would have stood little chance against one of his size by myself."

"You are to be commended, Talizar," the one in the center said, followed by a hum of approval from those gathered around him, "and do not be too hard on yourself for being led temporarily astray. The enemy has many tricks by which he deceives some of the best warriors. You were wise to see the deception in time to save the chosen one."

"Did the dark one return to search for his attacker?" the mighty Gebarour asked.

"No. I am in hopes that he may think it was one of his own trying to spoil his conquest. It may also be that he was acting without orders and dared not return. I have left watchers there in case a reoccurrence should take place.

"To our good fortune, the mysterious happening made the girl so frightened that she has beseeched her father to depart the city as soon as they can make ready. This will make protection much easier for us."

"Well done, servant. This will no doubt help further the master's plan," Gebarour agreed. Then, turning his attention back to the inner circle, he asked, "Mistrea is it true that you will be with us for some days?"

"Yes, worthy one," he replied. "The Master has given me leave from Mentridar to help here for a time. I will see to the placement of the Zensak at Nuwach's and await the reinforcements who will require the gift of wings."

"Excellent. It is always good to have one such as you among us," Gebarour complimented, making Mistrea's young apprentice nearly burst with pride.

At this point the concentration of the gathering was broken by a messenger who sailed through the cloud, between the rings of attenders and stopped just inside the inner circle. It was Hamayn from Armoun.

"Speak, my son," Gebarour addressed the new arrival, "I sense you have urgent news."

"Forgive my interruption, honorable one," the messenger began, "but there is a conflict at Armoun which requires more strength than our reconnaissance force can muster. The chosen ones are preparing to leave the city, but the dark host is taking great pains to prevent them."

"Thank you, worthy servant," the leader said, then continued, "Iadrea, take a small force and engage the enemy. We must defend them without appearing too protective."

"I understand," Iadrea replied, then lifted huge wings and rose slowly through the crowd and mentally called a small host to follow him. They held formation just inside the Zensak envelope and their captain gave brief instructions before they took wing to Armoun.

Before the detachment sailed away, Mistrea addressed Gebarour, "May I take my young pupil and observe? He has not seen a battle."

"Certainly," came the reply, "but hide yourselves; you are too valuable to be compromised in a skirmish such as this."

"As you wish," Mistrea respectfully answered. Then to Multar he said, "Come!" and they were off after the host flying ahead of them to the city below.

To the human eye things appeared normal in Armoun; people were about the normal business of a day which held no special significance. But from the perspective of the group of attenders marshaled over the walled city, something important was happening. At several places in the city small groups of dark beings were busily fluttering about the activities of the humans nearby. Occasionally dark forms could be seen sliding in and out of the windows of the temple, whisking back and forth with messages.

Iadrea was talking with the messenger who had interrupted the gathering and Talizar, the guardian of the city. "There is a commotion about something, Talizar," he observed.

"Yes, it looks as though the enemy is attacking on two fronts. The activity in the marketplace seems to concern the taxes Imanaq owes on his imports. At the house of Lamaq the purpose is less clear, but it is obvious they are trying to confuse the girl."

"I don't think we have time for a battle of wits with these forces," Iadrea suggested. "If we are to get the chosen out of the city, I think a frontal attack is our only choice. It is obvious that the enemy has his own plans for these people — at least for the girl. To delay now may cause them to be lost to the master plan."

"As you say," Talizar agreed. "How shall we proceed?"

The captain thought for a moment, then turned to Mistrea, who was observing from a distance. "My friend," he addressed him, "you can be of great service to us and fulfill Gebarour's wish that you remain more or less concealed."

"What is your command?" came the willing reply.

"Can you throw a screen over the temple to cut off their communications briefly?"

"Certainly," he said. "There are columns of zensak near the atmosphere which can be placed at my command."

"Good," Iadrea continued. "As soon as you can accomplish that, we will attack the forces on the ground."

"It will be done in a moment," Mistrea said. Then to Multar, "Follow me; you will see what value all your gardening on Mentridar can have in a battle."

With that thought, the two raised wings and rocketed out of the planet's atmosphere to a position where cylinders of zensak were awaiting transport to the surface. The master of Mentridar stopped before a large mass of the smoky grey creatures and held out his arms. The response was a quivering and hum such that sound and movement became one.

"Again we enlist their aid," Mistrea explained to his pupil. "No creature is forced to participate in a dangerous situation. They are willing to be used in any way we choose.

"Meld yourself to the after portion of the cylinder, as I will to the front," he continued his directions. "When I give the order, we will fly this mass back to Armoun and drop it directly over the temple building. Can you do that?"

"How will I stay with you, master?" the eager young one asked.

"Simply unite your thoughts with mine; stay focused on the target and our purpose," came the response.

"Very well," Multar said. "I am ready!"

As soon as they were in position, the unit blasted into the atmosphere of Araq and dropped precisely over the target.

Iadrea and Talizar, having positioned their forces for attack, went into immediate action as soon as the tower was shrouded. Swooping down into he city with swords drawn, several of the attenders took their foes so completely by surprise that they were dispatched without knowing what hit them. The others, thus alerted, drew their awful rods and began swiping at their attackers.

Iadrea had chosen to go after the monster who was working over the city market. Although Iadrea was larger than his foe, the dark one was quick and very skilled with his rod. He was able to block several smashing cuts of the attender's brilliant sword. Then, according to the plan, Iadrea began backing out of the city, as if being driven.

Meanwhile, Talizar and his group were attempting a similar tactic. The dark ones they engaged were somewhat smaller than the creature Iadrea fought. Talizar was accosted by two of them at once, and found himself very busy indeed. The dark ones swung their rods and followed with sweeping claws. They timed their attacks so that one hit from the front just as the other swung at his back. At one point, sensing their approach, he shot straight up and they nearly collided with one another. As they spun around looking for him, he dropped back into the fray and sliced a wing off one and narrowly missed taking the other's head off.

Hoping they had engaged a fight, Talizar called his troops to fall back and regroup at the wall on the northern edge of the city. The dark ones took the bait and followed. Seeing their approach, the attenders moved into the hills and once again, flashing swords met crashing rods of darkness.

From high above the city, Mistrea and Multar watched as the plan developed perfectly. As Talizar and his group backed out of the northern quadrant into the hills, Iadrea was effecting a similar move out of the east gate near the marketplace. It appeared that the dark host was running the attenders up the road out of town.

Talizar's group took a stand just beyond the hills and Iadrea's battle moved gradually in their direction. As soon as the struggle had moved them through the pass above the town, Iadrea took a position south of the opening and stood his ground. It was a difficult task, the rod of his opponent thundering dangerously close to his darting form, but as soon as the two groups were in position, a signal was given and the attenders on both fronts pushed their evil counterparts backward with all their strength.

Soon the bright creatures had the dark host surrounded in a pincer and began closing the jaws. Talizar began to show his true power and overcame not two but three of the enemy, slashing them limb from body. There were a great many cries from the dark ones for help, and they were astounded that no one came to their aid, the temple being full of worthy soldiers. Of course, no one in the temple knew anything was amiss, shielded as they were by the thick blanket of zensak.

Most of the lesser demons had been dispatched to Qavah Khoshek when the largest remaining one realized he was doomed. Taking one last lunge at Iadrea with his rod, he broke free of the surrounding enemy circle and bolted into the sky. His loop took him in a path back toward the city; his intention being to drop straight into the temple and get reinforcements. Directly in his path, however were two more attenders, one large and one quite insignificant. He drove fiercely at the smaller one, thinking to smash him aside and careen into the temple.

When Multar saw him coming he nearly froze; snatching his sword at the last second, he prepared to block the massive rod that was plunging like an arrow at him. Before his sword met the coming doom, a blinding light flashed between the two and the weapon and the arms that held it fell aside, not without bumping the small one and casting him some distance away.

As Multar turned to look back, he saw his master and Iadrea following the wounded monster toward the city below. Having been slowed by Mistrea's interference, the demon was overtaken by his pursuer and in one more flash was without a wing. He began tumbling out of control and was struck again by Iadrea's sword in his shoulder. Then, with a thunderous voice the pupil had never heard from his master, Mistrea shouted, "To Qavah Khoshek for eternity!" and the dark one lost his head and disappeared.

At this point Multar, shaken seriously by his brush with doom, noticed the one called Chantar streak in from the southeast. He drew beside Iadrea and began speaking, "There is more trouble, Master," he began. "The second son and the servant Naashah are being attacked by tree sprites. Doulas is trying to hold them back."

"Well," the large one nearly gasped," this is a day for battles and victories, I think." He immediately signaled Mistrea to pull the zensak from the temple and simultaneously called the others to withdraw from the remaining skirmishes.

"Retreat into the hills as if running away," he commanded. "Meet me at the compound for further orders."

CHAPTER EIGHT

Early in the morning Sharaq went to see her Father. She was disturbed by the dream she had experienced and could not shake the cold feeling it left with her. She found her father sipping a hot drink while looking out the window of the second floor room.

"Good morning dearest daughter," he sang as she entered, but seeing the look on her face, changed his tone and asked, "What is wrong?"

"Oh, Father," she began, "this seems so foolish in the light of day. I had a dream last night...at least I think it was a dream; it was so real, and yet so very strange."

Imanaq sensed the disturbance his daughter was feeling. "Come and sit here by the window with me. Tell me about your dream; perhaps it has some meaning for your future." He reached out his hand to take hers as she walked toward him and he eased her into the seat beside him.

"I don't know what it could possibly tell us, Father," she said. "It did start out with Lamaq...I think it was him. We were married; I remember the wedding...there were ceremonies and..." She struggled to recall the earlier part of the dream. "All I really remember clearly is the last part."

"Tell me that part; often it is the truth that remains from a dream," her father coaxed her.

"Well," she continued, "Lamaq came to me...we were going to...be together," she was slightly uncomfortable at this recollection, as the feelings of anticipation again began to well up in her.

"Yes, daughter; I understand. Continue."

"It's hard for me to explain. We were just lying together.... It seemed so wonderful for a moment, Father, then suddenly there was a noise and a flash of light and it wasn't Lamaq anymore; I don't know who it was...or what...It was very confusing."

"What is the primary feeling that remains?" he asked.

"Mostly confusion, that and fear. The last instant was frightening, but it happened so fast that I can't really describe anything clearly."

"Quiet your mind," he said soothingly. "Let the feeling guide you," he paused momentarily. "Do you want to return to the time of the dream?"

"No," she responded immediately, "I am afraid the awful thing at the end will come back."

"Then perhaps this means you are not yet ready to accept Lamaq's proposal of marriage?" he posed.

She thought for a moment, basking in the sunlight streaming through the window. It all seemed so distant now, yet a lingering aura of foreboding gave substance to the memory, making her reluctant to experiment further.

"Perhaps you are right, Father," she concluded, looking into his face. She saw again the depth of his love for her and the wisdom of age, but she hated to disappoint him, thinking he wanted her to wed Lamaq. "Will you think me a silly young girl if I beg for more time to decide?"

"Not at all," he insisted. "You must do what you believe is right for you."

"But you will lose out on all the business Lamaq has promised," she protested.

"I would give up all the money in the world to make you happy," he said as he stroked her temple with the back of his hand.

She leaned over and kissed him on the cheek before saying, "I am the luckiest girl in the world to have a father like you; there can be no better one."

"Surely I am luckier to have a daughter such as you," he responded.

He stood up, offering her his hand as she followed. "Have you eaten?" he asked.

"No, I was too upset."

"Go back to your room. Have some figs and bread. Get your things ready to travel. I will go to the market and make arrangements to leave today."

"Father," Sharaq looked worriedly into his eyes. "Will Lamaq be angry?"

"He will no doubt be disappointed, but we aren't saying no to his proposal, are we?" he searched her eyes for her answer.

"No, I don't think so," came the uncertain reply.

"Good. Then we can simply say we need time to consider his generous proposal before we settle down here." Imanaq led her to the door of his apartment and returned her kiss on the cheek. "Do not worry; everything will turn out fine," he assured her. His true thoughts were not so sure, however. Disappointing Lamaq again could try the relationship beyond the breaking point. He kept this from his daughter, so he thought.

She gave him a little hug and left for her room, not fully assured at all.

The marketplace was beginning to hum with typical daily activity when Imanaq strolled into the square. He sought out the money keepers with whom Lamaq had arranged his financial dealings. Under a small canopy near the middle of everything he found who he was looking for.

The banker saw him coming. "Good morning, prosperous one," he greeted him. "You are here early. A man of your position should sleep away the morning and not worry himself with work."

"Greetings to you," Imanaq returned. "I am an old man, and habits formed during a lifetime die hard."

"So it is with me," he said. "What can I do for you this morning?"

"I am preparing to leave on a trading journey; can you settle my accounts today?"

A brief look of surprise crossed the banker's face, then he recovered and said without conviction, "Surely, but what has brought about this decision. I thought I heard you were settling here."

"That decision has not been made yet," Imanaq replied.

"I see; well, give me some time and I will see what you have."

With this announcement, a dark figure, invisible to the men, flew swiftly from his position over the banker into the temple. He drifted through a window and into a central room sealed off from the outside, allowing not a trace of light to enter. There a large black creature sat with huge wings folded behind his back, the scaly fingers on the tips hovering ominously about his sides, deadly claws prominently visible.

"Master," the diminutive one spoke, "the trader has asked for his account at the bank to be closed. He is leaving on a trading journey."

The massive wings rose slightly and the creature in the center of the room growled softly in a sinister sigh. "These humans keep messing up our plans. Fauxxin was just here with a request from the high priest. It seems that the lugal's son has prayed for help in keeping these very ones here in the city. Go back to your post. I will send reinforcements immediately." The giant wings nearly swept the smaller creature out of the room.

With a thought, another small being appeared in the room. "You needed me, master?" he asked in a squeaky voice.

"Yes, find out what is going on with the woman who is staying in the lugal's house. Find some way to make her comfortable — make her enjoy herself. We must convince her that she would be better off staying here."

"Yes, master," the small one said and was off.

When Sharaq returned to her room, it was not without the sense of confusion she had felt earlier. It was wonderful to have the servants and comforts of a house after all the years of traveling. The sunlight flooding the room nearly swept away the feeling of fear she had experienced from the dream. She looked at the soft feather mattress she had spent the last few nights on and compared it mentally to the straw mat on the ground which was her typical bed.

Then the thought of her father's part in all this struck her. He stood to gain by her marriage as well. He could send others traveling the dusty roads while he spent his days in comfort here in the city. No more cold nights and constant fear of robbers; no more of the sand storms that were becoming quite frequent lately. Yes, she thought, her father would be better off if she accepted Lamaq's offer.

The oddity of this last thought struck her next. What girl in the world would have any say in who or when she married. Here she was keeping her father from his right to place her as he wished. This made her feel very selfish indeed, to the point that it almost brought tears to her deep brown eyes. Who did she think she was, taking advantage of her father's love in this way? Just because he cared for her she had no right to force her will on him. She began to feel very low and selfish.

Lamaq would be more than disappointed too; he may even lose interest in a girl who couldn't make up her mind. What girl wouldn't jump at the chance to join the family of the lugal. Lamaq was handsome and strong; he had the admiration of everyone in the city; he would probably be the next lugal. He wouldn't stay interested in a girl who kept him waiting without good reason.

All these thoughts flooded her mind as she stared out the window at the street below. She could hear the noise and bustle from the marketplace. Then she was startled by a soft touch on her waist and a little squeaky meow as the kitten which had adopted her moved along the window sill and brushed against her. She picked it up and held it lightly in her arms. Looking into its eyes she suddenly remembered the yellow eyes that had momentarily flashed in her face that morning. A chill raced down her spine. What was it that made that vision so real?

To wash it from her eyes she looked out over the plain stretching south as far as the eye could see. The road wound along the eastern edge of the plain, appearing and disappearing as it slid over the rolling terrain until it vanished in the distance. Three days down that road was another world, a world she had always looked forward to visiting — Sha'ym's world. What a contrast: peace; quiet; even a sense of belonging which she never felt anywhere else.

Once again she felt the incongruity of her situation. Two more different lifestyles couldn't be imagined. How did she get into this predicament, she wondered.

Sharaq was shaken from her reverie a second time by the kitten, this time as it bolted suddenly from her arms and streaked across the room as if being chased by some invisible dog. Its action puzzled her, but then, kittens never did act in ways humans could understand. They seemed to be in a world all their own. She turned back to the window and to thoughts of the distant hills where she had always been so happy.

Meanwhile, Imanaq was experiencing a struggle of a different nature. First there was disagreement as to the amount of his account. The prices guaranteed by Lamaq were not being allowed. Once this was cleared up, the count of Imanaq's merchandise was disputed. In the end, the trader had to settle for less than the quantity he had brought, but the price was higher than expected, so he was satisfied with the final outcome.

The dickering and bickering had taken nearly an hour, so news of their intended departure had reached Lamaq before Imanaq returned to his home to get Sharaq. When he arrived, the two were in the central courtyard having an impassioned discussion. Lamaq, his back to the entrance, had both of her hands in his as if to keep her from backing away. She was trying not to look into his eyes as she struggled to explain why she needed more time to decide.

"It's not that I don't care for you," she was saying as her father walked in, "I am attracted to you in many ways. And I know that it is unusual for a father to give such decision making power to a daughter. You must understand; I am all he has. Since my mother died we have grown closer than most fathers and daughters," she tried to explain.

"And there is another proposal," her father interrupted. The couple, surprised by his presence, dropped their hands and turned to greet him.

"Good morning," Lamaq offered. "Yes, Sharaq has told me that a farmer has approached you, but how can this be compared to my offer? Surely you would not weigh them on the balance evenly."

"Nuwach is more than just a farmer," Imanaq explained. "Our friendship spans many years..."

"I know of this Nuwach," Lamaq cut in. "He was a trouble-maker here in Armoun years ago according to my father. He was driven from the city when he refused to sacrifice to Inanna. He claimed some higher god held his allegiance. He still follows this old religion, I hear. In fact, the last time he was in Armoun, he tried to tell us that we would all perish if we didn't join him in his ancient ways."

Turning to Sharaq he continued, "Surely you don't want to be wrapped up with a dying old heretic like that."

Suddenly, this attack on her father's wise old friend stirred her in his defense. "Nuwach has always been very kind to me. I don't know about the religious differences he has with others. He seems harmless enough; he doesn't hurt anyone with his beliefs."

"It may seem that way to you now," Lamaq parried, "but when Dumuzi decides to crush his opposition, you will be better off standing here than under his hooves."

"Perhaps you are right," Imanaq countered, "but give an old man one last trip to say good-bye to the many friends he has made in many places."

"Fine. Of course," Lamaq responded impatiently, "but let Sharaq remain here with me...that is as a guest in my house until you return."

"Your offer is appreciated," Imanaq answered, "but she too has friends to greet, and she is my only comfort and best helper on the road. Let us return to you willingly in three months. Then you will have many years together."

Lamaq did not hide his disappointment well. He cast about in his mind for another argument, but was at a loss to dissuade them from leaving. Anger began to well up in him at the thought of losing this prize and he considered other options. They were in his own house; he could take her now...kill her father...of course she would only be property then; she would never agree to marry him. Did that matter? Lust and rage battled against reason.

Suddenly he felt that he wanted her for more than her physical attractiveness; he wanted her to be completely his. If he had to wait three more months, he would wait.

Almost without realizing what he was saying, he spoke: "Go then, and part with your friends as you have said. I will look forward to seeing you at the end of your journey as soon as you can return."

"It is not yet too late to leave today," Imanaq suggested. "We will buy provisions and be on our way.

Lamaq once again took Sharaq's hands in his and looked deeply into her captivating brown eyes. "I will be unhappy until you return to me," he told her, nearly believing what he said.

She saw the desire in his eyes as she returned his glance. "Until we meet again," she returned.

Father and daughter walked together out of the courtyard and left a disappointed and somewhat confused young man standing alone. The air overhead was clearer than usual, but his thoughts were muddier.

CHAPTER NINE

There was struggle going on in the young man's mind. A struggle against unnamed bitterness and unrest. As the second son of his father, he knew that his older brother Sha'ym would get the best of everything, yet he resented the way he was treated. Not that Nuwach was ever cruel or unfair to any of his three sons, he knew that, but the favors seemed to flow heavily to Sha'ym. This trip was a good example. Being sent with servants to the forests to harvest timber was slave labor, although Nuwach would have no slaves per se. There had been much talk and artificial importance placed on the value of this mission, but it was obviously nothing more than a trip for building materials which dutiful servants had long been harvesting.

The need for more timber was unclear to the young man too. None of the livestock nor vineyard buildings was being used to capacity. Nuwach had built them generously large to begin with. The walls around the compound were unusually tall, almost as high as the walls of a city. Indeed, it was as if Nuwach were constructing a city, the compound comprising multi-story buildings while most farmers lived in low huts or even tents.

The mysterious new urgency for the project had servants and sons talking. Sha'ym was the only one thought to know what the structure was going to be used for, but if he did know, he wasn't talking.

"Come Chamah," a voice interrupted his thoughts, "You must leave the shade of that fine tree and continue homeward. We can be back tonight if we travel quickly. Your father will be anxious to hear our report. It has been three days since he sent us here."

"Coming, Naashah," the young man responded as he rose.

Before he could move away from the tree, the servant stopped him, "Thank the tree for the rest and shade he provided, Chamah," came the command.

"You know Father does not approve of that sort of thing," Chamah answered.

"True, but your father is not here, and the Meslantaea is. I fear the gods here more than your father who is yet a day's journey away."

Chamah walked away from the tree.

"Forgive him, Meslantaea, god of the trees," Naashah intoned, "for he is just a boy and does not mean to offend. Do not take out your displeasure on him. We are grateful for the welcome shade you have provided."

Strangely, Chamah thought there was a stirring in the leaves of the tree in response to the servant's apology.

"You see, Chamah," the man continued, "we have taken from the forests and must not forget our duty of thanks to the ones who have provided for us." Again to the tree he said, "Thank you for your generosity. May your leaves not wither forever."

With this, he turned and moved toward the crude vehicles on which their harvest of timber lay. Little more than axles with rough wheels on either end, they served to transport the logs from the forest to the compound. As they bumped and rumbled across the surface, there was movement in the trees. It was as if a shadow of each leaf and branch was stepping aside from the substance of the tree and following the humans and their cargo.

This was in fact precisely what was happening. The spirits of the trees which had been harvested were claiming their right to follow the timber and inhabit the structure that it became; this was their directive from their leader, Meslantaea. They scoffed at the human's puny sacrifice of thanks for shade when he carted off numerous trunks that had been home to them for years. They had orders to exact their own price when the timber reached its destination and was put to use. Life in that structure would be miserable for the humans unlucky enough to use it.

While the evil presence was unnoticed by the humans, there was another group of beings watching from a position overhead. With the sun behind them masking their presence, Iadrea and several lesser attenders looked on as the dark shapes slid along beside the travelers.

"We must find a way to rid our charges of these pests," Iadrea was saying. "It would not do to have them stumble into the compound. Better we deal with them here, far from the destination of this important cargo."

"Shall we attack them now, Master?" an eager young warrior asked.

"No," the seasoned strategist replied. "I have a plan to insure our success. We must lure them into an ambush away from the humans, lest they attempt to use them as hostages. Maintain your position above them here until I return."

With this the huge rainbow wings on his back stretched to their fullest and he shot upward like and arrow sent into the sky. He nearly left the atmosphere of the planet before he turned and traced and arc back down to a place ahead of and to the west of the intended path of the travelers. As he whistled back down toward the surface he scanned the area until he sensed what he was looking for. There was water a few meters below the surface in a subterranean stream. He saw no signs of Ninazu's water spirits lurking about; he didn't want to disturb another host of dark ones. Dealing with the group from Meslantaea would be enough.

He did not stop his descent at the surface, but drove into the soil until he reached the water underneath. Once in position, he began to revolve, slowly at first, and stretched himself out until he reached from the water below to the surface above. Normally he could move through the material substance without disturbing its nature, but now he purposely became semi-materialized so that he ever so slightly stirred the soil he was spinning in. This reduced the density of it just enough so that the water began to flow upward toward the surface.

Once satisfied that he had gained the desired result, he returned to his normal form and pulled himself out of the soil. As he stood there, water began to pool around his feet and he smiled at his success. Again he raised his wings and backtracked his sky-trail to his waiting fellows.

When he was back in their midst again he said, "Now we are ready to mount an attack on these vermin." Those around him drew their swords and hummed together a beautiful note of agreement and readiness. "But we need a volunteer for a risky decoy mission," Iadrea continued.

"I will go," one of the smaller ones eagerly offered.

"Fine, Zechel. Come up higher with me." Saying this, he rose several hundred meters higher in the sky. "See that pool of water in the distance?" he asked the volunteer.

The small one looked to where his master pointed. "Yes," he replied.

"I have made sure it is free of evil spirits. You will go there and dance in the sparkling light as it reflects off the surface of the pool. Sing if you like; enjoy yourself as if you had no idea an enemy was anywhere around."

"I see master, and the evil ones will be lured into thinking they can snuff my light while I dance."

"Just so, my friend. But it is important that you keep acting until all of the fiends are drawn away. We don't want any to escape our trap. If one gets back to Meslantaea with news of the attack or takes possession of one of the humans, our success will be incomplete. You must keep dancing even if they appear to be coming quite close; do not take flight until we have revealed our attack. Trust me to protect you from them," Iadrea's tone was almost fatherly at this point.

Fearing of the risk to his friend, one of the others asked, "Can we be sure all the evil ones will be drawn away at once?"

"Think of their nature; if they see a chance to crush a seemingly helpless victim, they will tumble over one another to be the first to strike a blow," the leader responded.

"Yes, I'm sure you are right," the questioner conceded.

"To the dance then, Zechel," Iadrea commanded, "and may the Father of Lights be with you."

The little one followed his master's example and drove straight into the sun before slicing back to the surface in a grand arc. Once there, he began playing the opening scenes of the drama that he had chosen to perform.

It was not hard to enjoy the performance. The life-giving water bubbled into the small pool, quenching the dry earth. The afternoon sun struck the rippled surface and burst into tiny rays that lifted the dancer and twirled him in laughing pirouettes. Even a human can sense the magic in the sunlight as it splashes off sparkling water. It was even easier for one who spans four dimensions to glory in the mystical communion of earth, water and sun.

He imagined he was an unfettered tree growing by the edge of this sweet pool, reaching branch and leaf upward in praise to the one who made him. He became one with the water, light and air as he made his very essence vibrate in song and dance. He was so rapt in the beauty of the mystery of life that he did not notice that his dance was beginning to attract the attention of those who had claimed the trees as their domain.

The bait was taken.

The innocent attender was nearly engulfed in a dark cloud, just as Iadrea had predicted. The evil ones couldn't stand to see anyone enjoy himself so much. They poured headlong out of the trees toward the sound of the hated music. One of the demons at the head of the charge had just swung his rod of darkness at Zechel when Iadrea swooped in and sliced the attacker's arm off. The rod continued to fall on its course and struck Zechel, knocking him out of the rays onto the ground beside the pool. The blow was enough to bruise him, but good fortune provided that it saved him from the next attacker who could not swerve in time to bring his blow home on the toppling dancer. Nor could he avoid the sword of another attender who neatly severed one wing and scarred an arm.

After these initial blows, the battle was entered from all sides at once. Rods and swords clashed with ringing smashes. The dark ones tried to single out attenders who were smaller than they, but the more experienced warriors interposed themselves until the sides were nearly matched. It wasn't long before the swords of light were dispatching the dark ones one at a time, reducing their number significantly.

Two fiends at the outer edge of the foray separated themselves and fled back toward the humans while the battle raged behind them. The larger of the two attached himself to Naashah before his flight could be arrested. The man stopped walking immediately and grasped his head with a wail. Having no idea what was happening to him, he felt as if something was tearing into his skull. Before the smaller one reached Chamah, he was bisected lengthwise by the sweeping sword of the pursuing attender.

The attender then turned his attention to the dark one on Naashah's head. He clung there with his feet resting on the man's shoulders and his wing-claws buried in his skull. His rod was raised in defense, though his best hope against the light sword was the use of the human as a shield. He hunkered down and almost melded his body with the human's. He leered at his opponent, snickering foully at his victory.

Naashah's legs became heavy and his movements sluggish from the effect of the dark one's presence. He stumbled and reached out to catch himself on the logs beside him. The falling motion left just enough of the dark one behind that the attender could clearly see wings apart from the human body. Seizing the moment, he swept his sword at the dark form. He caught just enough wing to chop the middle section out. The creature screamed in pain and clung more tightly to his living shield.

As Naashah rested his dizzy frame against the logs, he cried out from the simple understanding he had formed, "Oh Meslantaea! Forgive us for our grievous trespass. Only free me from this horrible pain and we will forsake the trees we have plundered. Please, mighty god of the trees, let me be!"

This was all the dark one needed by way of invitation. He melded almost invisibly into the form of Naashah so that neither attender nor human could easily detect his presence. To attempt to dislodge him now would almost certainly kill his host. The disappointed attender turned back in the direction of the skirmish to see if other dark ones might attempt a similar tactic. His dark opponent took advantage of this momentary lack of attention; he reached out of his hiding place with his awful rod and struck the unwary attender fully upon the head, driving him to the ground. Another quick slam and the light one was all but extinguished. The victor slithered back into his body-shield.

By the time Iadrea was able to disentangle himself from the fray to follow the fleeing one and his pursuer, it was too late. He sailed onto the scene just as the vicious blow was struck and the enemy disappeared into his host.

The giant attender glared for an instant into the eyes of Naashah which now glowed supernaturally back at him. He knew what the evil one had accomplished, and he felt both anger and sadness at the loss. He hovered briefly with his huge wings outstretched. In the twinkling of an eye there was a multi-colored spark of light from the spot where his compatriot had fallen; then he shot from sight above the scene.

After a quick glance to see that none of the other foul creatures had escaped, he swooped back to the scene of the ambush. When he arrived, the last evil spirit was being dispatched. At their leader's signal the band raised their swords in unison, touching the tips together in victory salute. When Iadrea added his to the others, a stream of light bolted into the heavens accompanied by a sound that was so rich and so beautiful in its harmony that it can not be described.

"Glory to the King," they all sang in unison, "and power to his throne through the ages."

"And may the Father of lights receive our brother who has fallen," added Iadrea solemnly.

Naashah had collapsed to his knees with the pressure of the possession by the evil one. Chamah was kneeling beside him now, trying to ascertain the cause of his servant's distress.

"What is wrong, Naashah," he repeated for the third time.

A moment after the spirit had become engaged, Naashah found the strength to speak. "I have a tremendous pain in my skull. It feels as if an arrow has pierced my head."

Instinctively, Chamah looked for signs of a wound; of course there was none.

"I knew we should have brought something to sacrifice to Meslantaea. Now he will take my life in payment," the servant continued.

"My father has taken many trees from the forests and no god has yet taken his life. He says his god is stronger than all the spirits that dwell on the Araq. This is why he warns us against displeasing the Ancient One."

"I think your father's god is strong at the compound," Naashah countered, "but I do not know who rules in the forest. Besides, if this ancient god were so powerful, why has he not destroyed all those who speak against him? Is this not the way of the gods?"

"Perhaps; perhaps not," was all Chamah could think to say. There was contemporary wisdom in what the servant said, but his father despised the wisdom of the day, preferring the ancient wisdom. The boy was not at all certain what he believed.

"I say we leave the trees here," Naashah concluded.

"But what would we tell Father?"

The more Naashah thought of giving up the trees, the better he felt. He continued, "I think I'll not be telling your father anything. I've had enough of this work anyway — defying the gods — it's too dangerous."

"But Father would never..."

"Nuwach will never know," the servant interrupted. An idea was forming. "You've always wanted to see the city, haven't you?" He was looking intently into the boy's eyes, trying to read the impact of his treasonous suggestion.

The younger one returned his stare, finding something in the man's eyes he hadn't noticed previously; it made him uncomfortable at first, but momentarily he began to get an idea himself. "You mean we could go to the city from here?" he asked.

"When we journeyed into the forest, I noticed a pass not too far down the trail from here. We could follow it into the valley and find the road into Armoun." He could feel the boy coming with him.

The boy thought for a moment of his father, of his certain love for him and of his probable sense of loss if the boy didn't return. But the lure of the city was too great to resist. For years he had listened to the traders tell of exotic places and he had longed to see them for himself. Here was his chance.

"Father will no doubt assume that we were attacked by robbers. He always warns us about that, doesn't he?"

"Yes, my boy," came the smiling reply, "that he does."

Without another word between them, they picked up their personal things from the luggage and struck off down the path toward the pass.

In a short time they found the low spot in the hills Naashah had remembered and it led them to the valley on the other side. At the foot of the hills, there was a small pool.

"Look!" exclaimed the servant, "Here is a sign from the gods that we have been forgiven. Who would have expected to find water in a place such as this. Let us refresh ourselves and drink." Before he had finished speaking, he was kneeling to cup his hands and drink from the fresh water which sparkled in the afternoon sun.

When they had drunk enough and filled their water skins Naashah said, "If we keep the sun on our left as it drops in the sky, we will surely meet the Armoun road before dark."

Chamah took courage in the confident sound of the older man's words. The thrill of the adventure was still fresh upon him; he hadn't stopped to think of the very real danger of robbers nearer the road, nor had he imagined what they would do when they arrived in the city. Right now there was just something in moving, in putting space between himself and the life behind him.

"Let's go, then," he said, echoing the other's confident tone.

They strode away from the glittering pool towards adventure, and a small band of invisible creatures followed above them.

Mistrea and Multar joined the others just as the two humans began their descent into the valley. "Is not the boy one of the chosen?" Mistrea asked.

"Yes," Iadrea responded sullenly. "We were unable to stop the dark ones from inciting him to rebel. One of them bound himself fast to the servant and we can not break his grip."

Multar wondered at this lack of ability since the dark one involved was smaller than himself and downright puny compared to Iadrea.

It was Mistrea who caught his thought and answered the unasked question, "There is a connection between the light within and the vessel they use. When the dark one reaches beyond the outer shell and grasps the light itself, we can not separate them."

"But how can they do this, especially since they hate light so much?"

"They don't really like it, for as you say, they detest the light, but they will endure it for a short time if it meets their purposes."

Looking at the unfortunate man who still winced occasionally from the pain in his head, Multar asked, "Does the dark one control the human completely? Does he not have his own mind?"

"The human has allowed the dark one to speak to him," it was Iadrea who answered this time. "The enemy can have his way almost completely with the lower creatures, but the humans must by direct wish or indirect attitude create an opening for the dark one to enter."

"Perhaps I could show my young pupil how this works," Mistrea offered. "That is, if we are not needed immediately."

Iadrea looked again at the wayward humans and answered, "It looks as though we have some added complications to consider. It would be good for you to continue your lessons while we seek to understand what is happening here. I will call you when we are ready to proceed with the zensak."

"Very well," Mistrea bowed slightly, Multar imitating him a second later. "We will remain at your service." Then, "Follow me," to Multar.

Mistrea led them to a place on the east side of the hills, near where the men had been harvesting trees. "The sprites are momentarily cleared from this area," he began, "so I think we can have a moment's peace to practice something."

Multar was excited at the prospect of learning something new, even though he had no idea what it was.

Mistrea reached out with his senses in the immediate area until he found what he was looking for. Though not as skilled as Daman or Iadrea who spent nearly all their time on Araq, Mistrea had little difficulty calling to a small furry creature who was hiding under a pile of brush a few meters away. As Mistrea bent down in a squat, he also gradually became more solid, until he was almost as substantial as the elements around him.

The small animal seemed not to notice the change in the one who had called him out, as he hopped curiously to the stranger's feet. "Hello, little one," Mistrea said gently, making a sound that the creature could pick up with his tremendous, long ears.

Multar felt the vibrations of his master's speech, and looking at him realized suddenly that a perfectly normal human was bent before him. "Master!" he almost shouted in his thoughts. "How have you done this?"

"In a moment I will show you. First you must understand what it is to be solid." He scooped up the small animal in his large hands and turned with it toward Multar. "Remember the experience with the squirrel?"

"Yes, Master."

"This time we will go a step further. Look into the creatures eyes as you did with the other." He waited for Multar to comply.

"Can you see his inner self?"

"Yes, he is very much the same as the other one on the inside."

"You are right. Both are simple, peaceful creatures with simple desires and needs. Reach out with your mind and connect with the creature's thoughts if you can."

Mistrea waited while his pupil exercised this new faculty awkwardly. "Try placing your finger tips gently on the creature's head. See if this helps you connect."

Upon touching the animal, Multar immediately exclaimed, "Oh my! Oh my goodness! This is amazing. I can feel hunger and... pain, I feel pain in a leg and... oh... I don't know what this is. It seems like... pleasure... desire... it is pleasant but I don't understand it exactly. Some kind of union, I think."

"Good," Mistrea said. "Now you are getting the feel of being a rabbit. Take your hand away and try as hard as you can to imagine what it would be like to be a rabbit."

Multar concentrated very hard for a few moments and then said, "I can picture it. No! I can feel it! It... it... I can smell things and... yes, the wind... I can hear — and feel — the wind."

The young attender looked up at his master to suddenly realize that his view was from the ground looking up at him towering above. Multar looked to the side and found himself eye to eye with the creature he had moments before looked down upon. Then it struck him: he was a rabbit.

When the thought occurred to him to look at himself, he began to swell back into the size of his former self, his top half resembling a young attender and his lower half still rabbit, though greatly enlarged. Then he shrunk again back into the rabbit form.

"Mistrea! What is happening?"

The large attender, now a man laughed out loud. Multar felt the pulsations of the laughter, heard the rich tones and himself began to laugh with glee. Only his laugh became nothing more than a squeak as he morphed back into the rabbit form.

"Concentrate, little one," Mistrea instructed in bursts of laughing.

Finally the two rabbits sat side by side in front of the man in the late afternoon sun. "There now," Mistrea finally stopped laughing enough to think/speak. "We can still communicate the old way if you can concentrate."

"I can, I think," the one rabbit answered. "Can he hear us too?" he asked, indicating his furry companion.

"Not precisely. He senses something going on, but unless we make a suggestion that is very simple and within his natural character, he will not respond."

"Mistrea!" Multar suddenly thought. "How do I get back out?"

"Just the way you got in. Imagine you are an attender."

In a flash, one of the rabbits became first a tall pillar of light, then took the form of the young attender. "Oh master, that was an incredible experience. Now I understand what you mean about being bound by the physical form. It was like being squeezed into a very small space. Surely you are not so confined when you become a man?"

"On the contrary, any physical embodiment feels very restrictive. You see, it is not just the size that we must accommodate, but the time conformation as well. Space and time are as one with us naturally. We move through them without thinking about their relationship. For these creatures, the passage of time has been slowed, so to speak. For us to enter their material universe implies accommodating their time as well as their space."

"I can not understand everything you explain, but I have felt what you mean," the breathless young attender responded. "How is it that I was able to assume another form?"

"Perhaps I can clarify what takes place while we wait for Iadrea to return," the teacher said.

"Everything we know to exist is composed of various forms of energy. We are called creatures of light because light is the primary component the Creator used to make our bodies. The creatures on Mentridar are also mostly light energy. That is why you had no trouble adjusting to the work we do on that planet."

"Adjusting?" Multar questioned. "I don't recall doing anything special."

"Just so," Mistrea answered. "The Father has given attenders the ability to change form with relative ease. This makes us useful to Him in many different situations and in various places throughout His creation. The first time you arrived on Mentridar you instinctively took on the form necessary to accomplish your work there. You were able to do it effortlessly because the life forms there are simple and closely related to us in composition.

"Here on this planet, you must give your transformation a good deal more thought due to the complex foreign nature of these creatures."

"Is that why I felt so restricted in the rabbit's body?"

"That, and the added fact that the dimension of time is not as transparent here as we are accustomed to." Mistrea paused to look for an illustration of what he was trying to say. He pointed, "Look far to the north where the ridge seems to blend into the plain."

Multar turned in the direction indicated. "I see it."

"Because of our multidimensional nature, we can be at that point without the passage of time; if this rabbit ran as fast as he could, it would take him most of the day to get there: much of his "time" would pass making the journey."

"So do we travel outside of time?" the pupil wanted to know.

"Not exactly. Do you remember how I demonstrated the use of my wings on Mentridar?"

"When I beat you to the ridge...."

"Precisely. You beat me because I was traveling through space and time to get there; you traveled by thought, which moves you through a fifth dimension. That is as natural for us as moving through four dimensions is for these creatures. Although they don't realize it, they are moving relative to all four dimensions at each moment of their existence. If this rabbit runs toward the ridge, he senses that he is moving relative to the ridge, but at the same time he moves in his relationship to things beside, behind, above, and below. He also moves across the fabric of time, his fourth dimension as he completes his journey.

"You felt constricted by the rabbit's physical being because his form is more complex than yours. In addition, you were experiencing the passage of time in a way that is unusual for you."

Multar thought for a moment as Mistrea paused for his words to sink in. Then the little one asked, "This seems so complicated; how was I able to accomplish the change without understanding?"

Mistrea chuckled, "For anyone but an attender, what you have done would not just be complicated, but impossible. This is an ability the Father has placed within his attenders."

"Can the dark ones do this also?" Multar wondered.

"Yes, they have not lost this ability; they use it to create endless mischief, so I am told."

"Then they can take on the form of any creature of the Araq?"

"Yes, but they are lazy; they usually just take possession of an existing animal. I also think they do this because it gives them a sense of power or control over beings they see as weaker."

"But Iadrea said they had to have permission...."

Mistrea interrupted, "That is only true with humans. The Father has made the humans different from all the other creatures here. Their inner being is very much like ours, in that it is mostly light. They are bound to their physical bodies only as long as they are on this planet. As far as I know, they maintain control of their bodies, but can not leave them until their usefulness is ended. If they give over control to a dark one, they can be manipulated almost completely."

"But why would any creature wish to surrender control to another?" the pupil asked.

Mistrea thought for a moment, then replied, "I am not sure; I think the dark ones deceive them into thinking they will receive greater powers or other gratifying rewards. I must warn you, this is something the Father has forbidden us to do. It is an inappropriate situation for both the possessor as well as the possessed."

Tiring of the academic turn the lesson had taken, Multar asked, "May I experiment again becoming a rabbit?"

"Yes," Mistrea nodded. "When the time comes for you to join me on a mission, we will choose an appropriate shape for you to assume. Until then, this will allow you to grow in your experience and become comfortable with the process."

The thought of more embodiments was tantalizing. Multar could hardly contain his imagination. "Will our opportunity come soon, Master?"

"Soon enough, I imagine," came the reply.

As Multar was considering the change into a material form, his thoughts became confused and Mistrea caught his train of thought.

"I do not wonder that you are confused, little one; this is a great mystery. Come with me and I will see if I can make it more clear to you."

When they stopped, Multar realized that they were in an entirely different kind of atmosphere. They were once again in the presence of the soft harmony similar to the sound he had experienced above the planet of Mentridar. He sensed a peace and quietness even greater than he had felt there. In the distance he could see countless pinwheels of light organized in a spherical pattern around a definable center.

"Where are we?"

"I have taken us to a place beyond the measures of the stars and planets we have been working on. The Father of Lights created all that you can see," his hand swept the space where the spinning lights appeared. "Here we do not mark the boundaries of time or space as we must among the stars and their planets. I will tell you what I know of the Father's creation and then we will return to our work and find that no time has passed there.

"Let me start where your confusion began; you were wondering about the difference between our bodies and the material forms we will assume, were you not?"

"Yes," Multar agreed. "Here our bodies seem more... substantial, more dense than there. On the planet, it is the material forms which appear thicker. Why is that?"

"Let me begin by explaining that all things which appear were created by the Father of Lights out of a form of light or energy. Even though the things we see appear solid, they are in fact made up of concentrated energy which is itself always moving. To appear solid, dense as you have called it, the movement is coordinated in the measures of time and space. Within the material universe where we work, all things are moving through time and space in the pattern which has been ordained by the Father.

"When we enter the created universe, we arrest our passage to the same rate as the energy around us. The Father has given all attenders the ability to organize their own energy by the power of thought. When we choose to coordinate our movement with that of the things around us, we appear to be more or less solid."

Mistrea could sense that his pupil was struggling with this concept, so he continued, "Let me give you an illustration. On the planet we just left, a human standing by a road could watch another human pass by on a swift horse. "The rider would move quickly by the one standing beside the road, do you see.?"

"Yes, I understand this much," Multar answered.

"Well then, imagine that the man beside the road was also on horseback, traveling with the other; then the two would remain side by side and not appear to be moving at all, one compared to the other. In the same way, we can choose to come alongside a material creature and move through space and time at the same speed so that we appear to occupy their space and time with them."

"I can understand this too, but we do not always appear as they do; we are not as dense as they are."

"True. We are beings of light; we do not have the same substance that they have. We must adopt elements of energy from their world if we wish to appear as they do. This is what we mean when we refer to materializing. All living things are merely a coordination of the elements present where they exist. When we materialize we simply organize the material elements present there in a form which is similar to their own bodies."

"Can they change their forms as we can?" Multar asked.

"As far as I know they have not been granted the skill to do this at will. When a creature dies, the energy which has been maintaining its form is released. The elements then begin to slow and dissociate into their simpler forms. Humans do have a life energy which remains after they die. This energy is returned to the Father's control after it leaves the material body. At the Gatherings, many of these beings can be seen around the Father's throne."

"Yes," Multar interrupted, "I saw them when I received my sword. I thought they were more attenders like us."

"They are similar, but not identical. The Father created humans and attenders for different purposes. It is our solemn duty to see that all humans and attenders accomplish the purposes for which they were created. This is precisely why we have been called into service in the battle for the humans of the Araq."

"I see," the pupil said thoughtfully. "So the Rebellion is not really over, is it?"

"No, it is not. The dark ones continue to work against the Father's will and seek to enlist whoever they can in their evil plans."

"Do they do this by changing their form?"

"Sometimes they do. They can cast of their shadow forms and appear as one of us or any material being they wish. They can also exercise almost complete control over any being which surrenders its will to them.

"You see, everything in the material universe is controlled by the power of thought. Thought itself is like a form of energy which orders the energy around it. The Father created the universe as we know it by his thought and it is sustained and manipulated by thought, both by his and by the thoughts of the thinking beings he created, although his thoughts are far more substantial than any of his creatures thoughts. Just consider how we travel by thought. We simply think ourselves in another place, and we are instantly there."

After pondering this for a moment, Multar asked, "Does the Father appear in his universe?"

"This is something which I do not know. We attenders have had many debates about this. Some say that because the Father is pure energy, he could not appear without completely disrupting the elements around him. Others think that he could separate a part of himself, a kind of emanation of reduced power, that could appear in or near the material creation. We do not know for sure."

"I still do not understand why he has not crushed the rebellious ones and restored the harmony to his creation," Multar said, perplexed.

"This is something none of us understands. All we know is that he has some purpose for allowing the battle to continue. One day, we feel sure that all will become clear; until then, we must simply do as he bids us."

Multar looked at the beautiful swirling lights beyond them, trying to absorb all that he had been told. He felt so small and inconsequential when he contemplated the vastness of the creation and all that lay behind it.

"How will I know if I am doing what is required of me?" he asked humbly.

"Just do what is before you, and when that is accomplished, do the next thing. The Father always gives us what is necessary for the task at hand, whether skill or strength or knowledge."

With that, Mistrea signaled that they should return and in an instant they were back where they had come from.

CHAPTER TEN

A stoop-shouldered, gray haired man knelt on an old hillside. The once young shrubbery around him had the look of centuries of struggle to eke moisture from the soil. Craggy and twisted, the little plants measured out their existence by the available water. The process of aging in the fauna had crept in inexorably as it had with the man. Time passes imperceptibly, yet leaves undeniable footprints.

Humans treat the passage of time as if it were measurable. Sand flows through the glass one grain at a time like the wind-blown sands that move dunes in place. Each particle is meaningless, yet the cumulative effect is mammoth. What one grain is compared to the whole dune, one second is to eternity.

So the plants were looking older to the man on this day. He commented as much to no one who was visible. His next thought was that he too was showing the signs of time's passage. When the plants were young and robust, water plentiful, the sun screened from the planet's surface by protecting vapors, he too felt more energetic. Now as the vapors gathered into clouds, forming ominous gray masses, leaving the surface of the Araq naked to the burning sun, the old man questioned his longevity. He felt he had outlived his time.

The Araq was not the only thing to see changes. The man considered the vast differences in how people lived. No longer needed solely as herdsman or farmers, people began congregating in cities. Farmers carried their produce into the city to exchange for the growing number of technical advancements: metal for plow blades and scythes, specialists who worked in wood or pottery, and of course, brewers who had begun to turn grain into a drink that would make your head spin.

Then there was the spiritual condition of those in the cities. The old man blamed it on the lack of connection with the ground from which they came. In the city, one might not even own a piece of land; one was dependent upon another to provide bread and milk and wine. Worse, there was too much time on idle hands; this was the root of endless mischief, in the old man's opinion. Without the land to work, it became fashionable to be lazy. One even gave up the work of relating to god, leaving that to the priests who were only too glad to perform the service — but not without a price.

Religion had become so complicated that it took a full-time cleric to untangle all the inter-relationships between the pantheon of gods. The trees, the sky, the hills, the animals each had their spirit counterparts. They were constantly bickering and feuding with one another, fighting for territory. In his lifetime, the old man had seen numerous alliances formed and broken among the gods. Cities' fortunes rose and fell according to the fate of these alliances, so the priests said. The people were called to give tribute and homage to this one and then that one in an effort to appease and cajole the invisible powers. Not commerce nor politics nor private life was free from the tentacles of the priestly tribute system.

The old man had tired of trying to convince his fellow citizens that it was all futile; they only mocked him anyway. The priests labeled him a heretic and bade the people avoid him. He had finally left the city altogether to make his own life here in these hills.

This is where he truly began to commune with his god. This is where he first heard the rumblings of displeasure from the true god of the Araq. And this is where the plan to save the Araq had been revealed.

Nuwach was in his beloved hills on this particular afternoon, listening to the wind, listening for more than the wind. He worshiped this way, making himself quiet and at one with the Araq and her god. On this evening he saw the caravan approaching only after it was very close; his eyes had not been open much of the time. It was close enough to identify as the train of his old friend Imanaq.

This would be a good evening; he always enjoyed the visits of his friend, but he especially looked forward to his coming today, hoping he would be bringing a wife for his oldest son. Sha'ym had talked of little else since their departure some months ago. It meant a new stage in his son's life, and it meant another step in the father's plan was accomplished as well.

He stood slowly, stretching his limbs which ached from the long spell of sitting. He headed down the east side of the ridge, planning to make preparations for his guests who would arrive shortly after he did. When he reached the compound he spoke briefly to his wife and then went on to make ready for the animals with his servants.

When the animals had been cared for and the evening meal finished, Sha'ym and Sharaq were excused to stroll in the compound and the men sat around the fire in the center of the comfortable little house. Sha'ym was glad for the opportunity to be alone with his friend. He had been feeling unnamable things since she had left, and he was anxious to talk to her. Strangely, though, he found he could talk of everything but what he was feeling.

He watched her as she walked slowly around the perimeter sketched by the log stockade. Occasionally she would reach out without thinking to touch the logs, almost as if to caress them. He noticed her hands as if he had never seen them before. He saw the combined strength and gentleness of their fine, delicate shapes. He wondered at their softness in contrast to the rough logs she touched. Impulsively he reached out at one point and took her hand gently in his.

"What is it?" she quizzed him with a smile, taking his hands with her free one so that all four were cradled together.

"Um," he stammered, "they're soft."

"Well of course," she laughed, "compared to one who works with the soil and timber."

Her laughter both embarrassed and fascinated him. He raised his glance from her hands to her face. It was the same face he'd known for years, yet he was seeing something he had never seen before. Her silky brown hair fell in gentle waves beside her face. Again on impulse he reached out and stroked the hair slightly aside. He watched as it slid softly away from her collarbone at the opening of her tunic. Her seductive feminine form caught his attention as it pressed the tunic into a graceful shape. The sight had the effect of finding a hot coal when stirring the gray ashes of last night's fire. He was first surprised, then excited, then somehow embarrassed that he was looking, so he returned his gaze to the relative safety of her eyes.

But there too he began to drown in feelings he could not name. There was depth in those eyes one could swim in for centuries. They sparkled; they teased; they hypnotized.

Now it was her turn. Not at all on impulse she slid her right hand from his gentle grasp and pushed aside a strand of hair that had fallen into his eyes as he tilted his head down to look at her. Then she deliberately lowered their still engaged hands as she raised herself on her toes and leaned just close enough to touch her body against his as she kissed him gently on the lips.

By this time stars had begun to litter the darkening sky, but there might just as well have been sun, moon and stars all dancing in the compound, the way the young man felt. He let her left hand go and took her in his arms and returned the kiss, with more passion this time. When their lips parted after a moment, they remained in the embrace, reeling at the emotions that were unleashed by such a simple act. He bathed in the silky softness of her hair against his face.

"Sharaq," he began hoarsely, keeping her pressed gently against himself, keeping his face in her hair. "I...I..."

"I know," she sighed, stroking the curly locks on the back of his head. "Me too."

They stood awkwardly yet so comfortably in one another's arms for a long time. Finally she said, "We should go in now; it's getting quite dark."

"Do we have to?" came the disappointed reply.

"I think we should."

He moved his head away from hers far enough to dive into her eyes once more. He kissed her again, more gently this time, but longer. He reveled in the soft sweetness of her kiss as if it were nectar to a bee.

Reluctantly he slid from his position in front of her to her side, keeping his arm around her shoulders and her body pressed against his. Thus linked with her arm around his waist, they moved slowly across the compound toward the house.

The conversation in the house had moved through the usual pleasantries and reminiscences on the past months when Imanaq reached the chronological point in the tale where he and his daughter were on the road from Armoun.

"I met your son Chamah and your servant Naashah on their way to Armoun as I journeyed here, Nuwach."

The old man straightened quickly and looked disturbingly at his friend. "On the road to Armoun?" he questioned in disbelief.

"Why, yes," came the somewhat puzzled reply, Imanaq having seen the distraught look on his friend's face. "They said you had sent them on an errand to Armoun for some woodworking equipment. What's wrong, my friend, were you not expecting us to see them?"

"Whether you should or should not have seen them is not what disturbs me," explained Nuwach. The old man was becoming visibly agitated now. "That they were on the road to Armoun is the puzzle. Not many days ago I sent them to the northern forest to cut trees for a project I am undertaking. They should have been back here soon."

Darkness having enclosed the compound, the young couple entered the room at this point. Nuwach stood as they appeared, looked from his guest to his eldest son and began a sigh which evolved into a guttural moan that spoke of a sadness and fear too deep for words. As he wailed, he tore his tunic from the neck down to his waist.

"My son! My son! You are lost!" he proclaimed to the ceiling.

A look of bewildered terror flashed onto Sha'ym's face. "Father, what have I done?" was all the boy could think to say.

In a move somewhat uncharacteristic of recent years, the father stepped towards the son and took him in an embrace. The terror left the young man when he felt his father's compassion, but the bewilderment remained.

"Peace, my son," he said, control returning slowly to his voice." "It is not what you have done, but your younger brother's deeds which destroy me."

As he was saying this, his wife stepped into the circle of light cast by the fire, having returned from other business outside. "I came when I heard you scream; what is this about our Chamah?"

Stepping back from his eldest he took the approaching woman in his arms and said, "He is lost, wife; he is lost!"

What do you mean?" she asked, fear creeping into her voice. "Beasts? Robbers? What do you mean, 'Lost'?"

"He has defied me and gone into the city with Naashah; I never should have let him go with that one; I shouldn't have trusted that one with my son."

"Oh," she sighed, pulling herself gently from his embrace. "I thought he was dead."

"He is, wife!"

"Nuwach, my husband..." she began, only to be interrupted.

"Has he not been told since he was old enough to listen that the city is forbidden to him? Can one defy the command of the Father and remain a true son?" Anger was beginning to replace the nascent grief of moments before.

"When your heart softens I will sew up your rent garment and we will speak of finding our 'lost' son," she said quietly, landing firmly but gently on the word "lost."

By this time Imanaq had risen and all were standing somewhat awkwardly between the door and the fire. Sha'ym finally found his tongue, having been drawn pell mell from the heights of splendor to the depths of dread and confusion.

"I will go and rescue him from the city, Father."

"No!" came the thundered response.

"But Father, I am certain I can convince him to return; he will listen to me," he reasoned.

"One son already lies in the clutches of death; I will not send another meet the same fate."

"But, Father..."

"No," the interruption came, still firm as mountain rocks, but with a pleading compassion added, "it will not be necessary for you to risk your life.

"The sky has long been filled with the stars of night. we must not speak of this again until another day." The earlier emotions were overtaking the anger. "Let us sleep now; perhaps the light of morning will cause us to see more clearly."

"Yes, good rest to all," Imanaq said somewhat awkwardly.

The young couple looked into each other's eyes an said good night without words.

"Peace on this house and all who sleep in it," Nuwach intoned, "and may the god who made us and all that is watch over us until the sun rises."

When they were alone the woman spoke softly to her husband, "Did you and Imanaq speak of the offer?"

Lying on his side, his back to her he answered, "No. We were interrupted by the news of Chamah." He let out a huge sigh. "Why would he do this to us?"

"He is a child," she said wistfully. "It is not strange that he should act like a child."

They listened to one another breathe for several moments. Then she put her hand on his shoulder and gently massaged it as she continued, "He may yet return to us; you have trained him well..."

"Not well enough if this is how he behaves when given a man's responsibilities," he complained.

"Boys sometimes struggle with their first efforts at a man's responsibilities," she consoled. "Don't be too hard on yourself; every cub leaves the den sooner or later. We can only do our best and leave the rest to god."

He turned to his other side in order to face her and put his free arm over her. "Again you upbraid me with your gentle wisdom, woman. Surely you are a gift of the gods."

"I only speak as you have taught me, master."

"You have not called me 'Master' in many seasons, wife."

"But I always think of you as Master."

"As if you were a child?"

"Was I not a child when you took me as your wife?"

"This is so." He paused to look at her in the dim glow shed by the dying fire in the next room. "How long it has been, yet it seems like only yesterday."

"Then much has changed since yesterday."

They closed their eyes and lay in each other's arms for a while. Then she said, "Sha'ym and Sharaq have changed since the last sunrise."

"Do you think so?" he asked, opening his eyes to discover hers looking into space.

"I am certain. When I was outside earlier I saw them walking in the compound. Their behavior has grown into that of adults. They are ready for the ceremony."

"Let us hope that is the reason for their visit. It would be most unfortunate if Imanaq has chosen to give her to the lugal's son."

"If Imanaq were another father, and Sharaq were someone else's daughter, that would be expected," she reasoned. "But he cares for her better than many sons; he will do whatever she wants"

"How do you know she wants Sha'ym?" he asked.

"How can you ask?"

"Perhaps it is something a woman knows."

"Anyone with eyes could know this; she shines like the sun when she is around him. I can feel her love for him."

"Perhaps she has this same feeling for the lugal's son," he began to tease her.

Still serious she responded, "No, this is something a woman only feels for one man."

"You know this?" he asked, looking directly into her eyes.

She looked back into his eyes and smiled at the hidden question behind his words. "I know this."

She kissed him, and they closed their eyes and slept.

CHAPTER ELEVEN

After a breakfast of bread and goat cheese the two men were preparing to go outside. Sha'ym addressed his father, "May Sharaq and I walk in the hills this morning; I have finished my chores."

The man stole a glance at his wife who closed her eyes and nodded her head almost imperceptibly. He looked back at his son and hesitated momentarily.

"What is it, Father?"

"Take your staff, and be back before the sun begins its descent. There is work to be done this afternoon," he said, ignoring the puzzled look he had received.

The two left the house and strolled from the compound toward the western ridge. While they climbed, they talked of things they had done as children, shared memories they had built over the years. Even though they had been together only a few weeks out of each year, they had a friendship that was founded on hundreds of insignificant shared moments and one significant shared grief. Strong relationships have been based on less.

As soon as they reached the top of the ridge and looked into the valley, Sha'ym stiffened and took Sharaq by the hand. "Look there," he said, pointing with his free hand to a place near the road."

"What? I don't see...Oh my!" she gasped, gripping his hand tighter. "Do you suppose its robbers?"

"There they are again!" he said as several shapes moved from one concealed position to another. From their vantage point on the hill, the two could tell a small force of men was advancing on the pass. Exactly how many was uncertain, as they never showed themselves all at one time.

"Let's move into my watch position. My brothers and I used to play here all the time. There is a protected ledge near where the road enters the pass. We can see what they are doing and still stay hidden."

They crept partway down the hill, staying behind the rocks and small shrubs until they reached the overlook Sha'ym had discovered.

"Sha'ym, if there are no caravans, what are they preparing to ambush?"

"Perhaps they think someone might be coming through the pass unseen, or perhaps...." He stopped dead in his thoughts as the impact of what he had been about to suggest hit him. He looked straight at her, trying to conceal the fear that was stealing into his mind. "Perhaps they are going to attack the compound?" he asked, hoping she would tell him he was being ridiculous.

The stockade had been built primarily to keep the domestic animals from wandering afield, and to keep wild animals from helping themselves to the food within. It was not built to repel an attack, nor had it ever been tested. Except for rigorous men trained in the use of the staff for self defense against the ever-increasing threat of robbers, there were no experienced warriors or weapons at Nuwach's compound.

The mysterious band was getting closer now, almost close enough to hear had they been talking. Of course, they were not. It was obvious, however, that they were armed.

These were something closer to warriors than Sha'ym had ever seen. Most carried battle clubs or fighting staffs. Two or three appeared to have swords, a relatively new instrument of battle.

The metal smiths of Kamaresh were beginning to turn their talents to more destructive ends than previously. Imanaq had told of seeing cutting instruments and spear heads made of metal in recent years. Originally, the gods of Kamaresh forbade the distribution of such weapons outside their city. But inevitably, wars and treachery spread the tools of death to surrounding kingdoms.

These new contraband weapons were extremely costly, so only the wealthiest warriors carried them. The thought did not immediately occur to Sha'ym that this made the approaching force the more mysterious. What would the wealthy want at a farmer's settlement?

The troop was coming dangerously close now; the faces of the closest were taking recognizable form. This brought Sharaq to attention as she peered around the rock and through the bush which sheltered the front side of it from the road. Something about the men seemed familiar, though they were still too far away to know why.

Sha'ym crept on his hands and knees to a position where he could see as far into the pass as possible from his location, just to see if indeed anyone were coming. Not to his surprise, there was only the slight stirring of the dust as the breeze tunneled through the narrows created by the encroaching hills. As he turned back toward their hiding place, he was terrified to see Sharaq's mouth fall open, her eyes wide as she stood up in plain view of the closest attacker before he could stop her.

"Lamaq?" she said incredulously.

The leader froze in his tracks not twenty meters from the pair. The sun was behind the speaker as the armed man stood beside the road. He could not be sure whom he saw, but he was quite sure he recognized the voice. "Sharaq?"

"What are you doing here?" she asked with genuine curiosity. Sha'ym had still not revealed himself.

There was a brief pause from the tall young man. "We are on maneuvers," he explained matter-of-factly. Saying this he signaled to the men behind him to move forward and he began ascending the hill to reach her.

At this point Sha'ym stood, and Lamaq instinctively reached for his sword, but held up, only placing his hand on the leather bound handle. Sha'ym took a defensive stance beside Sharaq and repeated her question. "What are you doing here?" He had not the curiosity of the girl's question in his voice, but a protective challenge.

"Oh, we are just practicing." He continued to move slowly closer, as did the men behind him. "You see, we don't have any mountain passes to practice on in the valley." With this he swept his left hand across the vista behind him, not taking his eyes off his prey. "You must be Nuwach's son."

Sha'ym was completely taken aback by this piece of intelligence. He had no reason to suspect this stranger would have ever heard of him or his father. Again, had he reasoned immediately what this might mean, he might have run for his life.

Trying to maintain some sense of defense he retorted, "If I were the son of this 'Nuwach', what would that mean to you?

Lamaq had reached a point just below the ledge where they had been hidden. He was standing a meter or so lower than they, so his full height was not yet apparent to Sha'ym; indeed, the stranger stood nearly a full head taller than he. Had Sha'ym realized this, he may have been more frightened than he was already.

Behind his back, Lamaq signaled to his men to begin to move around the rock position held by the two. Unknown to

Sha'ym, one of the attackers had already moved in a circular route to gain high ground above him, and the trap was now nearly set. As the lone attacker stood, preparing to leap down on Sha'ym, his shadow fell across the rock between Lamaq and Sha'ym. When he raised his battle club and jumped, Sha'ym realized what was happening just in time and turned to defend himself.

The attacker was himself taken by surprise as Sha'ym landed a blow on his neck — a missed swing at his head — which threw him off balance. As he regained his footing, Sha'ym was delivering his second blow. The intruder was able to block it with his club; otherwise it would doubtless have split his head. At this point his battle instincts took over and several interchanges pitted his club against the skillfully handled staff of the younger man.

Lamaq circled the rock while the men fought and coming from behind, grabbed Sharaq, placing one hand over her mouth and the other firmly around her waist. His other men also took up positions nearer the ledge where the fight was going on. One of them slipped past Lamaq and was about to take a swing at Sha'ym. Sharaq let out a muffled scream through Lamaq's hand just in time to see Sha'ym turn and block the attacker's blow. Now, however, he had opponents in front and behind and rock on either side.

He jabbed at the new attacker and spun in time to thwart the roundhouse swing of his original foe, but the force of the club against his staff and his waning strength made him falter slightly.

This was the only advantage the trained warriors needed. From Sharaq's direction a blow struck Sha'ym across the chest, only partly blocked by his rod. Then the other attacker brought his club down on the top of Sha'ym's unguarded head. He slumped to his knees. Another blow to the back of his head drove him face-first into the dirt, and he did not get up.

Sharaq was sobbing behind the large hand that throttled her. Tears ran down onto the rough fingers of her captor. As Sha'ym's original attacker placed his foot on the neck of his vanquished opponent, he raised his victorious club to the sky and let out one whoop of conquest.

Sharaq fainted.

Things were not going well in the unseen world either. When Lamaq's head cleared of the confusion he experienced the day he let Sharaq go, he cursed his own stupidity. He could not imagine what came over him causing him to be so kind. It was definitely not what he wanted. When he decided to follow Sharaq two days ago, Talizar, the guardian of Armoun, sent a warning by messenger to Iadrea, who had returned to the fortress of Nuwach after helping deliver the innocents from the evil forces in the city.

As Lamaq and his men traveled hastily toward Nuwach's, it was obvious that the dark forces were going along.

Iadrea listened intently to the messenger's account. When the speaker paused Iadrea asked, "Did you number the forces which are accompanying the men?"

"At least two dozen had followed by the time I left, Master," came the reply.

"What level are they?"

"Several appear to be ranking officers, among whom is Glaxxin, who was assigned to the girl. They are under the command of Fauxxin."

There was a hum from those gathered around listening. Iadrea acknowledged their reaction. "Yes, this is more serious than we thought. Things have been building at Armoun ever since the council there recently. The evil ones apparently have designs on Lamaq; why else would the second in command leave the city with him?

"We must plan very carefully. Fauxxin must not be allowed to reach the fortress if we can stop him. He may be perceptive enough to recognize the zensak defenses. That would surely trigger an investigation which we do not want.

"If he does approach this position, we must have some legitimate reason to attack him with equal force; it must not appear that we are simply defending the chosen ones. I have an idea, but it will require Gebarour's approval."

He stopped speaking to those around him and retreated within himself. He sent his thoughts ranging to his master. Because the two were of such great power, they were never out of instant communication anywhere around the planet. However, they dared not relay important thoughts over great distances as the enemy spoke the same language and could intercept thoughts under ideal conditions. When he contacted Gebarour, Iadrea relayed a vague sketch of the situation and proposed that he send a messenger to him. Gebarour agreed instantly.

"Chantar," Iadrea was again speaking to those in his presence.

"Yes, master"

"Go to Gebarour with all you have heard, and tell him my counter-measure involves a sacrifice requiring his approval. Return to me as soon as you can."

"As you command." He immediately raised his wings and was gone.

"Doulas," the huge attender looked to another of his troops.

"Master?"

"Take wing to Mistrea. He is preparing zensak to strengthen the fortress here. Tell him he must bring whatever is immediately ready."

"It is done," he replied and disappeared just as Chantar reappeared at Iadrea's side.

"Have we permission to use a sacrifice?" the commander asked the returned servant.

"Gebarour gives the operation to you to do as you see fit," he reported.

"Good. As soon as Mistrea arrives, I will outline the strategy. In the meantime, Chantar, take a reconnaissance flight over the approaching forces. Report their position immediately."

With a nod and one stroke of his wings he was gone.

Momentarily Mistrea and Doulas dropped out of the sky trailing a cargo of zensak herded to the surface by thousands of cxings. Multar hung expectantly at his master's side. Turning to Iadrea the giant Mentridarian announced, "These are all I have immediately ready; I am at your disposal."

"May the Father of Lights give us strength today, my brother," Iadrea greeted him. "We must strengthen the dome here immediately. A force is approaching, led by the second to the Prince of Armoun. They are either leading or following an attack force of humans led by Lamaq, the son of the city ruler. He has been most troublesome to us in our shepherding of the chosen ones."

"Was it not he you struggled with just two days ago?" Mistrea asked.

"The same."

"Do you know why a dark leader so strong as this accompanies him?"

"No. This makes the situation more difficult. We dare not make a frontal attack without apparent provocation. For this reason I have devised a plan to create a reason to attack them with some force."

At this point Chantar returned from his reconnaissance. Iadrea stopped speaking and looked to the arriving servant.

"The report is accurate. Fauxxin leads three lieutenants and some twenty lower peons. The humans are moving quickly on horseback; the dark ones are keeping pace with them."

Iadrea considered the situation for a moment, then spoke. "It seems reasonable to assume then that the host will stay near the humans when they camp for the night. This will give us a chance to reduce their number without drawing attention to ourselves."

Turning to the messenger from Armoun he said, "Go relieve your master and tell him to report to me."

"Yes, sir," he said and flew off. Momentarily Talizar appeared.

"Welcome, guardian of Armoun," Iadrea saluted him.

"What is your command, Master?" he replied.

"The en-lil will undoubtedly carry the news of Fauxxin's presence in the valley to Meslantaea. No foray into the tree god's territory goes unnoticed for long. There will no doubt be skirmishes during the night. Some of their number will be wounded; this is doubtless why there are so many. Fauxxin won't want to be bothered by tree sprites, and Meslantaea won't honor the Dumuzi's second by stooping to attack him. If we remain under cover, we can perhaps help to increase the number lost if the battle ranges far enough away from the camp so that our intervention remains unnoticed.

"Then with their number reduced somewhat, we will initiate the counter-measure with the sunrise. This is what I need you for, Talizar, should you choose to accept the mission.

"As soon as the sun has made them quite uncomfortable, I want you to attack them with one or two others."

"This I will gladly do, Master," the eager attender replied.

"That is not the end of the matter." He looked compassionately at Talizar. "We need to manufacture a reason to attack Fauxxin in force to keep him from getting too close to the fortress here."

The point to which Iadrea was coming began to dawn on Talizar and some of the other seasoned attenders around him.

The commander continued, "If you go willingly, you are instructed to fight valiantly, taking down as many dark ones as your light allows, but at the critical moment, you must allow yourself to be vanquished." He paused, measuring the attender's reaction.

Only a moment passed before the valiant Talizar responded. "For you and the cause of the Mighty God of Light, I am prepared to commit the sacrifice."

"I do not need to tell you, righteous warrior, that you must take great care not to be captured, but to lose in fierce battle at all costs. Do not let them take you captive to torture you. You well know that they may draw so much light from you that we may never recover your essence."

"This I know, Master."

"Very well, then. The planet has already turned far towards night here. Let us take up positions around a large circumference of their camp. Stay undetected at all costs. At their leader's last words, the small group disappeared skyward, tracing arcs to distant positions around the approaching menace.

"Mistrea, if you and your apprentice will remain with me, we will discuss how you can best help us."

"I am at your service, my brother."

"First we must distribute the zensak you have brought," he began. "Can you and Multar accomplish this alone?"

"My young apprentice is unfamiliar with the process, but we will have no trouble; it will be a good lesson in battle tactics away from the front line."

"Good," Iadrea agreed. "When you have finished, come to my position and we will talk further."

"It will be as you have said," the one from Mentridar acceded.

After they had distributed the fresh zensak around the fortress, Mistrea and Multar followed Iadrea to a position on a small rise several kilometers from the encampment of the Armounians. The commander began by explaining to Multar some of the techniques of fighting the dark ones.

"They will sometimes try to avoid direct combat by melding with a material substance," he began. "Different sects have different objects in which they feel most at home.

"These from Armoun will doubtless shelter themselves in rocks or the earth itself, as they were formerly of the mountain god. They joined forces with Dumuzi, the ram god, originally, and then followed him when he in turn joined the one the humans call Inanna.

"When they leave the safety of their territory, they revert to their old ways. You will see the smaller ones clinging to the rocks away from the fire (they despise the light, you know.)"

Though he was still humbled by the fact that he was in the presence of so great a general, Multar was feeling comfortable enough now to ask a question. "It does not appear that Fauxxin or the other officers are cowering in the dirt."

"True," Iadrea replied. "There are probably two reasons for that. First, Fauxxin is of the Dumuzis, as are one or two of his lieutenants, if I'm not mistaken. Furthermore, they are strong enough — Fauxxin is at least — that they feel more or less secure in the open. Remember, if as Talizar reports, Fauxxin is second to Dumuzi, that makes him only one step down from Inanna."

Slightly puzzled Multar asked, "Is Inanna a great one with the dark host?"

"Indeed! The one they call Inanna, the moon goddess, is second only to the Prince of Darkness himself. He...that is Inanna (Only the Araqans see Inanna as having female gender; he is as we are: genderless.)...he dwells on the dark side of the Araqan satellite they call the moon. It is appropriate that they ascribe the title of moon goddess to him."

"And Dumuzi has joined with Inanna?" Multar asked.

"Yes, in the Araqan mythology Inanna took Dumuzi as one of her husbands. It seems the enemy is looking with favor on those whose territory encompasses a city. The old nature and agriculture gods are losing favor. This is why so many are making alliances with the city gods.

"You have heard of Meslantaea?" Iadrea asked.

"Only in passing; I do not know anything about him."

"He is the god of all the tree sprites. Actually he has equal standing with Inanna, but the Prince of Darkness has lately favored Inanna, so there is friction between him and Meslantaea who feels slighted. That is why I expect a challenge tonight; these Dumuzis will irritate the local en-lil who will carry the message to Meslantaea. Unless I am mistaken, strike forces will be assigned to harass the intruders."

It was beginning to approach true darkness, and Iadrea turned from Multar to Mistrea and said, "There is a lesson you can teach much better than I, my brother. As the Prince of Mentridar you are also the master of zensak cloaking. This is a skill we may have need of before this campaign is over.."

"How can I serve you, Iadrea?"

"If you are willing, I would like you to be our rear guard at the fortress. Even if we stop the dark host (a formidable task with the likes of Fauxxin in charge), the humans may yet continue on their quest.

"If they do attempt an attack on the fortress, you can be of great value in protecting the chosen ones. Of course, we must still keep our protection covert if possible. This is why your presence and great skill in cloaking will be so invaluable."

"I thought all attenders could cloak themselves," Multar interrupted without thinking; he was feeling too comfortable at this point.

"You are correct," Iadrea patiently responded, "but an attender's powers increase as he grows in wisdom. Because your master is a prince, he has abilities surpassing most of us, especially where the use of Mentridarian forms is concerned."

Once again Multar felt a sense of pride as he heard his master referred to in such a way.

"The same increase of powers applies to our enemies. This is why we must be so discreet if Fauxxin approaches the fortress of Nuwach. His powers of perception are very keen. We can only hope we have added sufficient zensak to deceive him, or to cloud his mind at least."

At this point Doulas appeared in their midst. "We have sensed the approach of dark attack forces on several fronts, Master," he reported.

"Good," Iadrea smiled slightly. "It is as I thought. You know what to do, Doulas; may the Wings of Mentridar preserve you."

"Inasmuch as the Father of Lights is my protector, it will be so," the warrior responded liturgically, but with deep feeling. Then he flew into the night.

Turning to Mistrea, Iadrea asked, "Would this be a good time to give your pupil some battle lessons?"

Multar stiffened instantly to attention.

"Yes, I think it could be ideal," his master responded.

"Very well," Iadrea looked approvingly at the young one. "Fight well, young warrior; your teacher will give you the best of counsel, and the Father of Lights goes with you.

"Guard against escaping ones at all costs, Mistrea," the commander looked to the tall one.

"Have no fear; none will live to see the morning light if they engage us."

Multar could hardly contain himself; he was sure that the sense of song he felt in his soul could be heard to the stars above. When Mistrea rose and motioned for him to follow, raised his wings with a sense of purpose which was something from a dream. Finally he was going to join the battle he had heard about on Mentridar; he was going to raise his new sword against the dark ones. He felt thrilled beyond his greatest imaginations.

As they attained a position far above the plain, Mistrea came to a stop and spoke. "Now you fully understand the great strategic use to which our beloved cxings are put, no?"

Multar nodded in excitement.

"Our move to this position would have resembled a huge two-pronged lightning bolt had we thought-traveled. And below, you would see arcs of light streaking across the surface were the attenders not carried on the Wings of Mentridar."

The mention of the on-going battle caused the young one to look down toward the valley they had just left. Even with his limited powers, the pupil could make out the shapes of his fellows moving about as the eagle sees his prey when soaring high above it. With their true light cloaked in zensak battle uniforms, the attenders were only slightly more visible to him than the dark ones. To an enemy foot soldier, they were all but invisible.

"Master," the smaller one asked, "the form of the dark ones is so vague in the night; how do we see them at all?"

"It is true that they are little more than a vapor even in the daylight, but it is not so much sight as sense that allows us to locate them precisely."

Multar's face showed the puzzled thought he was struggling with.

Catching this, Mistrea continued, "Remember the sensation you felt from this vantage point over Mentridar?"

The young one smiled slightly and nodded as he recalled the rich music he had experienced coming from the small planet.

"What do you feel here?" his teacher asked. After reflecting for a moment he shook his head. "There is feeling, a sound of sorts." He paused to sense it more fully. "It is as a ringing or high humming, almost a whine. Nothing of the intensity or beauty of the sensation at Mentridar."

"This is one of the effects the Prince of Darkness has had on this poor planet. The harmony of the spheres — that which you felt a portion of at Mentridar — is stifled by his darkness. There is such absence of light in him and his minions that they virtually absorb all light and beauty around them.

"The weapon they carry, the rod of darkness, is the epitome of this phenomenon. It is the exact opposite of the sword of light we use to battle them. What they are swinging is the power to suck the very light out of us and hence our life.

"This weapon, added to their own darkness, is the very thing that makes them discernible to us. We can sense the absence of light just as easily as its presence. When you look at them, you are not so much seeing them as seeing the absence of all light and beauty in the space they occupy. This evil presence is detectible from a great distance if you are trained to perceive it."

"Does this explain why I feel such repulsion when I look upon one of them?" the pupil asked.

"Certainly. Because you have been created to dwell in the presence of light, its absence is discomfiting; and given the connection with the enemy that this bears, all creatures of our Master feel some sense of this repulsion."

Mistrea had been watching the movements below as he was talking, and at this point he directed Multar's attention to a scuffle that had begun between two dark ones. As they watched, an attender slid unnoticed towards them, and when he was just outside the circle of their flailing wings and rods, he shot into their midst and with two strokes — something of a grand figure-eight — he dispatched them both.

An involuntary cheer went up from Multar at the demise of the two dark ones. "Chantar is an excellent swordsman, is he not?" Mistrea asked.

Then in a combination of fear and excitement he asked, "Will you teach me to fight like that?"

"You will be surprised at how easily it will come to you, Multar. These tree sprites are perfect training for you. Their rods are little more than twigs — no match for your sword."

"But I have never wielded it in battle, except for the sad effort to defend myself at Armoun earlier." Multar began to feel almost ashamed as he remembered being bested by the dark one days ago.

Sensing this Mistrea chided him softly, "Stop this useless guilt. You can not expect to take on the mighty ones until you have gained some experience. And that is what we will do right now." He pointed to another skirmish between two dark ones. "See those two?" Multar nodded. "Follow me," Mistrea commanded, and swept off in an arc to a position near them.

When they were settled there, Mistrea said, "Just do as you have seen Chantar do; I will be right behind you."

Multar looked at him almost with disbelief. All the zeal he had felt on Mentridar had vanished and in its place was something as close to anxiety as he had ever felt. But there was such a look of confidence on the face of his teacher, that trust in his master's opinion took over where uncertainty of his own abilities had been.

He glided slowly toward the tiny combatants. There was a kind of electricity flowing through his being. The cxings were nearly humming on his back in anticipation of the need for sudden movement they sensed from him. His left hand tingled as he began to call for the sword that magically dwelt in his ring. For a moment he wondered foolishly if he would be able to draw his weapon quickly enough when he needed it; Mistrea calmed him with the assurance that there would be no passage of time between his need for the sword and its appearance in his hand.

When the two demis were facing one another directly in front of him, he chose to make his move. In one movement he flowed at them, raising his left arm above his head as the wings on his back thrust him forward. He tried to imitate the move he had witnessed earlier. His first sweep was right on target, slicing the demon nearly in two. However, the other saw a faint glimmer of his new enemy's sword as it appeared behind his dark opponent. This gave him just enough time to duck the return swing of Multar's clumsy figure-eight move. The sword nicked the tip of a wing that didn't get pulled down quickly enough.

The little dark form immediately thrust his puny rod at his new opponent, catching him in the mid-section. Multar fell back slightly, feeling a sensation not unlike a human who has had the wind knocked out of him. This apparent advantage was encouraging to the dark one who used it to make another lunge. Flying full speed with his rod above his head, he drove at Multar before the attender fully regained his balance. The rod swung down at Multar's head, only to be blocked by his risen sword.

The little one's momentum carried him fully onto the attender, bowling them both onto the ground. Multar was immediately struck by the stench and repulsiveness of this mass of dark clumsiness that had attacked him. As the dark one struggled to get up, he found himself standing on the chest of his enemy, much the way a child might stand on his father's chest. But the sight was kept from being funny by the apparition Multar beheld. Yellow eyes glared out of a black face; fangs dripped something on him as a shriek rasped out of the ugly mouth.

The dark rod was poised to come down on Multar's head as the sword of light swept from above Multar's head through the attacker awkwardly, taking off the arm and then the head of the putrid creature. The small pool of darkness that had been the enemy vanished, leaving only a momentary stench behind. Multar stood quickly, thinking he would have to brush something off his chest, but nothing remained.

Mistrea was immediately at his side with a hand on his shoulder. "Well done, Multar," he said with pride.

"Surely I must have looked clumsy, Master," the young attender replied.

"You look like the winner," was the only answer. "Let us seek another lesson for you," he continued as they moved slightly above the scene.

There were no more lessons for Multar that night. Several other attenders were successful in dispatching unsuspecting pairs of battlers, however. By morning there were significantly less forces gathered around Fauxxin as the sun began to light the eastern sky. He was amazed and disappointed that his troops had made such a bad showing against what he supposed was a puny attack by the tree sprites. Only his over-riding interest in the movements of his human pawns kept him from wondering more deeply how he had suffered such losses.

With the rising sun, the humans began to move toward the pass which lay several kilometers distant. Before they had followed very far, Fauxxin and his troops were surprised by a flash coming directly out of the sun. One of the lieutenants was bisected before he even knew he was a target. As Talizar swooped back into a position between the enemy and the sun, he shouted, "For the glory of the Father of light!"

Menacing growls rumbled from the throats of every dark creature there. The only thing they hated worse than light was the mention of the Creator of light.

"Talizar, is that you?" Fauxxin shouted.

"Prepare to be dispatched to Qavah Khoshek, Fauxxin," came the reply.

"It will take more than your puny light to make me go anywhere, my long-time foe." The words drooled off his giant fangs with disgust.

They were somewhat ready for the next dive Talizar made. While they couldn't see him until the last moment, knowing he was coming placed them in a defensive stance.

The large attender came at them out of the sun and swept toward their outer ranks on the north flank. His glistening sword managed to slice off half of one wing as he rolled and spun past the semi-prepared warrior. Two other dark ones immediately cut off his retreat into the sun this time, so he was forced to do direct battle.

At first, he was amazingly successful. His sword clashed again and again with the rods of the two closest defenders. He swirled and twisted, dodging their sweeping rods deftly while he continued to keep them in peril with his flashing sword. Quickly others slid in around the combatants and before long, Talizar was hopelessly outnumbered.

He carefully chose a spot to attack the sphere of darkness gathered around him. Diving towards a smaller one in the lower portion of the group, he held his sword in front of him as if to impale his foe as he drove at him. Two giant rods met him from either side and crashed into him with such force that he was sent reeling towards the earth. The awful rods had impacted with enough direct body contact that he was almost extinguished. The cxings on his back instinctively continued to carry him away from the fray. Even though he was virtually unconscious, they took direction from his last thought and brought him to rest near a small bush on the valley floor.

"I've been waiting a long time to crush that stinking wretch," Fauxxin growled. "This adds unexpected pleasure to this trip. However, we must be on guard; this victory of ours will not go unnoticed by the enemy. A reprisal is certain.

"Take up defensive positions immediately."

In the glow of the rising sun a large host of attenders paused momentarily to give homage to their valiant peer. There was depth to their feeling, yet not exactly like human sadness at a similar loss.

Sensing this new emotion of reverence, yet mystified by the lack of mourning, Multar posed a question to Mistrea. "Why are they not mourning Talizar's passing?"

"Passing?" Mistrea responded. "He has not passed anywhere yet. True, his light has been diminished almost to non-existence, but we are eternal creatures. There is no such thing as death for us. After we have finished with this wicked horde, you will see how we deal with one of our own who has fallen in battle."

Multar wanted to know more, but just then Iadrea spoke. "Now is the time; fly to victory on the Wings of Mentridar for Talizar and for the Father of Light."

A dozen swords were raised in salute as their voices blended together in the chant, "For Talizar and for the Father of Light!" They then dove out of the sun onto their waiting foes, spreading out so as to confront them at every angle. Most of the small demis fell almost immediately, being outmatched even by Multar who was the smallest attacker. He took out one of them but was immediately challenged by a larger foe who forced him to back away with blow after blow of his rod. Multar managed to block each swing, but he was losing strength very quickly. Just when he thought he would not be able to withstand another blow, another much larger sword swung mightily against the rod of his opponent as it fell upon him.

He watched as Mistrea returned blow for blow with the dark foe until he was the tired one. Then a beautifully executed diving swing slashed off the arm holding the rod. With a scream the brute swept at Mistrea with his clawed wings, but the attender was too fast. He returned with another stroke that left only a partial wing on the dark one's left shoulder. This was enough advantage for Mistrea to finish him easily.

The other warriors of light were similarly successful, sustaining only minor wounds except for the blow of Fauxxin's rod on the back of Doulas as he faced another of the dark host. He was sent spinning into the sky, but before Fauxxin could pursue him to finish him, Iadrea lunged at the dark lord and kept him fully occupied.

It soon became apparent to Fauxxin that the battle would go to the enemy, so the dark captain struck out in the direction of Armoun. Naturally the two lieutenants who remained wished to follow, but they were so badly outnumbered by this time that only one of them made it back to the fortress/temple in the city with his master.

As the flight towards Armoun began, the humans, oblivious to what was taking place just above their heads, were moving into stalking position near the pass. Mistrea swung to Multar's side and arrested his flight after the fleeing enemy. "Come," he said, "We have charges to protect."

CHAPTER TWELVE

A tall, muscular man with sandy brown, shoulder-length hair stooped next to a young man lying face down on a dusty ledge near a pass on the road to Armoun. He was dressed in simply tailored animal skin clothing consisting of a mid-thigh length breech cloth and a vest. His ample hair was held in place by a woven leather thong tied around his forehead, and the ends, which hung at the side of his head just behind his right ear, were finished with several colored beads and a curious silver ornament.

A large reddish brown dog sniffed at the side of the fallen man's face, then looked up and whined quietly at his master.

"Yes, he's still alive, my friend," the man said to his dog. He carefully turned the young man over and slid him closer to the rock face behind the ledge where he could prop him in a sitting position. He took a skin of water he was carrying and poured some into his hand which he had cupped over the unconscious head. The water spilled out of his hand, into the hair and onto the young face. Gradually the eyes began to move under their lids and then one opened briefly. A groan escaped the lips of the wounded man as consciousness brought him awareness of the pain in his head.

"Sharaq..." was the first word out of the young man's mouth, spoken before he was even fully conscious. When both eyes opened, squinting from the light and the pain, the young man started slightly at the sight of the stranger, thinking he may have been one of his attackers.

"Fear not, my friend," the stranger said kindly. "I am here to help you."

"Sharaq," the wounded man began again, "where is Sharaq?"

"I do not know of whom you speak, friend. When I found you here, there was no one else in sight."

A look of horror spread slowly across the face of the seated young man as realization gradually overcame him. "Sharaq is my..." he tried to find the word for exactly what to call her. "She is my betrothed," he stretched the truth.

He began to get up, thinking to look for her, to go after her, but pain stopped his movements. One of the blows of his attackers had glanced across his temple, breaking the skin and causing a slight trickle of blood to run down the side of his cheek. The real damage was done by the thump to his crown; it had driven consciousness from him while mercifully leaving little noticeable wound apart from a lump the size of a goose egg.

"Don't try to get up; just rest, the command came firmly but with concern. "Were you traveling with her?" the tall stranger asked after a moment.

"No, we...I mean I live just beyond this ridge," he replied with a nod indicating the rise behind him, the nod sweeping serious pain through his head and neck. As he winced in response, the stranger held out his water skin again, offering a drink.

While the young man sipped, the stranger said, "Then let us get you home straightaway."

At this moment the dog bristled and stiffened, looking up the ridge and to the south. He had heard something moving among the rocks. He raised his snout, testing the air for scent, but the unknown sound-maker was downwind, giving no hint of its identity. The stranger also looked in the direction of the dog's interest and asked, "What is it, Jireh?"

The animal responded with a soft, low growl which was quite normal from such a beast in that circumstance, but which in this case said to his master, "I heard something moving up there; I sense that it is human, but I can not confirm anything with the wind at my back."

The man thought, "Go quietly and investigate; I suspect it is someone from Nuwach's come looking for the boy, for I too sense its human-ness."

All the boy perceived from this interchange was the growl and the master pointing up the ridge and saying quietly, "Go!"

The dog slipped silently in the direction of the sound it had heard, guided additionally by another sense telling it that a human life form was approaching from a certain position ahead of him. In only a moment he had reached a point where the approaching man became visible. He stopped short of revealing his presence. "I see him," he thought to his master. "He is one alone, carrying a staff and dressed as a farmer."

"Good," the stranger returned in thought. "He is doubtless, as I expected, a servant of Nuwach's. Reveal yourself in a friendly way and bark. I will then call to you and you can lead him to us."

The animal obeyed immediately, causing the approaching servant to recoil in a defensive stance at first, but seeing the wagging tail and absence of any sign of an attack, he relaxed. Then when the servant heard a strange voice call, "Jireh, what is it?" he again became somewhat defensive. The dog barked repeatedly, jumping slightly off his front paws excitedly. When there was no movement from the subject, the animal took several turns toward the location of his master and then back toward the servant, trying to indicate that he wished him to follow.

"He is not moving," the dog thought to his master.

"Very well," came the return thought, "I will come toward you and speak to him." The stranger turned to the young man, still seated against the rock and said, "I think someone from your settlement may be coming to look for you, yes?"

"Oh, yes," he replied. "I...I mean we... were supposed to be home by now." He placed special emphasis on the "we" because as he thought of Sharaq's abduction, the pain it brought to his heart rivaled what he felt in his aching head.

The stranger gave him an understanding look and stood, stepping out from behind the outcropping. "Jireh, what is it?" he said again, although he knew exactly what it was.

He only had to walk a few meters in the direction of the excited barking before he could see the man standing on the hill fifty meters away, the dog in between. Once again the servant stiffened, instinctively bringing his staff into a defensive position. He examined the stranger, noting that he was apparently unarmed although he was dressed not unlike a bandit might be expected.

"Fear not," the stranger said as he moved closer to the servant. "I mean you no harm. There is a boy here who is wounded and needs attention. Is there a place nearby where he may receive assistance?"

Of course, the stranger knew precisely how far beyond the ridge help lay, but he condescended to the situation.

"Sha'ym?" the servant cried, temporarily ignoring the question. "Is the boy badly hurt?"

"I do not think so, although he is not able to move without some pain at the moment."

Suddenly it occurred to the servant to ask, "But is he alone; is there not a young girl with him?"

"No, I'm afraid something happened to the girl. He spoke of her, but she is not here. I believe his attackers abducted her."

The weight of this revelation slammed onto the servant's mind as he pictured how the news would be received by the girl's father. By this time the two men and the animal had hurried back to the ledge where the boy lay.

"Oh, Sha'ym, may the god of all Araq preserve you," the servant said as he saw the boy. "Are you alright?"

"Ben'Sedek," the young man nearly cried, "they've taken Sharaq!"

"I know, young master," he replied. "The kind stranger has told me." He knelt down at the boy's side and placed a hand on his shoulder. "Can you walk? We must get you home; your father sent me to find you...oh, he will be both glad and sorely distressed, will he not?"

The stranger and the servant began to help Sha'ym stand. The boy finally realized just how huge the man was who had been his helper. He stood more than a head taller than the boy, and the servant as well. His shoulders were wide and strong as those of an ox, and his biceps were nearly the size of the boy's thighs. In spite of the obvious power present, there was an uncharacteristic gentleness about the man.

With Sha'ym between them, the two men began to lead him toward the road. While it would be slightly longer taking the road, the stranger reasoned that the climb up then back down the hill would be more difficult than the boy could easily manage.

At the edge of the road, they stopped briefly for the stranger to pick up a large skin bag with a strap which allowed him to carry it on his back and a large staff which he carried in his free hand. Thus loaded, they proceeded through the pass toward the compound with the dog trotting alertly behind.

"Stranger, forgive me," Sha'ym began, "but I have not thought to ask your name. I am Sha'ym ben'Nuwach and this is my father's servant ben'Sedek."

They paused momentarily and repositioned themselves with the stranger facing the other two. "I am called El Channah," the tall one said. "It is my pleasure to be of service to you."

Standing on his own however briefly, Sha'ym began to sway slightly and both men immediately resumed their positions on either side of the wobbling boy. As they began walking again, El Channah returned to the painful subject of the girl. "I believe I may have seen your betrothed's captors this morning." He was not lying, for he knew exactly who they were, and where they were even now. However, he added details to the truth so that it would fit the understanding of his eager listeners.

"I saw riders approaching as I came this way early this morning," he continued. "I feared they may be bandits so I hid myself, even though I have no purse to attract such; it is my experience that one can be harassed these days for reasons other than money, and I wished to be left alone."

Sha'ym considered the big man's use of the word "fear" in his explanation, thinking that a man of his size and obvious strength surely wouldn't know fear, but he kept his thoughts to himself.

The sun was at full strength and heating the day to its peak, but Sha'ym did not feel quite warm. Although he didn't know it, he was still suffering slightly from the shock of his attack. The men helping him along the road were becoming quite warm before they reached the entrance to the compound.

Nuwach and Imanaq, who had been watching for the return of the servant with their children over the rise, were suddenly aware of the people approaching on the road. They rushed out to meet them when they were still over a hundred meters away, greatly concerned that Sharaq was not with them and Sha'ym was obviously hurt.

When they had covered half the distance between them, Imanaq shouted, "Where is my Sharaq?"

The three were silent momentarily, not knowing exactly how to break the news to the unfortunate father. Ben'Sedek finally spoke up, "Dearest friend of my master, we do not know what has become of her; she was not with the boy when we found him. This traveler says he may have seen the men who attacked them heading toward Armoun. Perhaps they have taken her there."

"Oh! Of course!" Sha'ym exclaimed. "Why did I not remember before now? They are certainly going to Armoun; it was Lamaq of Armoun who attacked us — he and his soldiers."

By this time the two older men had reached the party on the road. "How can you know this, my son," Nuwach asked. "You have never met the one called Lamaq."

"No, Father, but Sharaq called him by name, and we spoke briefly before one of his men ambushed me from behind.

"May the gods forgive me for being such a fool!" Imanaq cried. "I knew something like this would happen when we kept refusing Lamaq's proposal. He is a man who takes what he wants, regardless of the cost or custom."

"Then we must take after him and reclaim what is ours... I mean yours...I mean..." The boy was still struggling with the newly discovered relationship he and Sharaq now had. Finally he gathered his thoughts at what he considered the critical point. "We must go to Armoun at once!"

"First we must see to your needs," Nuwach proposed, "then we can discuss how to proceed."

During this interchange El Channah had fallen slightly behind the other two while they spoke. Now Nuwach remembered his duty as the host and grateful father. "I am called

Nuwach," he addressed the tall traveler, "and I believe I owe you a great debt."

"I am called El Channah, noble sir," he replied respectfully, "and you are no more in debt to me than any of us are to one another."

Nuwach immediately liked the tall stranger, both for what he said and for some unnamed subtler reason. "What you say is truth, kind sir, but there are not many today who will behave as you have, despite the debt you speak of."

"Sadly, this is true," El Channah responded, "but it is still my purpose and my obligation to help those I find in need."

"A noble attitude, indeed," Nuwach continued. "But what can your purpose be, traveling so light and far from your home?"

"Which of us truly knows our purpose until it is discovered in doing it?" El Channah said strangely.

Uncertain how to respond to the cryptic remark, Nuwach suggested, "Come, let us seek the shade and tend to my son. We can discuss all these things then."

With Sha'ym now aided by Father and servant, the group headed toward the compound. Imanaq and El Channah walked behind the others and the older man took the opportunity to learn more of the situation from the stranger.

"Did you see a young girl with the riders who passed you this morning?" the concerned father asked.

The tall one delayed for a moment before answering, waiting for an indication that discretion might be in order. Sensing no need to withhold this information he responded, "Yes, I believe there was a girl in the party. She did not appear to be bound, although she was riding on a horse with a man. Perhaps it was this Lamaq our young friend referred to."

"Doubtless it was he," Imanaq returned with despair. Then he repeated his cry, "If only I hadn't refused his offer of marriage, this never would have happened."

"Good sir," El Channah interrupted, "if he is this kind of man, would you have wished your daughter married to him?"

"No, no, you are right," the poor man sighed in desperation. "I both feared to say yes and feared to say no."

Further discussion was precluded as Sha'ym's mother had seen them coming and had now rushed to meet them with a cry, "Oh Sha'ym, my son! Are you all right?" Then noticing Sharaq's absence asked with horror, "Where is Sharaq?"

"Let us see to our son's wounds, then we will make prayers for Sharaq."

"Oh no! She is not dead!" the woman interrupted, "Please tell me she is not dead!"

"We think she has been kidnapped, mother," Sha'ym explained. "Lamaq of Armoun has taken her."

"Remember, my dear wife, that Imanaq has told us of this man's desire for his daughter," Nuwach continued the presumption. "Sha'ym heard Sharaq call the leader of the attackers by the name 'Lamaq'. We assume he has stolen her when proper requests were thwarted."

"So you see Mother, we must leave for Armoun immediately," the boy impulsively inserted.

"We will speak of our course of action later, my son. Haste is not always wise in delicate matters."

"But Father," he whined, "they are already half a day ahead of us — and they are on horses. Surely..."

"We must still plan our actions carefully. We have been preparing to travel to the city on account of your brother. Now the stakes are even higher. The sun will soon be setting and neither they nor we will be traveling. Have peace while we dress your wounds and discuss what to do."

The boy's mother took the father's place and she and the servant led him into the house. Imanaq, El Channah and the dog followed Nuwach to a point beyond the house, out of hearing. Turning to the stranger Nuwach began, "These men you saw on horseback — they doubtless were armed?"

"One or two had the new metal swords the devils in Kamaresh have created for killing; the others had war clubs and some flint knives."

"Even if we could overtake them, we are no match for warriors. I know our god will fight for us when we protect ourselves, but I must truly seek his wisdom in this affair.

"Imanaq, my friend," he said turning to him, "Do you still cling to your belief that all gods share power on the Araq?"

There seemed to be some urgency in this request from an old friend. They had talked for many years of the interplay between the gods. Nuwach always held that the Ancient One he worshiped was sovereign over all gods, whereas Imanaq felt doubtful that one power could rule such a vast territory as the Araq with so many deities vying for control. He had seen demonstrations of power by different gods in the cities he traded in.

"I am confused," he confessed.

"I think it is time you determined where you allegiance belongs, my old friend," Nuwach gently suggested.

"I too have seen power displayed in many places," the tall stranger added. "But I have noticed something else." He raised an arm and indicated the arc of the sun saying, "The sun travels the same path each day; the moon keeps her appointed rounds; the stars appear night after night in the same courses.

"And here on the Araq," he continued, "the animals, the plants, and even men in most cases fall into a pattern of life. If each god in every place were independent, could such order exist?" With the question he looked deeply into the old man's eyes.

Imanaq struggled with the obvious answer. In defense he argued weakly, "But what of the changes in the Araq? The sun burns hotter year by year; the ground dries into parched dust in some places. Can this be possible if one god controls all?"

El Channah looked briefly at Nuwach and sensed that this was not the first time this argument had been used. "Has not your friend told you that this too proves the power of the Maker of all things; this is his judgment upon men for following their own way in rebellion against him?"

Nuwach looked intently at this stranger who echoed his deepest thoughts in simple words.

"There is much wisdom in what you say," Imanaq replied after a moment's thought. "Nowhere on the Araq can these gods cooperate for long; it would be foolish to imagine they could bring about the order we see in all things." Turning to Nuwach he said, "Perhaps I have been blind all these years, my friend."

"Sometimes it takes a harsh light to reveal those things that lie in the corners," Nuwach said with compassion. "Come, let us pray to the Ancient One. Perhaps he will smile on us with wisdom for this difficult decision."

Again the three walked together a short distance across the compound to a spot behind an outbuilding. Here they stopped near a large rock, insignificant but for its size. One might have guessed that it had remained there because it was too heavy to move. In fact, there were a number of smaller rocks roughly encircling it which had obviously been placed in their positions. One might also have noticed that the rock was stained in a curious way, as if dark liquid had flowed down its sides.

"Wait here a moment," Nuwach said as he stepped into a nearby building. He reappeared in an instant carrying something and walked past them to a pen opposite the building. Lifting the gate aside, he stepped inside and looked at the sheep gathered within the corral. In a moment he selected one and placed a rope gently around its neck and led it back to where the others waited.

When he had returned to the circle of rocks, he stopped, knelt down beside the animal and stroked the top of its muzzle briefly. He seemed to saying something, although it was unintelligible to them. After a moment he scooped the animal in his arms and lifted it onto the nearly flat top of the rock in the midst of the circle of rocks. He deftly caused the sheep to kneel then sit on the rock with its head up and its legs under it.

Placing one hand on the sheep's head, the old man raised his face to the sky and began, "We are all your creatures, oh Maker of the Araq and all that is upon it. We bring this sacrifice to you as an offering. Take this innocent one in payment for all our wrongs. Accept this blood and incline your ear to our voices."

With this he produced a long, curious flint knife and with one stroke drew open the throat of the unsuspecting creature. There was no sound, no struggle; the animal lay down almost as if sleeping except for the stream of blood cascading over the sides of the rock and soaking into the dry ground at its base.

Nuwach now raised both arms to the heavens and continued, "You know our days from the beginning; nothing is hidden from your sight. You have seen the evil of this day as well. We must now beg for your mercy and your wisdom. We beseech you to guard the life of the precious Sharaq; show us what to do."

Imanaq's gaze had unconsciously been drawn upward when Nuwach began to pray. He now noticed that the stranger was in a similar pose, arms uplifted, face turned skyward. He couldn't be sure, but it seemed in the fading light of day that there was a stream of light flowing down on the tall sandy head. The more he looked, the more convinced he was of a certain liquid presence enveloping him. Though he couldn't see the upturned face, he sensed a serene confidence and strength that was beyond explanation. Suddenly he realized that the feeling was within his own heart as well. Never before had he felt such peace.

No words were spoken, yet both men dropped their arms slowly to their sides. Nuwach was almost imperceptibly nodding his head as if in acquiescence to something unheard. The stranger broke the silence, "Our god has heard your prayer." Nuwach nodded. "I will leave at once to rescue the girl."

At this Nuwach seemed to come to a realization that this was what he had expected, yet immediately he began to have second thoughts. "But you have no..."

"You heard as clearly as I, did you not?" the tall one interrupted.

"He said, 'I have sent one to help.'" Nuwach responded. "You are that one?"

"So I am."

"But travel at night is dangerous..."

"I have no fear when I go on a mission for the Mighty One," he replied. "There is no darkness is his presence."

"Do not cease to pray, however," he continued. "In this way you may participate in the success of the mission."

"This we will do," Nuwach agreed, placing his arm on the shoulder of his friend. "We will not fail in this," he said, emphasizing the word "we."

Imanaq looked at his old friend and nodded with a new confidence in his wisdom.

"Peace to you and all within your house," El Channah said formally, with one hand stretched toward the men. "I will be back as soon as the god of all gives me success." With this he turned and walked out of sight around the building.

When the boy learned of all that had happened, it was all they could do to keep him from running off after the tall stranger. By late morning the next day, he took his staff, water and some bread and slipped out the gate when no one saw him. He flew through the rocks and bushes over the hill and down to the road to Armoun. He too had a mission.

CHAPTER THIRTEEN

As the young man trotted down the road he wondered at the storm-tossed sea of feelings he was experiencing. His newfound affection for Sharaq was now overshadowed by a sense of protectiveness and loss like nothing he had ever known. Or was there something in the past, something similar yet disguised by youthful innocence. He wracked his brain to remember what it was that seemed familiar in the distant past.

At each turn in the road and crest of a hill Sha'ym scanned the distance for a sign of the tall stranger who called himself El Channah, little expecting to catch him, yet hoping against hope. In the middle of the afternoon, when the sun was at it's hottest, he stopped in the shade of a small tree to eat his bread and drink some water. As he ate his meager meal, he began recalling snatches of conversation, then the whole scene reopened in his memory. It was immediately after the death of Sharaq's mother. Even though quite young, he was feeling genuine sympathy for his friend's loss. He had asked his father why life presented such an ugly face, not willing or perhaps yet unable to call the visage death.

"What is in the cup?" his father asked, directing his attention to one of the vessels remaining on the dinner table.

Puzzled at first by this obvious question, the boy returned quizzically, "Wine, Father?"

Ignoring his son's initial confusion he continued, "And where does wine come from?"

"Grapes?" the reply came still without any hint of the meaning.

"And where do grapes come from?"

"From the vine, Father, but I don't..."

His father interrupted with gentle understanding and began the real point of the lesson. "The vine, my son, takes elements of earth, water and sunshine and fashions young fruit. It glistens with morning dew when it is firm and green. When it is plump and begins to blush, what do we do?"

"We pick it."

"And then?"

"Some of the grapes we eat and some we crush and draw the juice into casks to make wine," the boy answered almost impatiently.

"Yes, and after time we can enjoy the wine as you see it here," he gestured to the cup on the table again. "Can you see that the life of a grape is a picture of all of life?"

The boy thought silently for a moment, then his father continued, "Just as the grape gets its particular flavor from the elements of the Araq on which it feeds, so life is made up of the elements we gather from around us. We blend them into our experience, sometimes in joyous sunlight, sometimes under crushing pressure. But always in time, there is a sweet product. In time, we taste the goodness and forget the bitterness."

The boy glimpsed what his father was trying to say, and after a few moments of contemplation asked, "Yet Sharaq loved her mother very much and now she is gone. Why can't we keep the things we love?"

"This is the time of crushing, my son. The sweetness and the crushing can not share the same moment."

The young man under the tree realized that in his reverie he had finished all of his bread, despite his plan to save some for tomorrow. This made him realize more urgently his need to find the stranger. Uncertain as to why he felt so, he was confident that the tall warrior could solve all of his problems. With this in mind, he struck off down the road with renewed vigor, and with a resolve to find his way through this moment of "crushing."

At one point as he walked along the road, searching the plain for signs of his friends, he stopped suddenly. He thought he saw something move a great distance ahead of him near where the road bent out of sight. He froze as he tried to make something out of the movement. It refused to materialize into anything definite, but the boy was sure he saw something. After remaining still for several moments, he decided it must have been a sort of mirage, the kind of thing he had seen dozens of times before as the heat created images in the empty desert air. Just as he was about to move on, he imagined he saw it again, almost definite enough to call a color or a shape, but before it resolved into anything real, it was gone as quickly as it had come. He waited, but after several minutes, resumed a brisk walk along the road. It must have been the heat, he thought.

As the sun began to set that evening, Sha'ym was not surprised that he had not overtaken the stranger. He found a large rock that had absorbed some heat from the sun and afforded a protected spot to rest, and leaning his weary body against it he drank a few sips of his shrinking water supply. By midday tomorrow he would be in the city where food and water were plentiful, but he was by no means certain how he would obtain them unless he located El Channah.

That afternoon in the city, not only water, but wine had flowed liberally at the temple tavern where Lamaq and his friends toasted their victory. Lamaq sat talking with his number one lieutenant, Delzar, curious as to why the black bearded warrior seemed distant.

"Forgive me, Lamaq. I was thinking of my wife."

"I had almost forgotten you once had a wife, my friend. Batinah, wasn't it? Lost her in the last raid by Kamaresh, didn't you?"

Batinah. Delzar hadn't heard the name in almost two years. "Yes, I was defending the pass when a small detachment scaled the cliffs and circled around to attack the settlements south of the city. I should have been there." His tone revealed the guilt he still harbored for having failed to defend his wife from the marauders.

Lamaq was not entirely sympathetic to his friend's plight, unable as he was to understand why he had not simply replaced his lost wife with another. Not too drunk yet to see an advantage in Delzar's mood, Lamaq offered a suggestion. "Since you are not interested in drinking, perhaps you can undertake a little mission for me."

"What do you wish, my friend?" he asked, glad to be delivered from the celebration.

"Earlier this afternoon, after briefly questioning the girl, the meddling priest, Gishnan, approached me with some strange questions. After asking how long I had known her and some other trivial information he asked if the girl had ever said anything about the condition of her womb. Does the high priest think young girls talk to men about their wombs? You were in his sect once, Delzar; what in the world was he getting at?"

Mildly curious, Delzar asked, "Did Gishnan specifically ask if you knew whether the girl is a virgin?"

Now Lamaq's eyes took on a look of understanding. "Is that what he wanted to know? Why didn't he just ask.... Wait a minute. What is he thinking? He's not going to try to steal her for the temple, is he?" He looked directly at Delzar with piercing eyes, "Now I know I want you to look into this. This could be more serious than I thought."

Although Delzar had little use for the priests anymore, he was not anxious to get in the middle of a power struggle between the lugal's son and the high priest. The balance of power was always tentative, shifting back and forth depending on the personality of the men in power and the circumstances. If the issue had to do with crops or weather or predictions of who might attack whom, the priest was more in demand. If the commerce or government of the city was threatened, the lugal and his army were on top. Since he didn't see how he could deny his friend's request he decided to assent, but to stay as uninvolved as possible.

"I will see what I can learn. Do not hold out too much hope. Remember, the priests were not happy when I chose the way of the warrior over the priesthood. They saw it as a defection of sorts. To them, I was putting my trust in the sword instead of the gods."

Delzar didn't say that this was precisely the case, but left unsaid what he hoped would be irrelevant to Lamaq.

"Good," the other responded, as if the matter were already taken care of. "Let me know what you find out."

"I still have some respect among the temple guard; they understand my choice to become a warrior. Perhaps one of them will know something that will help you," Delzar said, emphasizing "perhaps" so as not to sound too promising.

"Yes, yes. Do what you can; I have great confidence in you." As he spoke, his eyes drifted towards a girl who was looking intently at him with startling dark eyes. She had the unmistakable demeanor of one of the temple girls, yet there was a presence about her which placed her in a class above the mere prostitutes who surrounded most of the men in the tavern. Seeing her gave Lamaq an idea. With the barest of nods he summoned the girl. She set down a cat she had been stroking and floated over the floor towards him.

"Delzar," he said as the girl came within earshot, "I have a present for you. It will help you forget Batinah." The girl immediately understood and slid around the table past Lamaq and sat lightly on Delzar's lap.

Her arm circling the strong neck, she sat upright so that her breasts were mere inches from his beard. "You need to forget someone?" she asked in a musical tone.

Delzar was involuntarily taken in. The girl had obviously bathed in the scented water they used for ceremonial cleansing. The scent brought the image of his beloved wife crashing unwanted into his consciousness. The girl's light tunic was open slightly so that the curve of her breasts tantalized him. As she turned the movement drew one side away so that the full round form was half revealed. She kissed him lightly.

"Take her. It will do you good." With these last words, Lamaq was rising from his chair and turning away from Delzar.

She stood, allowing her hand to slide slowly up the muscles on his neck and momentarily cup his bearded chin as she rose. Her eyes never left his as she seductively paused for him to rise. They walked through the crowded room into the hall which led to the private chambers in the rear.

Once in her room, Delzar let down the wall he had erected since his wife died. The girl pulled him firmly to her body and kissed him more passionately. He closed his eyes and thought of Batinah. He kissed her madly. Soon they were taken with the passion. He slipped the tunic off her shoulders and remembered the softness of Batinah's willing body. Then they were on the bed and he kept thinking, "Batinah. Batinah," until once in the heat of the ultimate moment, with the girl moaning softly just the way Batinah had, his lips parted beside her neck and he mumbled in a hoarse whisper, "Batinah."

The girl thought nothing of it, if she even heard through her increasingly loud, long moaning sighs. It was customary for the faithful to repeat the name of one god or another when they performed the ritual acts of worship.

Some time later, Delzar sat on the edge of the bed, the girl naked beside him, her hand resting gently on his thigh. He felt relieved, but not fulfilled. Stroking his black beard absentmindedly, the warrior's eyes looked off into nothing as he thought of the conversation he had with Lamaq. The man's request interested him for reasons he would not admit to anyone, least of all the lugal's brash son. He thought to himself that the confidence the young man placed in him was less deserved than it once was. He would look into the matter, to be sure. But he was not at all certain what he might do with the information he obtained.

As Delzar left the interior room, a familiar face appeared; familiar, though not welcome. "Donar," he said as they met, "I trust all goes well with you."

"No, Delzar, all does not go well," he replied in his usual negative tone. "I have just been to see Gishnan again. The high priest was very interested in what I had to share with him. I have learned that there is quite an interesting connection between the old man we visited and the trader his son asked about." His face had the look of one who has far more interesting tidbits to share on the subject.

Initially Delzar was genuinely uninterested in Donar's temple politicizing, until the plump one continued, "The daughter of the trader is one of the girls Lamaq wishes to take as a wife. I told you there would be a connection to the old religion; I told you..."

Donar's voice continued, but Delzar's mind was racing ahead to plan a way to make use of this chance encounter. So this wasn't just another pretty face the lugal's son was after, but the friend of his imagined enemy. At this thought he regretted all the more having helped the spoiled young ruler capture his prize. Yet perhaps he could make amends some way by spoiling the plans.

"You see it is just as I told you.... Delzar, do you hear me?" the puffy face was entreating him.

"Just as you told me when?" Delzar asked, grateful that a reasonable sounding question allowed him to reenter the conversation.

"On the road the day we visited the old man," the whining voice continued. "I told you the religious implications would not be lost on Gishnan. He wants to make special use of this virgin." His eyes sparkled at the thought of whatever use may have been intended.

"And strike a blow at the lugal too, no doubt," Delzar remarked, seeing the political as well as so-called religious implications.

"Neither the lugal nor his impudent son can dispute the priests' right to choose a virgin for the Sacrifice. Since the beginning it has been the priests' right..."

"Yes, Donar, the priests' right," the black beard interrupted. "But you say the Sacrifice; Gishnan wants to use this girl for the Sacrifice?"

"That is what I have been trying to tell you, had you been listening," he retorted importantly.

Now it was clear why the priest was hurrying the preparation rites. It had nothing to do with Lamaq's desire to marry quickly; the crafty priest was orchestrating a power play with the lugal and using the girl as the innocent victim. The rush was no doubt on account of the approaching feast of the new moon.

With no need to feign interest now Delzar asked, "So Gishnan has the girl in the inner chambers for the final rites of initiation, then?

"Yes, and won't the lugal be surprised?"

As Delzar nodded, deep in thought, the woman he had been with stepped out of the chamber they had shared and stooped to pick up the cat that had apparently followed her. She gave only the briefest look at Delzar as she passed, knowing better than to interrupt two men having an official sounding conversation. As she reached the point in the hall where she would turn to re-enter the tavern, the cat wriggled free and jumped to the floor. With typical feline detachment he sauntered to a far corner of the hall and curled up. The girl cast an overly dramatic wave in the cat's direction and said loudly enough for the men to hear, "Well! If that's the way you want it, I shall just have to look for another male companion." She disappeared around the corner, leaving the three males to themselves.

Earlier that afternoon, another romance had begun, but far more innocently. Chamah and the servant Naashah had slipped into the city with the throng of traders and merchants that flowed freely in and out of the gates most days. As long as there were no immediate threats from nearby adversaries, the guards were fairly relaxed, looking only for obvious signs of weapons or commotions. Naashah indicated that he wished to offer penance to the gods for the slight they had suffered in the tree cutting expedition, but in truth, he had more lusty intentions for visiting the temple. To his relief, Chamah asked to be excused from the ministrations so that he could take in the marketplace. Naashah was only too glad to give assent, as it nicely solved the problem of how to explain his temple activities to this young lad, and reduced the possibility that Nuwach, who loudly decried the whole temple scene, would ever hear of his escapades. That is, if he ever saw his old master again.

On his own, Chamah wandered among the stalls of those selling baskets, bread, and tools, and ventured into the foreign section where more interesting curiosities were found. He felt the fine cloth and sniffed the spices that had been brought from distant lands. He marveled at the fine workmanship of the metal workers. It was this new industry that fascinated him most. Although he had admired the metal objects Imanaq occasionally brought on his regular visits, his father still worked almost exclusively with wooden and stone tools; but here were bowls and ornaments and even blades made from fire-hardened materials dug from the belly of the Araq. It was the last of these that most drew the young man. He could not take his eyes off a small dagger with a handle carved from bone or antler. It seemed to him to be the finest piece of workmanship he had ever seen. The thought of sliding it in his belt gave him a feeling of power and security he had only dreamed of. Who would dare challenge a man with such a weapon close to his side?

As Chamah stood dreaming, the man in the stall startled him from his reverie by asking, "This dagger was made just for such a strong warrior as you, young master."

The compliment went directly to Chamah's head, as was intended. He actually blushed, a fact which immediately embarrassed him, deepening the hue in his face, which only made him feel more awkward than before. "I... uh... yes," he stammered, "it's wonderful." This remark sounded so childish, so unwarrior-like to the boy that he nearly turned and ran away. However, the merchant continued his pitch, stopping the retreat.

"Wouldn't you like to feel it in your hand?"

Chamah's hand nearly trembled as he accepted the wondrous implement from the man. He held it loosely at first, then gripped it tightly, as if preparing to brandish it at some foolish bandit.

Looking the boy over carefully for signs of a money sack, the merchant baited him with, "No price would be too much for such a fine dagger as this, yes?"

At the word "price," Chamah was brought back to reality harshly. The search for a money sack would of course turn up nothing, as the trip to the city had been quite unplanned.

Even if the lad had planned it, his father had little use for the convention of exchanging coins for goods. Barter still seemed to him the only fair method of obtaining the few things he couldn't make, forage or grow himself. In an attempt to save face, the boy blustered, "I didn't bring my money today. I will come back tomorrow."

Reluctantly he handed the dagger back to the man, whose smile had left his face with the admission that there was no money to be had. In truth the boy's remark only confirmed the canny seller's initial suspicion that he would not profit from the encounter. With a faint reappearance of the smile he said, "Very good; you do that," doubting that he would see the boy again, but keeping that hint of optimism that sustains merchants through the dry times.

Nothing else held any attraction for him after that. He continued to imagine the sleek blade snugged under his belt, making him the object of envy and fear as he strode through the city. Before long, though, something else under his belt distracted him: he was getting hungry. Having no idea how they were going to buy bread, he headed back towards the temple where he had agreed to meet Naashah.

Without any real purpose in mind, he felt compelled to enter a street he had not taken when he earlier passed through the marketplace. All at once he smelled, then saw a stall with a few round cakes of bread stacked on a board which served as the sales counter. Without thinking he instinctively drifted towards the booth. Before he reached it, he noticed the young girl tending the loaves seated under the small canopy against the wall of the building where she had staked her claim. Within a few steps he realized that he hadn't noticed her at first because she was wearing a dark cloak with a scarf of similar hue over her head. The hair that showed under the scarf was a mass of dark curls surrounding a strikingly beautiful face. Her skin was dark too, darker even than Chamah's, a fact which gradually dawned on him as he stared, since girls usually didn't spend as much time in the sun as boys, their chores being more domestically sheltered.

Almost in front of the booth now, he could make out her strong chin, full pouting lips and the deepest dark eyes he had ever seen. She was altogether unlike anyone he was used to seeing, yet he had an eerie feeling he had seen her before. He decided it was the eyes, or perhaps the combination of the dark eyes and the broad nose that reminded him of someone, yet he was certain he had never seen a girl of such unique beauty in his life.

It suddenly became obvious that the two were staring at each other, so they both averted their eyes at once. When he returned his gaze after an instant, she was looking at him too, and to his wonderment, she spoke in a soft, almost husky tone with a trace of an accent he did not recognize, "Would you like some bread?"

"Yes!" he blurted without thinking that he was without the means to buy it. "That is I... I was thinking of bread... I mean I was hungry for bread..." His voice trailed off and he realized he was once again staring into her beguiling face.

She looked at his belt and seeing no money sack surmised his predicament. "You are welcome to some; it is late and these few remaining loaves will probably not sell. Most of the people have already gone home."

With this last comment, Chamah realized that it was indeed far less busy in the marketplace than when he had begun his explorations. As he looked down the narrow street, she surveyed his non-city dweller's clothes and asked, "Do you live in Armoun?"

"No, I..." He paused, trying to think of how to explain just what he was doing there. "I am a traveler," he concocted.

The look on her face instantly told him that she was trying to imagine him as a traveler. It occurred to him that she probably saw hundreds of travelers every day, and he certainly did not appear convincing in that role. "Really,

I am just visiting the city," he began again apologetically. "I was just looking for my servant." Again the attempt to elevate himself failed in her eyes. Noticing this he added, "My father's servant."

"You are visiting the city with your father?" she asked.

Somehow it seemed useless to attempt any more fabrication with this girl. He had never had trouble getting away with his little stories before, but she gave him the uncomfortable feeling that her intriguing dark eyes were seeing straight through to his backbone. "No, I am here alone with my father's servant. We were cutting trees in the hills (he gestured in the direction of the forest) and decided to sneak into the city for a..." Here he stopped because he truly did not know what he had expected.

"For a visit?" she completed his sentence.

Realizing that he had already told this stranger more than he had expected to reveal, he pressed on as if driven by some magic spell she had cast upon him. "We never get to the city. We live three days journey south, but Father never lets us come to the city," he noticed to his dismay that he was almost whining.

"Where did you plan to stay tonight?" she asked as she looked at the lengthening shadows on the street.

"I don't know," he said with complete honesty, something that felt quite rare to him, yet not uncomfortable in the presence of this girl.

"I am sure my father would not mind two guests for the night. You are welcome in our home," she waved toward the south gate as she spoke. "We have a house by the south wall near the gate."

"Oh... well I..." he didn't know quite what to make of the invitation. "We are strangers; you can't..."

"I am Delyah. What is your name?" she interrupted.

"I am Chamah," he replied weakly.

"There," she continued. "We are not strangers now. And since we are friends, I can't let you just sleep in the street, you know; it isn't safe. Besides, it is getting cold at night again."

He thought for a moment of what other options they had; there were none. "I guess that would be alright then, if you're sure your father won't mind."

"Not at all," she smiled assuredly. "He loves talking to travelers." She put a little emphasis on "travelers" making him wince slightly, but her quick laugh dispelled his fears that she was mocking him seriously. Teasing would be a better word.

Later that night, after Chamah and Naashah had finished a meal of not just bread, but a delicious vegetable soup and some wine, a tall dark man appeared suddenly in the doorway. "Well daughter, I see we have guests."

The two at table turned to see the same bearded face that had glowed in the firelight a Nuwach's table on that strange night only a short time before. Suddenly Chamah realized why the girl had looked familiar.

Later that night, in the shade of a rocky overhang in the hills outside Armoun, three spirits held counsel out of the pale moonlight. It was not unusual to find dark ones lurking in the shadows; nor was their conversation rare: they were traitors plotting a Rhuyh Klaxxin. What made this meeting different was the fact that two of the creatures followed Dumuzi, and the third was of Ningirsu's army.

"How do I know you aren't setting a trap for me — or for us all?" the one from Kamaresh asked.

The larger of the two from Armoun spoke up, "You don't. But if it is as you say, and an attack is already planned, you have nothing to lose." He glared at the foreigner with one yellow eye, his other lost in battle long ago. "My friend here is in charge of the guard on the road to Kamaresh," he continued. "He will see that your troops' approach is not noticed. Should you encounter resistance or cause an alarm, you will know we have failed. In that case, what have you lost?"

"But if I tell you when we plan to attack, you will increase your defenses," he countered.

"We are always on alert for your attack; your only chance to succeed against us is with our help."

"Alright then, I will tell you," the traitor relented.

A wisp of a cloud passed across the moon as the three hatched their rebellion. When they finished, they slid into the night, shadows floating among the rocks.

CHAPTER FOURTEEN

When El Channah left Nuwach's compound, he walked only far enough to be certain he was completely out of sight and then ducked behind a large outcropping of rock. Instantly, he and his dog vanished, or rather metamorphosed into their true selves again. They flew quickly to the west, knowing that a gathering of their peers was sure to be underway already.

In seconds they located the group hovering above the plain where the battle had recently been fought. As they glided into the perimeter of the circular gathering, they immediately joined the chorus of reverent thanks to the Father of Lights for allowing them this small victory. They sang several ancient hymns of glory and praise. Without any obvious signal, the tone began to shift as everyone began to focus on the losses that had been suffered.

"We must form the Star of Twelve," Iadrea spoke the thought everyone was having. At his signal, the six highest ranking attenders separated themselves from the rest. Then as an indication of honor, six lower ranking participants heard themselves called by the first six. They then positioned themselves so that the six junior fellows formed a ring, their wings outstretched so that they were tip to tip. Then the senior ones formed two triangles, one slightly above and one just below the ring of six. They too stretched their wings fully so that the points of the triangles corresponded with the positions of the ring of six just above or below them.

Although Mistrea was a visitor to the planet, his rank and more especially the purpose of the Star of Twelve assured that he would be involved. As Multar watched, the whole geometric assembly began to move in formation, seemingly spinning on every conceivable axis, yet never losing its precise shape. The Star, as it now truly appeared to be a glowing form, moved over the plain where the battle had been fought earlier that day until it came to rest in one spot. Multar could sense that the group was uniting in some purpose when suddenly a shaft of multi-colored energy began to radiate from the bottom of the formation. The ray swept smoothly over the surface of the planet until a small glint reflected off something in the dirt.

Gradually, the tiny sparkle became larger and then was absorbed into the ray that had lighted it. There was the sense of something traveling upwards within the ray until it stopped in the precise center of the Star of Twelve. What happened next is impossible to express adequately in words. Multar sensed, more than saw, an opening in the sky above the Star, as if a door or window were suddenly thrown open. The radiance from the opening was unbelievably bright, yet because it was not simply light, was not blinding. In fact, it gave Multar the same sense he had felt when he had received his sword — a palpable sense of heat and light and rich musical harmony all rolled into one feeling.

When the sky window closed and the beam retracted — Multar couldn't tell whether it was seconds, minutes or hours — the glow in the center of the Star was gone. The whirling, pulsing congregation coursed smoothly over the scene of the battle, stopping once more and repeating the process when the ray caused a glint of light to appear on the planet's dusty surface. Again, as the spark of light reached the center of the Star of Twelve, the sky opened and it was as if a glowing ash were being lofted heavenward from a blazing fire, riding on waves of sound and color. After hovering for a few more moments, the Star slowly resolved itself into twelve floating attenders once again.

As the participants retreated to their places in the larger congregation again, Multar was about to ask precisely what he had just witnessed, but before he could begin, a messenger appeared at the center of the group near Iadrea. Multar recognized the new arrival as the second in command to Talizar, the guardian of Armoun. After a brief exchange with the messenger, Iadrea summoned Mistrea and Multar to his side.

"Hamayn has news that concerns your mission in the city, Mistrea," the general said as they glided into the inner circle. "Tell them what you have learned," he continued with a nod toward Hamayn.

"I was doing a reconnaissance in the temple when I overheard Lamaq speaking with one of his warriors in the tavern," the attender began. "When I recognized him as Delzar, I decided to sit in on the discussion to see how our promptings are coming."

At this point Multar's curiosity was so peaked that Hamayn stopped speaking and all three turned to look at the young apprentice, having caught his thoughts as if he had spoken out loud. "I am sorry," he apologized, "I didn't mean to interrupt, but I couldn't..."

"No apology is necessary, small one," Iadrea said with understanding. "You were brought here to learn; asking questions is one of the best ways to do that.

"You were wondering how a being of light can stroll through the tavern of the dark ones' temple?"

Multar nodded.

"Just as you have experienced an incarnation as a native beast of the Araq, Talizar and Hamayn often wander the city of Armoun in the form of a beast (Talizar's favorite being a cat, if I am not mistaken.) Cloaked in zensak, they can move freely about without drawing attention to themselves from either the humans or the dark ones. This same effect will, we hope, allow you and Mistrea to secure the rescue of the chosen one without drawing undue attention to our involvement."

"You mentioned promptings," Mistrea now interrupted with a nod toward Hamayn. "Is this the same warrior you have enticed out of the dark priesthood?"

"Yes," the guardian answered. "Talizar long ago noticed a searching heart in this one. He never gave himself totally to the dark ones, so we were able to lead him in his decision to withdraw from the training. To this day he has serious misgivings about the dark view of the world. We still hope to win him to our side eventually."

"And you heard something today which bears on the rescue of the chosen?" Iadrea resumed the inquiry.

"Lamaq asked Delzar to look into the condition of his captive bride," he continued. "It was difficult to read his thoughts precisely, as he is still somewhat confused. But it was clear that he is not completely in favor of the way Lamaq is forcing himself upon the chosen one. We may be able to use his indecision to our advantage when we attempt the rescue."

"Perhaps we should orchestrate a meeting between El Channah and this Delzar," Mistrea suggested.

"Perhaps," Hamayn agreed, "although it is hard to say how he would respond to a direct choice at this point."

As he finished these words an attender flashed into their presence from the east. "I have urgent news, Iadrea," he announced.

"Speak," the general ordered.

"The one they call Sha'ym is preparing to leave the compound and attempt to rescue those in the city," he said in a grave tone. "We did not understand his intentions at first because we were occupied with some tree sprites who were stirred up by the earlier battle involving the other boy."

Nonplused, Iadrea considered this new turn of events with the same confidence he felt when seeing his own plans unfold. He had been at this post for too long to feel any distress. He had an unshaken trust that whatever happened had been foreseen and his only chore was to put his cunning to work to fold events into the grand scheme as best he could. This was the way with the attenders. The younger ones might get excited or feel outmaneuvered occasionally, but by the time one rose to a general's position, unswerving trust that all would flow into the desired end was second nature.

"It appears that we will have an operation on a grander scale than we had first thought," he said after a moment. "I will go to counsel and seek the name of the wife of the second son. We know already that she is among those in the city of Armoun. This situation may be construed a means to extract both sons with their intended wives.

"We know that Nuwach can no longer conceal what he has been doing for these many years. It seems that the time for the cleansing may be approaching. If that is so, the wives of the sons must be brought into the compound."

"Is there word on the third wife?" Hamayn asked.

"No, the Master has yet to reveal her identity or position, but this must not concern us. If we are needed on her behalf, we will be told what we need to know. I sometimes think it is better to leave the chosen ones alone as our attention only causes the dark ones to increase their thwarting actions."

"But what if something happens to one of them?" Multar interrupted.

Several of the attenders chuckled softly. "Mistrea..." Iadrea looked to the teacher.

"Little one," Mistrea said kindly. "Remember how we watched the mintus rush to the zensak when we planted it on Mentridar?"

He nodded.

"The mintus went about doing what mintus do with no idea that you and I were watching them. In the same way, the Father of Lights watches over all his creation. Nothing can happen that He does not see; nothing happens that He has not foreseen."

Multar contemplated this for a moment, then Iadrea continued with his outline of the upcoming campaign in Armoun.

"Before we make further plans, I will seek to know the identity of the second wife." Saying this, Iadrea closed his eyes and to Multar seemed to become even less corporeal than attenders are by nature. His essence remained as it was, but it was as if he grew less substantive for a moment. Then, there was a quick change, not quite a flash, and the general returned to his former state and opened his eyes.

"Praise to Him from whom all things flow," he began. "The Master has seen fit to reveal to me the identity of the girl Nuwach's second son will marry." All eyes fastened on him. "She is the daughter of the one who is called Delzar."

This brought a response from each of the attenders in the circle; some nodded while others said various words of praise to their all-wise Master.

"You see, Multar," Mistrea said, "Even though we knew not the reason, the Master had already begun to enlist our aid on behalf of this important chosen one."

"But did the Master choose his daughter because you were leading her father, or did you engage the father because the Master would one day choose the girl?" Even as he spoke the question, Multar realized that it could not be answered.

"Did we place the zensak in the soil because the mintus would come, or did the mintus come because we placed the zensak in the soil?" Mistrea replied.

The question hung on the air for a moment, then Iadrea continued, "It is good that you have brought more zensak, Mistrea, in any case. I believe we will have need of a sizeable cloaked contingent of attenders in this engagement.

"Hamayn," the general addressed the attender, "go back to the city and attempt to arrange a meeting between the young wanderer and the girl. It will be easier to extract them if they are in the same part of the city when the operation begins. Keep a close watch on them if possible. The more we know in advance of our campaign, the better."

"It shall be so," the attender responded as he raised his arms and the cxings formed the rainbow colored wings taking him back toward the city.

After considerable discussion, a plan was formulated which would allow for the rescue of the chosen ones using minimal overt supernatural force, so that the dark ones would not grow overly suspicious as to the importance of the human subjects. As they were preparing to move to the city, Multar asked if he might know the purpose of the Star of Twelve.

"Do you recall my telling you on Mentridar that the cxings have a use even more valuable than their gift of stealthy flight?" Mistrea asked.

"Yes, Master."

"This is what you have witnessed," the teacher continued. "When an attender falls in battle as Talizar and Doulas have fallen today, the wound is seldom fatal; however, it may leave an attender unable to consciously direct the cxings. Since they have no will or purpose here except as we direct them, they lie with the fallen one until they are summoned."

"Summoned?" the young one asked.

"In His wisdom, the Father of Lights has taught us to use the Star of Twelve to focus our energies and our wills into a single mighty force. Hovering above the battlefield, we direct our power to the surface of the planet and the slightest light, even the tiny energy of the cxings is made obvious to us."

"And the window in the sky, what was that?" Multar interrupted. "I felt an intense... I don't know what to call it; it was similar to the feeling I experienced when receiving my sword."

"And so it should," Mistrea announced. "This was indeed a window to the very room where you were for that ceremony."

"But Master, we traveled a great distance to come here from that place. How can..."

"Little one," he gently interrupted, "what seems a great distance to us is no distance at all to the Father of Lights. As easily as a man opens a window in his house, the Father looks into the farthest corner of His creation. Remember that while we operate in this four dimensional plane, the Father remains outside of all dimensionality. As I said, nothing happens that He does not see."

"So the Father of Lights saw the Star of Twelve?"

"And He carried the fallen one back to Himself," Mistrea completed the thought. "There is another, even more dramatic use of the Star, but I hope you do not have to witness it, for it would only be employed in the most dire circumstances."

Multar longed to hear more of this, but the press of preparations requiring Mistrea's expertise forestalled any more lessons at this time. As several other attenders under Mistrea's direction busied themselves with the zensak, Multar tried to imagine what his Master had hinted at. It sounded foreboding and alluring at the same time. Even though it was spoken of in such grave tones, he hoped he would one day see the mighty Star in operation again.

"Mistrea," Iadrea motioned the attender to him and continued, "there is something else you must do before we attempt the rescue."

Multar was keeping his distance from the two, not certain if he was welcome in the conversation; Iadrea spoke a welcoming thought to him and he floated next to his master as the leader began his request. "As you know, we have been superintending the migration of the animals for some time now." Mistrea nodded. "Since it appears that we are coming closer to the appointed time, the herds and flocks are getting closer to the gathering area and this presents a problem."

"I think I understand, Master," said the one from Mentridar. "From what I have seen, the spirits of the Araq will become more and more discomfited as the various families are brought closer to one another."

"Precisely. And as you know, this was a major reason you were called upon to supply more zensak at this time. My question for you now is whether there is an efficient way to use the protective qualities of the zensak for larger areas. Until now, we have had relatively well-defined areas to secure. Now, however, the need is for more generalized diffusion. Naturally, we can not afford nor do we wish to have a full security level on all migratory paths. Still, it may buy us some extra time if the local sprites are kept in the dark, or at least confused."

Mistrea thought for a moment then responded, "Where the tree sprites are concerned, we can simply plant some zensak among their roosting trees. This will keep all but the higher principalities disoriented." After a pause he went on, "As for the various families, pardon my trespass into your area of expertise, but would it help to keep them separated as much as possible?"

"Yes," Iadrea answered, "and we have done this as much as possible. The problem comes at the watering holes. All species need to drink, and it is difficult to maintain segregation at the water."

"Is it true that the warring among the families and the general disdain for authority keeps the spread of information at a minimum on the lower levels?" Mistrea asked.

"It is as you say," Iadrea agreed. "They seldom share anything unless they feel it has some benefit to them directly."

"Do you think it would be sufficient, then, to plant groves at the watering holes for maximum security and confusion, and then to place periodic plantings along the expected route with a thin cover stretched from each to the next? The Araq's sun would dissipate the cover quickly, but it may provide enough distraction to accomplish our purpose."

"This sounds like our best hope for now, Mistrea," the leader opined. "I will direct the deployment as you have suggested."

"By your leave, Master, Multar and I should be preparing to make our move in Armoun with the others," Mistrea respectfully said.

"This is so; go, and may the light be with you," he said as he laid his hand on Mistrea's shoulder. "I too must make preparations for my part in the operation."

The two raised their hands as in a salute and then lowered their eyes and sent a prayer upward before they moved apart.

Deep inside the private chambers of the temple, another underling was hoping for an enemy engagement. Glaxxin of the dark host had been given guard duty over the young innocent who had recently been captured by Lamaq. Evidence of his failed Rhuyh Klaxxin had never been discovered so he retained his rank among the dark ones. His good fortune had been multiplied when his superior ordered him to take charge of the young girl. He burned with lust for this human creature, so much so that he even felt jealous of her human suitor, Lamaq. This was extremely unusual since humans were considered no better than the rest of the animals of the Araq. If anything, humans were more detestable because of their free will to choose whom they would serve. In their natural state, all of the life forms of the Araq were neutral towards the cosmic struggle that raged around them. The dark ones could take control of any of them for his own purposes — any of them except the humans. This ability to choose not to be controlled is what incensed the dark ones. They hated anything that infringed on their absolute power, and this innate right of the humans to choose their own destiny aggravated the dark ones beyond measure.

As he stood watch over the girl, Glaxxin's lust filled the room to the extent that even the human guards felt it. They maintained their self-control only because they knew that if they were caught molesting their charge, they would be stripped of their rank and possibly be executed. This was fine with Glaxxin; in any other instance he might have enjoyed tempting one of the humans to violate her, especially if he could watch. But this was different. To advance in rank he would have to do more than prompt a human misdeed. The essence of the Rhuyh Klaxxin was the boldness with which one overstepped one's normal authority. The orders to guard this girl came from the highest levels, so to assert his own will in this matter could be a grand enough achievement to merit a considerable increase in rank. Of course there was always risk in attempting the Rhuyh Klaxxin; if the act confounded an important plan of the superiors, one might be terminated for the insubordination rather than commended.

It was this very uncertainty which motivated Glaxxin and fueled his desire. His lust for the girl combined with his lust for political power strengthened his will and drowned his fears in a sea of imagined benefits. He watched the girl as she lay on the straw mat which was her bed, or as she paced aimlessly about the tiny room. The only opening was the door to the hallway, outside of which stood a temple guard. There was no window since the room was several flights of stairs below the level of the street. The only light in the room filtered through the small opening in the door or came from the small oil lamp which sat on the table in a corner of the room. Glaxxin sometimes crouched in the shadow beneath the table, as the darkness there was all he needed to cloak his presence. From there he could watch her as she slept restlessly on the straw mat, dreaming her own dreams of escape from her prison. He only hesitated taking her physically because of his memory of the painful interruption the last time he tried. He intended to watch for a few days to see who else showed an interest in the girl.

So far the only other interest seemed to be that of the priest. Several times he had ordered the girl taken to another room in the temple where various ceremonies had taken place. It seemed to Glaxxin that this young girl had been given more baths in the last few days than most humans took in a year. This was the nature of the ceremonial cleansing: ritual ablutions and priestly incantations spoken over the carcasses of various dead creatures.

As Glaxxin was musing over how he might take best advantage of the girl, the sound of shuffling feet drew his attention towards the door of the cell. The face of the guard appeared in the tiny opening near the top of the door. After a brief glance, the face disappeared and a conversation began.

"I told you she was still here; look for yourself if you wish," the guard said in a somewhat defensive tone.

Immediately another face filled the opening. Glaxxin saw a dark skinned man with a full black beard look into the room, cast his eyes to every corner in turn, then pull away.

"See," the guard continued, "everything is as I told you."

"Of course," the bearded one replied, "but you can understand Lamaq's concern. After all, he hopes one day to marry this girl, and he is anxious to know that she is being well cared for."

"Delzar," the guard began in a more familiar tone, "you were once among us; you know that the temple virgins are pampered. They spend more time in the temple with the priests than in their rooms. And you know they eat better than anyone else in the city."

"Yes, of course I know all that," Delzar interrupted. "But I wasn't sure if this one was considered a temple virgin, as you have said." Delzar's mind raced to find a way to ask if the high priest had any special plans for this girl. He continued with a slight probe, "After all, not every one of them is destined to be the wife of a lugal's son."

"This one is getting no special treatment, better or worse, as far as I can tell," the guard explained. "In fact, I knew nothing of her destiny until you mentioned Lamaq's interest just a moment ago."

Delzar let the import of this revelation sink in for a moment. If the guards knew nothing of any special arrangements, it might mean that Gishnan was behaving as the high priest should, treating all the ceremonial virgins alike. Or, it may mean that he was hiding the special nature of this particular girl to keep enterprising underlings from using the situation for political advantage if indeed he intended to steal her from Lamaq. What they didn't know couldn't be used for leverage with city officials in the constant tug of war between the secular and sacred rulers. Gishnan knew that his temple guard was infected with those who would like to better themselves by moving into a position of privilege in the city government.

Glaxxin listened to the conversation through the cell door. They were speaking quietly so as not to be heard by the girl, but the dark one was able to combine his mind reading ability with the partial voices and make sense of the conversation. He was not able to fully read a human mind yet. His powers extended to placing suggestions and giving nudges, but overt control was beyond his capability. The discussion he overheard caused him to wonder just what the plans were for the girl. If she was being prepared for the Sacrifice, as he suspected, his Rhuyh Klaxxin would be the more bold; if she were only to be the wife of the ruler's son, there was less to be gained by her violation. He decided to press for more information from his superiors before taking any action. With this in mind, he slipped invisibly from the room.

He slid into a large room in the center of the subterranean complex where Fauxxin was speaking with another dark being. At his entrance, his superior demanded, "What are you doing here Glaxxin; you are supposed to be guarding the girl."

"With your permission, imperious one, I have news you may wish to hear," he responded weakly.

"What is it then," he asked impatiently.

"One of the young ruler's men was at the girl's chamber inquiring into her condition, my master," he responded. "I thought it may be of interest to you that I heard him say that the boy is planning to marry the girl. I thought she was..."

"You thought!" the large creature shouted. "You have no business thinking about anything except your duty to do as you are told."

"It is my only wish to do as you command, Master," Glaxxin continued with what courage he could muster, the wounds on his neck not yet healed since his last confrontation, "but if the boy mates with her she will be lost as..."

"You are a mindless fool if you think this boy can thwart our plans for the girl." While speaking he moved towards the fawning Glaxxin so that he now stood towering over him. "Furthermore, if anything does happen while she is under your watch, you will be in Qavah Khoshek by the stroke of my rod. Do you understand?"

"Certainly, my Master," he wheezed. "I will return to her immediately."

The cowering shape slid quickly out of the chamber before any more threats could be made. He had learned what he needed to know. An assault on this girl would be a fine Rhuyh Klaxxin indeed. The stakes were such that he would gain either great reward or great destruction. These were just the odds he longed for.

CHAPTER FIFTEEN

As the sun crept over the ridge east of the city, the rays swept down the wall to rest on a small house nestled against its south face. A young girl was working at an oven just outside the house preparing bread she would offer for sale in the market.

Having finished a simple breakfast of fruit and bread, the owner of the house was preparing to leave. "I have some business in the city this morning; after I return, perhaps our guests would like a tour," Delzar directed his comments to Chamah and the servant.

"Thank you; we would like that," Chamah responded, turning to see a less than enthusiastic look of assent on Naashah's face.

"Very well then; when I return we will see what Armoun has to offer, but I must tell you that I remain steadfast in my opinion that you must return to Nuwach as soon as possible. After you have seen the city, we will make plans for your return home."

"Yes," the boy said with some dismay, "we will speak of that too."

"Until I return, then," he said as he swung out the door and moved into the flow of traffic headed toward the gate. "Good luck today, daughter," he called as he strode off.

A few minutes later when the girl entered the house with her day's produce she found Chamah and Naashah spatting with each other. "I thought I heard something going on in here; what are you two arguing about?"

They both went immediately silent and spun toward her in one motion. "Nothing," Chamah said trying to sound nonchalant.

"Oh, I see," she replied smiling coyly. Again, Chamah discovered that there was no keeping secrets from this girl.

"Well," the boy began lamely, "Naashah wanted to go back into town before your father returns and I said we should wait here as planned." This was only half true, because he too had reason to revisit a certain stall in the market unaccompanied.

Much to their mutual delight she said cheerily, "I see no reason you couldn't go with me to my stall. Father will have to pass by there on his way back here and everything can be done as he suggested from there. Besides, if I know my father, his so-called business will probably take the better part of the morning anyway; it would be a shame if you had to sit around here with nothing to do while you wait."

This announcement met with grins and nods of approval from both of them. Seeing their agreement she directed each of them to take a basket of bread. "It will be nice to have two strong men to carry my load this morning," she said with a look that Chamah was sure hinted at a wink in his direction.

When they arrived at her assigned spot, the two baskets were set on the small table and Naashah immediately spoke, "I wish to have a few moments to myself; I will return shortly." There was no tone of request in his voice, but rather a clear statement of his intention. Chamah began to object but before a word could be formed, Naashah was already walking down the street.

"And what about you," the girl said teasing him. "Are you going to abandon me as well?"

"Well," he began haltingly, "there was something I saw yesterday that I would like to take another look at."

"I suspected as much when you were so eager to follow me here," she responded with a knowing smile. Again the boy felt that she had some uncanny power to read his very thoughts. "I suppose it wouldn't hurt as long as you are back here before Father comes."

"Oh, I am certain I will be," he nodded energetically. "The merchant is not far from here; it was one of the last things I saw before meeting you yesterday."

"Alright, but don't get lost. My father will be quite angry with me if he returns and you are both gone."

"Don't worry; I know just where it is," he said over his shoulder as he headed down the street.

Naashah's mission turned out to be one last trip to the temple for reasons that were far more carnal than spiritual. He had sold a few trinkets yesterday to gain the price of admission. Over the years he had collected a number of coins and some modest jewelry due to the generosity of Imanaq, who had taken a liking to Naashah's leather work. Although Nuwach was aware that his servant was sharing his works with Imanaq, it would have surprised him to know how much money had changed hands over the years. Nuwach detested what he called "useless metal disks" in favor of straight barter where the value was easily determined. More to the point, coins meant cities to Nuwach and this made them doubly hated. It was precisely this aspect that had appealed to Naashah as he had long harbored a secret desire to escape the dull simplicity of Nuwach's compound and flee to the city. Thus he had stealthily packed his treasure when he was told to accompany the others to the forest in hopes that his escape might be possible. And so it was.

Chamah had no such trove, so his mind was conflicted as he approached the street where the metal vendor displayed his alluring knives. He milled about some of the nearby stalls, feigning interest in various items while keeping one eye on the glistening wares that had captured his imagination. His only course seemed to be to steal the knife, but his inner heart knew this was wrong due to many lessons he had from his father. Little things had gone missing from time to time around the compound and once or twice he had been discovered in possession of the articles.

On one occasion a new metal axe disappeared only to be found hidden under the mat Chamah slept on. The theft was quite pointless since all things were held essentially in common, but this very situation seemed to fuel a desire in the boy to have something of his own. Nuwach's discipline was swift and stern, although at first the boy didn't recognize it. His father told him that if he wanted the axe so badly he could have it, but only on condition that he split all the wood necessary for the cooking and heating of their home. The boy was sent immediately to the wood pile to chop a supply for the next few days. He soon learned the folly of his fortune when he came to the house for a meal.

"Are you done already?" his father asked.

"No, Father," was the reply, "I have stopped to eat."

"Not so, son," came the stern reply. "Since you loved the axe so well, it can be food to you until you have finished the chore."

By the end of the day, Chamah came sulking to his father, blistered and hungry. "Please, Father, I am sorry I stole the axe. I don't want it anymore. If I return the axe may I have just a piece of bread?"

His father eyed him closely searching for signs of remorse and asked with compassion, "Have you learned the true value of things: tools, work, bread, trust?"

"Yes, Father," he said with all the sincerity of the moment.

But that lesson was lost on him now as he admired the blades which sparkled in the morning sun. A plan began to form in his mind how he might obtain his lust-object. He stood in the shadow of a building adjacent to the metal merchant's stall. If he waited until the merchant was occupied with another customer, perhaps he could walk by and grab the knife unnoticed. The shadow around his head began to cloud his thinking and he actually congratulated himself for being so clever.

The moment came when in fact the merchant did turn his attention to a customer at the other end of the stall. While his back was turned he didn't notice the boy strolling by the stall and snatching his prize. But the customer, who was facing the knife table, did a double take when the boy walked by. His curiosity spiked, the merchant turned just in time to see the boy moving away. A quick glance gave an account of the missing weapon and he screamed, "Stop, thief!"

Perhaps if he had presence of mind enough to simply keep walking into the crowd he could have escaped, but Chamah panicked and broke into a dead run. Several stalls down the street, a fellow merchant, keen to see thieves brought to justice as a commercial principle, stepped into the fleeing boy's path and tackled him.

Again, had the boy been practiced at his vice, he might have used the newly gained weapon to obtain his freedom. But he was after all just a boy and not accustomed to the practical use of the object he had so earnestly desired. So, rather that brandish the knife as a threat, he let it fall to the ground in an effort to separate himself from it and the consequences. To his misfortune the blade struck a stone with a clang and advertised itself for all to behold. The merchant tightened his hold on the struggling lad and began to drag him back up the street to the scene of the crime.

"Say," the knife's rightful owner scowled, "I remember you from yesterday. You thought you'd steal my knife, did you? You will soon see how we deal with your kind." He turned to the rear of the stall where a mangy looking man was observing the proceedings, "Altair," he bellowed as the man stepped forward, "run to the magistrate's and tell them we have need of an officer here."

With that order the man hurried through the sizeable crowd which had gathered to watch the commotion. As the servant left, the merchant returned his scowling look to the thief. "Show me your hands," he demanded. Chamah raised his empty palms into the dire gaze of the merchant.

"Well, it appears that this is the first time you have been caught." A look of puzzlement overshadowed the fear in the boy's face. "Since you still have all your fingers it is obvious that you have not met with justice for your thieving ways," he continued. "That will soon be rectified. If you are lucky the magistrate may only take a finger or two, but I will press for the whole hand. An example must be made to all your kind. Thieves pay a dear price when they are caught in Armoun. The lugal will teach you to mend your ways."

Having made his speech, the merchant bent over to rummage in a crate that was near his feet. When he straightened up he had a leather thong of some three feet in length. "Here," he told the man who was holding the boy, "set him here and I will bind him to this post until the officers come to take him to jail."

The despondent lad, looking anything but the dastardly villain was roughly shoved to the ground near the rear of the stall and lashed to a post to await his fate. With the commotion more or less settled down, the crowd went back to the duties that had drawn them to the marketplace. With a look of abject dismay etched into his young face, Chamah was beginning to wish he had never laid eyes on the knife or even the city for that matter. Above him, in tones undistinguishable to human ears was the sound of gleeful laughter.

Back at the bakery stall, the young girl was beginning to worry. It had been over an hour since the two had left and she was concerned that her father might return and discover their absence.

"I see you are doing well this morning," came the familiar voice. "You have sold many of your loaves already." She looked up to see her father approaching with a smile. The look on her face immediately turned his smile into a frown. "What is troubling you, daughter," he asked. "You look as if you not pleased."

"Oh Father," she began, honesty always being her first response, "Chamah and Naashah came with me this morning and wanted to walk through the marketplace while waiting for you, but they have been gone for quite some time; I am worried that they may have gotten lost." Truly she had no more dire thoughts than this at the moment.

"I see," he said, reaching out to take her hand and give it a reassuring pat. "Perhaps they have found their way back to the house. I will go look; you remain here in case they return." With this he strode quickly down the street toward the gate.

Just moments before, Naashah had stumbled out of the temple tavern with a look of slightly inebriated satisfaction on his face only to be met by a small crowd following two officers with a young boy in tow. When the boy's eyes met his they shared a look of terror momentarily until the Chamah shouted, "Naashah, help!" In a split second the man stupefied himself by turning away to look for the person whom the boy had called.

"Naashah!" he cried once more as the entourage trouped by.

Guilt immediately overcame the servant's paralysis and he began walking quickly in the opposite direction. He found himself passing out of the city gate just as Delzar was returning from his fruitless search of the house. "Naashah, what is wrong?" the bearded one called.

Still somewhat muddled from the drinks he had consumed he could think of no plausible story and blurted out the truth. The story was related so quickly and in such slurred speech that Delzar was unsure exactly what had happened.

"Chamah taken by officers, you say?" Delzar asked in amazement. "Whatever for?"

"I don't know, master. We were not... uh...together and I was coming... I saw him down the street..." Even though he was innocent as far as Chamah's plight was concerned he felt somehow responsible due to his own feelings of guilt. He failed to mention that he had ignored the boy's call for help.

"Were they taking him to the jail?" Delzar prodded.

"We were... that is I was in... near the temple and I saw them moving down that street," was his stumbling reply.

"Delzar! Is that you?" a strong voice called from behind them. The two turned to see three men and a large ruddy colored dog approaching from the direction of the house.

"Who is it who asks," he answered guardedly.

"I am El Channah, but of course you would not know me. I fought with you in the last battle against Kamaresh. I was just a foot soldier, one of many who came to assist in the defense of Armoun. These are my friends Ramah and Giltar."

"Well then I greet you as friends," Delzar responded, reaching out to clasp the offered arm of the newcomer. "But I am afraid I can offer you no hospitality at the moment. We have a serious problem that this one here called Naashah is trying to explain to me."

"Perhaps I can once again come to your aid. I have business in the city, but I would be glad to offer assistance to a fellow warrior if I may," came the calculated response.

Delzar tried to explain the situation as best he knew it, with occasional injections from Naashah to help clarify when he could. When the predicament was fairly well outlined, the group was once again interrupted by a hail from the road. "Naashah, is that you?" They all turn to see a young man approach and continue, "Where is Chamah?" Before anyone could answer, Sha'ym recognized El Channah and said, "Oh, I am so glad I caught up to you, kind sir. I am determined to help you free my Sharaq."

"Free Sharaq?" Naashah said in puzzlement. "It is Chamah we must free; he has been taken by the officers of the magistrate."

Again there were explanations passed around until the whole dismal scene was before them all. El Channah was the first to speak: "Then it seems our missions coincide, my friend," looking carefully at Delzar.

"Strangely so, it seems," Delzar mused. "I know where Sharaq is being held, in fact I saw her yesterday..."

"You saw her?" Sha'ym interrupted excitedly. "How is she? Is she alright? Did they hurt her? If they..."

"Calm down young friend," Delzar spoke reassuringly. "she is being cared for like a queen, albeit a captive one."

"Thanks be to God," Sha'ym heard himself echo his father.

Once more it was El Channah who spoke, this time more as one in authority than a chance visitor. "It appears that I am in need of your help as much as you mine," looking to Delzar again. "But be assured, there is much for you to lose even if our mission is successful."

"You are correct, my friend, but my concern is more for my daughter than for myself. I have had my fill of the corruption of this city for some time now. I would have left sooner, but I could think of no place to go." El Channah nodded, measuring the sincerity of the man's tone. "If you will promise to see that my daughter is taken safely away — assuming we are successful, as you say — see that she is taken somewhere that she might be brought to womanhood apart from this dark place, I will offer my sword and my life if need be."

"As I have seen you use your sword, it is doubtful that any man will better you in a fair fight," El Channah complimented the warrior. "We are a small number, but I have others already in the city who will come to our aid as necessary." He did not elaborate on the nature of the "others" and Delzar took him at face value. "First, let us assure your daughter's safety," he continued, "and then you can show us where the two captives can be found. After we assess the situation, I am sure a plan can be devised which will accomplish our goals."

"So be it," Delzar said with confidence as he placed his hand on the tall warrior's shoulder. "Come. We can speak of plans as we go to get my daughter." With this the band entered the city and made their way to the bakery stall.

Hamayn, newly promoted as guardian of the city, was at the head of another band of warriors posted in the sky above the scene, the sun at their backs to avoid detection by the hosts in the city. Not that many would be about during the full sun. They mostly lurked about in the shadows and held to the temple rooms unless there was some specific business they were forced to attend to. Today there were several smaller dark ones hovering about the officers and their captive, enjoying the misery they had helped to inflict.

Glaxxin was at his post, guarding the girl he wanted so much to take carnally. He was hanging in a dark corner of the room when he heard footsteps in the hall, then a slight scuffle as the human guard was dragged into the chamber and dropped onto the floor unconscious. Sharaq, who had been sitting on her bed rose upon their entrance and gasped as she realized what was happening. El Channah stepped immediately to her side and covered her mouth to prevent her from screaming. "Be at peace; we have come to rescue you from this place."

His words were at once comforting and alarming to the girl. Before she could respond, Glaxxin charged from his corner intending to knock both humans to the ground. To his surprise, a dog leapt into the air and arrested his flight, careening him onto the bed. The dog had him by one arm, which totally surprised him since he thought himself to be invisible to all flesh. Multar was truly no match for Glaxxin's superior strength, but before the dark one could completely overpower him, El Channah drew his sword and swung at him.

Completely confused now, the evil one would have liked to flee, but the dog was still attached and the effort to block the human's sword took all his attention. Glaxxin thrust once with his wings and rose into the center of the room, the dog dangling from his left arm and his rod of darkness thrashing to and fro against the onslaughts of the human sword. He was dumbfounded how these carnal beings were making such a pointed attack. Had he time to think, he would have surmised that they were not what they appeared, but the zensak both cloaked the attenders and muddied the thoughts of their enemy.

When it became apparent to Mistrea that no other dark ones were in the immediate area, he shouted in thought, "Multar! Release him!" Instantly, the dog dropped to the floor and there was a brilliant flash as the true weapon of the being of light swept across the room and severed Glaxxin's head and right arm. Mistrea sheathed his weapon and turned back toward an amazed Sharaq to say in the voice of El Channah, "Come quickly!"

As man, dog and girl stepped into the passageway there was a loud blast from a horn somewhere nearby. The horn was followed by the clanging of one gong soon joined by several more throughout the city. "Someone has issued an alarm!" El Channah exclaimed out loud. "They can't have discovered us yet; I fear Delzar may have encountered a problem," he thought this to Multar. As they made their way toward the exit, people were rushing everywhere in response to the alarm, but no one seemed to be paying any attention to them.

Moments before the alarm sounded, Delzar had in fact met with serious trouble. The plan had been for he and Ramah to gain the release of the boy by explaining that the lugal had sent them to bring the boy to the court. The guard hesitated long enough for the dark spirits who were in attendance to send for orders from their superiors. Delzar was in the process of opening the cell after throttling the guard when the dark ones returned. Suspecting that their entertainment in seeing the boy maimed was about to be cancelled, they quickly looked for a human agent to intervene. To their good fortune, Lamaq was just passing down a nearby corridor, having just left one of the temple prostitutes. Imitating a human voice, one of the dark ones called to Lamaq for help.

Turning at the sound, Ramah discerned the presence of the enemy just as one of them moved in his direction. The little demon was surprised to find himself struck by something the supposed human swung at him. Realizing too late that Ramah was not human, the dark one lashed at him with his rod, only to be countered by the warrior's sword, an instrument which glowed surrealistically in the dark corridor.

Ramah began backing his opponent down the hall just as Lamaq entered the space behind him from around a corner.

Incredulous at the sight of an armed man swinging a sword in mock defensive moves, Lamaq stood motionless for a moment. Then a noise behind him caused him to turn and instinctively draw his dagger from his belt. What confronted him there was almost as confusing as the man dueling with the air.

"Delzar," he said in recognition of his friend, "What are you doing here?" His eye fell to the strangled guard at his friend's feet, and the open cell door. Only now did he notice the young man cowering behind Delzar.

With more force in his voice he repeated, "What are you doing?"

Ignoring his question, Delzar posed one of his own, "Are you in fact keeping an innocent girl imprisoned here for your use?"

"What if I am?" he answered. "You may have her too anytime, friend." The word "friend" was laced with a tone of interrogation.

"Well, you will not be 'having' her, if I can help it, and I am going to leave with this boy as well."

A scuffling sound from the direction Ramah had gone caused Lamaq to turn quickly. Delzar seized the moment to move toward the open hallway, but Lamaq turned immediately back when nothing appeared to be coming from the other direction.

"I don't think I can let you do that," he said, lifting his drawn dagger.

"Don't make me fight you," Delzar said. "This is something I have to do and I will kill you if you make me."

"That's no way for a friend to talk," Lamaq said, and once again was momentarily distracted by the noise behind him.

Delzar lunged for Lamaq's dagger and grabbed his wrist. The two men struggled as Chamah watched helplessly. Both were strong and well trained in hand to hand combat. Lamaq shoved his free palm under Delzar's bearded chin and dug his fingers into the flesh as he attempted to drive his attacker away. Delzar, now with both hands on the dagger wrist, tried to force the blade into Lamaq.

Meanwhile, Ramah had almost completely uncloaked himself while battling the two smaller demons. When he finally dispatched one of them, the second drew back momentarily, unsure of what was taking place. Ramah used the brief withdrawal to dash to the aid of Delzar. He took a roundhouse swing at Lamaq, intending to smash his jaw. Instead, the wild struggling of the two caused his punch to land on Lamaq's forearm, knocking it off Delzar's chin. The release of his chin propelled Delzar toward Lamaq and drove the dagger through the ribs and directly into its owner's heart.

The second of Ramah's opponents, finally realizing who he was dealing with, had gone for reinforcements. Three demons now flew directly at Ramah from his back. Sensing their approach, he wheeled to face them. Because the corridor was too narrow for three abreast, two were at the floor level, and one charged from near the ceiling. Ramah ducked and swung at one of the lower attackers, slicing off an arm and wing. The other two sailed past him, the lower one crashing into the unsuspecting Delzar with otherworldly force. He felt himself lifted from the ground and thrown across the hall against the wall. Before he slid fully to the floor, he was again lofted into the air and sent crashing into the wall six feet away. This time he collapsed on the floor and blood could be seen on the stones beneath his head.

Realizing he would soon be outnumbered, Ramah snatched the incredulous Chamah by the arm and hustled him out of the jail before the dark ones finished their attack on Delzar. When they saw the wounded man slump unconscious to the floor, they turned just in time to see the others leave. As they pursued the two humans into the daylight, the alarm sounded and people began running in all directions. They were about to overtake their prey when suddenly they were faced with a small band of cloaked attenders, nearly invisible even to them, but for the drawn swords of light which cut them down before they could raise a defense.

Delzar's house outside the gate had been the intended point of rendezvous so both of the released captives were being herded in that direction as crowds of panicked people ran in the streets. The flight of the captives was completely unnoticed in the total mayhem caused by the alarm. It was not until both groups of escapees were nearing the gate that an attender spoke to them from above.

"Warriors from Kamaresh have attacked the northern gate of the city. You must get out of the south gate before it closes." It was Hamayn who warned them to hurry, not that they could go any faster if they wanted to. As the streets from the jail to the south gate were less busy, Chamah and Ramah reached the gate first. Guards were in the process of ushering frightened citizens into the city and preparing to swing the gates shut just as the escapees were making their way against the crowd. To the amazement of the guards, the two insisted that they wanted to go out as the gates were closing.

"Fools," they were shouting. "We are under attack. You will have no protection outside."

They ignored the shouts and stepped through the gate as it shut them outside.

El Channah and his charges were not as quick negotiating the crowded streets. They found the gate shut and no amount of entreaty would cause the guards to lift the bars. El Channah feared to make too much of the request, lest they be discovered, so he sought another escape. "Come this way," he said to the two, approaching a building that backed onto the wall. "To the roof!" he commanded, seeing an outside stairway.

They climbed the stair to discover that the wall which formed the back of the house and the city defense stood only five feet above the roof of the house. Seizing a table he slid it against the outer wall. "Onto the table!" he ordered. The girl dutifully obeyed. From atop the table, they could see over the wall to the ground some twenty feet below. "I will go over first, then you must jump and I will catch you."

She looked at him in amazement. Even if he did survive the jump, she was not at all sure she could muster the courage to follow him.

The tall stranger turned and looked at her with incredible compassion and peace and said, "You must trust me." And he stepped over the wall.

She looked down, half expecting to see a crumpled body lying in a heap, but was amazed to see instead El Channah reaching up with his arms saying, "Come."

The dog barked behind her. The din of the horn and the gongs rose around her. People all over the city were shouting alarm. Again she looked down at the amazing stranger who implored her to trust. She was about to decide she couldn't do it when Sha'ym, Chamah and the others appeared, running to the place where El Channah had landed. They immediately recognized what was taking place and joined in entreaty to jump.

"Sha'ym," she cried. "I thought I would never see you again." The presence of her beloved was all she needed. She closed her eyes and stepped into the air.

What happened then was quite indescribable. She felt the movement of air as if she were falling, and yet it didn't feel as is she was falling at all, rather floating to the ground. When she opened her eyes again, she was in the arms of the tall stranger, being placed gently on ground. As she was wrapped in an embrace with her beloved, she saw over his shoulder the dog leap from the top of the wall and land like a cat on all fours, barely stirring the dust around his paws.

"We must get away from the city immediately," El Channah was directing. The attackers may intend to surround the walls. We will be safer on the plain when night falls."

Suddenly Delyah cried, "Father! Where is my father?"

El Channah looked to his fellow soldier.

"We were overpowered. I was forced to run with the boy. I am afraid he was lost," Ramah answered softly.

A loud wail erupted from depths of the girl's soul as a freezing gale rushes through a crack in a door. All stood momentarily stunned by the thought. Then Sharaq stepped to her and cradled her in her arms. "Come," she whispered. "There is nothing to be done. We must save ourselves. That is what he would have wanted you to do."

With this strange mixture of sadness and joy in the air, the sun cast their shadows behind them as they quickly moved away from the writhing city.

CHAPTER SIXTEEN

Lifted by unseen currents, the eagle drifted purposely back and forth across the blue morning sky. In the distance, above other peaks his neighbors were on similar patrol, seeking the first meal of the day. Below the craggy peaks where they built their nests, the forest was alive with small game that would serve to keep the eagle population strong for yet another season. In a small clearing on one of the foothills a wary rodent browsed for his breakfast, unaware that he was being watched from high above. When he did hear the slight rush of feathers behind him, there was time only for a sharp squeal as the talons pierced his flesh and he was lofted helplessly into the sky.

As the small squeak of the rodent echoed through the trees, a softer sound, something between a cry and a moan answered. A young woman squatted low to the ground with her back against the trunk of a large tree. With a soft cloth she had brought for the purpose and the water from a skin she had been keeping close to her body to warm it she was gently wiping the protective coating from the small creature that had just taken its first breath. When it no longer pulsed with life, the cord which had sustained the newborn until now was cut and carefully knotted. Having finished the cleansing, the mother wrapped the baby in a clean cloth and lifted her lovingly to her enlarged breast. Cradling the child next to her warm body, she squeezed a drop of milk onto her finger and put it into the tiny mouth. Instinctively the baby began sucking on the finger. With great satisfaction, mother replaced finger with nipple and the first meal began.

Even though this was her firstborn and she was barely fourteen, she knew exactly what to do because her mother had carefully rehearsed the procedure with her every month ever since she had begun to be a woman. The lessons were all part of the ritual which helped to explain the changes that were taking place in her body month by month until the day when the chief noticed the changes and called for her. She was special and had been taught from an early age that one day the chief would take her to himself. When that day came, she accepted it as a matter of course.

Although she called the woman who taught her all this Mother, she had never known her real mother. While she was still a baby at her mother's breast, a stray arrow had taken her mother's life during one of the frequent attacks on her village by rival clans who roamed the forests. Normally she would have been clubbed or left to die, but she was special. Her hair was flaxen and her eyes blue like her mother's; this was held to be a sign of deity bestowed upon the fortunate few by Hursag, the patron god of the tribes inhabiting the forests around Kamaresh, so she did not suffer the fate usually reserved for captive orphans. She was taken as spoil by the chief and nursed by one of his wives in the hopes that one day she could provide him with a son of the gods. It was hoped too that this child could remove the curse which had fallen upon the tribe as retribution for killing her mother, the mother of gods as they thought.

She was nearly overcome by dread when she discovered her baby to be a girl, but as she gently cleaned her tiny scalp, fine wisps of pale hair appeared as a helmet of protection.

She would be allowed to live at least long enough to be sure that the eyes stayed blue and the hair blonde. Dark haired slave girls might not live through their first day, but her baby had the protection of the gods. Knowing this, the young mother sang softly as the tiny mouth sucked hungrily at her breast. She could finish her delivery and return to her tent to complete the days of purification with a peaceful heart. The chief would rather have a boy, but she felt sure that he would be pleased with the sign of the gods adorning this little one.

Later that day as she made her way down the trail to the encampment, for it was too insignificant to be called a village, and too temporary, she was blithely unaware of the dangers she had overcome. Had there been complications during childbirth, both she and her baby were at risk of death. There were numerous animals which made the forest their home and might have found the young girl easy prey, as she had only her small rucksack and a staff for protection. This one was lucky her time came in the spring, for many in her situation had succumbed to the elements during prolonged labors in the colder months, which had for years been getting increasingly more harsh. Finally, there were always roving clans who lived off the fruits of their violence. If a local band discovered her, she would be a prize capture; but recently, incursions of bandits from the south had been more frequent. These people saw golden hair as a sign of their rival's god, and would have taken special delight in ceremoniously torturing and finally killing the poor girl as a sign of their superiority.

As she caught the first whiff of cooking smoke, lifted to her by the gentle currents flowing through the trees, none of these thoughts occurred to her. She didn't consider the fact that countless generations of wisdom had dictated the ritual of secluded, unassisted birth to assure that only the strongest survived. She only thought how happy she was that her child would be kept alive because of the touch of the gods on her crown. She could not have imagined the true value that golden touch would have for her daughter.

A satisfied smile subconsciously settled on her young face as she considered her good fortune. She took only casual glances at the forest ahead because her eyes were concentrating on the animal trail she had followed to her chosen delivery spot. She knew she could retrace the narrow, but well-worn path to the ridge above the meadow where her people were camped, then leave the trail and make her way down the gentle slope into the clearing.

Suddenly she froze in mid-stride, hardly daring to place her bare foot down on the moist earth. Something had moved in the trees to the right of the path. Instinctively she clutched her precious bundle closer to her breast as she peered at the spot where the movement had been. Something gave the impression it was an animal, but she was far enough away and sufficient undergrowth intervened to make certain identification impossible. As she watched breathlessly, it moved again so that she was able to confirm her suspicion that it was alive, but the brush between her and the creature prevented a clear view. It seemed to have dark fur — she thought perhaps a large bear cub — yet something about the head was strange, as if the bear were bald. Then too, as she continued to stare, it became apparent that the shape was not right for a bear.

When she had almost decided to take a few steps further down the trail to get a better look, a twig snapped ahead and to her left, sounding roughly as far away as the creature on the right. Without a conscious thought, her head spun in that direction. Immediately, she felt a wave of panic because she knew that quick movement would signal her position, but her reaction had been reflexive. It became apparent that her movement had caught the attention of the second creature, as it reacted by rising up. To the young girl's horror, it reached at least two meters in height; again, she was not able to see the whole figure, nor determine what it was. It might have been a full grown bear, but the chest, which was all she could see clearly, was dark brown and bare.

Just then the second creature extended an upper limb, appearing to make a waving gesture in the direction of the first movement she had seen. In the corner of her eye she detected movement on her right again as the first creature slunk out from behind the tree he had been crouching near. Not willing to make the mistake of moving herself again, she lost sight of the first creature altogether. However, the second creature, at which she was still staring motionlessly, began to move across in front of her, apparently following the first, not aware of her after all.

It was only then that she caught a brief glimpse of the entire shape of the thing. It was a human. What she had mistaken for fur was an animal skin tunic, badly matted and scattered with hanging leaves. When the men crouched, the lower reaches of the garment dragged on the ground. The man she saw now had coarse black hair not unlike the fur he wore, thrusting disheveled from under a dark brown leather helmet. Under the tunic he wore a leather breastplate of similar hue. His legs appeared to be bare, but the brush was too thick to see them until his progress took him onto the path in front of her. As he crossed, she finally saw a fairly large man half bent over so that his tunic barely cleared the forest floor as he shuffled back into the brush on the right of the path. His legs, although bare, were apparently smeared with mud so that they were as dark as his fur covering. In his hand he carried a sizeable war club.

He never looked in her direction, but kept his gaze riveted in the direction of her family enclave as he stole back into the forest, eventually stopping at the same tree where his fellow had been moments before. She had just begun to think she might escape totally unnoticed when movement to her left again stopped her heart. The spot where she had noticed the second man was now occupied by a third similarly cloaked warrior.

After what seemed an eternity of waiting frozen in fear, she watched the third man rise and motion to his left. It was hard to be sure, but he appeared to be extending his arm and waving it slowly up and down. When he dropped his left arm, he repeated the same motion with his right. By moving only her eyes, she could cast her glance to both of the men, noticing that they each remained crouched behind his tree. It now became clear to her that these men, dressed for battle, skulking about the forest were preparing to attack her clan. The rise above their encampment was only a few meters beyond where they were positioned.

Her thoughts immediately turned to how she might warn her people. If she stole quietly towards the enemy position, then burst into a full run just before they could see her coming, she might outdistance them and reach camp before they caught her. But as her newborn squirmed slightly in her close grasp, she was reminded that even if she could normally outrun them, her condition now was one of pain and weakness from her birthing experience. Carrying the child and overcoming the dull ache she felt in her lower abdomen would slow her to the point that an old woman could doubtless outpace her. These seasoned warriors could move like the wind; she would not outrun them.

As her mind raced to come up with other options it became obvious that the men were no longer moving. They had apparently reached their desired attack positions and were awaiting some signal to charge. The thought that they were waiting for a signal gave her an idea. Perhaps remaining undetected was important enough to them that they would let her walk past unharmed. After all, she reasoned, if they intended to surprise her people, her screaming at this point would rob them of that advantage. She certainly couldn't just wait for the attack to begin, nor was a retreat into the forest a good option. She would either be left to fend entirely for herself or be captured if her people were vanquished. Or she would have to face her people after the battle, knowing that she could have warned them.

Although unsure she had the courage to complete it, she realized her course was determined. Not willing to wait another moment, lest fear should change her mind, or the attack should commence, she began to make her way down the trail toward the ridge and toward what might be her death. She burned with fear and a curious need to look at the attackers to see if she had been noticed. As she approached them from behind, she decided that her ruse would only be successful if they were certain they were undetected. So she fought her urge to glance into the forest, keeping her eyes glued on the opening ahead where the trail veered along the top of the ridge: the point where she would leave the path and descend toward the relative safety of her village.

As it happened, the gods smiled on the young woman a second time that day. By chance, each of the men had positioned himself so that the tree around which he peered was between him and the path. Thus they were unaware of the girl's silent approach until she was well past their position, almost to the crest of the ridge. Both men saw her at the same instant, turning simultaneously to stare at one another in disbelief, then back up the path to see if she was alone. They couldn't be sure from their crouched position, so one cautiously stood to peer over the growth of ferns and seedlings. Taking several moments to be sure no one else was approaching, they were surprised to find that the girl had vanished by the time they looked back. Assured that they were still unnoticed, the man to the right again motioned the other to lower himself into position and wait.

It was all the young woman could do to continue walking after she left the trail. Every cell in her body wanted to break into a panicked dash for safety. Once she was clear of the trees and into the meadow where the camp was, she dared to call out to the village. She could see two women tending the cooking fire and several men standing outside the chief's tent talking. At least one of those men should have been standing watch and noticed her coming. Instead she decided she would have to make her presence known. Maintaining her ruse, she simply asked for permission re-enter the camp with her new child. Technically, the chief would have to examine her and the baby before she would be allowed back. In this instance, however, since it was the chief's offspring, and since they were all awaiting the verdict as to the child's appearance, everyone who was outside turned toward her call and almost in unison shouted cheerful, yet somewhat strange greetings. Without catching all they said, as many spoke together, she could perceive several words: favored... chosen... prophecy. None of it made any sense as the words tumbled across the clearing and echoed off the trees behind her. In any case, her present state of mind made deciphering their words unlikely at best.

One of the women near the fire stood up and began walking immediately toward the girl. The chief also started toward her, followed by the men he had been talking with. As the group got nearer, both she and they realized there was an unexpected look on everyone's face. Hers was naturally the look of fear owing to her unique knowledge of the impending attack. Their faces puzzled her, however, much as the unusual type of greeting they offered.

When they were only a few meters apart the group had reached the boundary of the encampment. At this point the girl recognized the woman as her adoptive mother, but realized that there was a stranger among the others. He was a very old man, and it was on account of his shuffling speed that she had traversed most of the clearing before the group reached the edge of the camp.

"Forgive me, Father," she began, using the customary woman's address for the chief, "I know it is not my place to speak, but if I may be permitted a word I must warn of great danger."

"Have no fear, Marah," he said, reaching out to take her shoulder as the distance between them closed.

The chief took a breath to continue speaking when he was suddenly interrupted by the old stranger. "Let her speak first," he said with such authority that it startled the girl. "When I rose this morning to greet the sun, I felt a disturbance in the forest. This young one will tell us what about to happen."

Puzzled by this strange communication, she continued, pressed by the urgency only she knew. "I saw three men dressed for battle hiding in the forest as I returned."

At this their faces all mirrored hers in fear, except for that of the strange old man. He simply nodded with no apparent change to his visage. "They are from the South," he said with certainty. Looking toward the forest and scanning the treetops he went on, "Dumuzi is here. This is what I felt at the sun's rise. The creatures of the forest have gone almost silent. There is an unnatural power abroad."

He closed his eyes as if he had suddenly fallen asleep, but his hands slowly lifted from his side, palms down, so that the people nearest him had to step back. When his hands were at the level of his waist, he slowly waved them from beside to in front of himself, then back. He broke the respectful silence by continuing, "Yes, the en-lil whisper of an intruder." He opened his eyes again and said again, "They are from the South."

"You say you saw three, Marah?"

It was not her, but the old man who answered, "There are many more." He closed his eyes again briefly, then spoke ominously: "Some from water; some from wood."

At this the chief furrowed his brow momentarily, then shot a knowing look at the opposite side of the clearing from the forest. There was a small brook below a bank shaded by willows — perfect cover for the other half of a two-pronged attack force.

"From the South, you say, Seer," he pulled on his long beard as he always did when thinking. "From water..." he looked at the stream bank, "...and from wood," he finished by turning his gaze to the forest. "Then we have no time to lose; they may attack at any moment.

"Listen carefully, everyone; there is no time to repeat my instructions. "You women go back to the fire and tend the food as if nothing were happening. Men, we will all walk back into camp and go to our tents. Every man gird yourself for battle and stand in your tents with weapons in hand. Wait for my signal." He looked intently into the men's faces. "Hear me: no one is to step outside armed until I call."

They all nodded their understanding.

"Come, let us go to our tents as I give one further instruction." They pivoted and began walking into camp as the chief continued, "If I yell 'Wood!' those of you camped with your backs to the forest," he motioned toward the five tents, "come out and repel the force from the forest. The rest of you, remain in your tents. If I yell 'Water!' those on the other side defend the approach from the brook and the others remain in their tents."

By this time they had reached the point where the first men were lifting the flaps of their tents. "Do you understand, all of you?" the chief asked. "Only half of you must appear when I first call. The men nodded, though some looked perplexed. To answer their unspoken question he went on, "they will attack from one side until they think we are committed, then the others will overrun the camp. We will make them think we are committed, then when the second attack begins, we will be the one's with the surprise."

Crouching in the dense cover at the stream's edge, a soldier watched the people move back into their morning routine. When he had seen the girl step into the clearing, he imagined for a moment that his fellow warriors were not yet in position. He waited while the people gathered and then broke up again. Similarly, those in the woods watched the scene, unsure if they had been detected, but quite certain they were safe, given the girl's casual behavior. Their suspicions were confirmed when the meeting at the camp produced no apparent alarm. As soon as it became obvious that their surprise was undiminished, one of them had made the sound of a bird call, the prearranged signal that they were in place.

In an instant the peaceful morning meadow erupted with ominous and frightening sound. Twelve creatures, looking half man, half beast, burst screaming from the lush growth that separated field from brook and raced toward the quiet circle of tents. Long spears tipped with sharpened flint cut through the morning air as they were flung ahead while the men rushed at full sprint behind them. Clubs almost the size of small logs circled above the heads of the attackers after they launched their spears. A few of the men had short metal swords at their belts, prizes of earlier victories. The rest carried short flint knives which, handled skillfully, could rip a fatal gash across the enemy's throat in hand to hand combat. With their open goat-skin tunics flapping aside, their leather breastplates and helmets, some with small ram's horns attached, all hiding their humanity, the hoard resembled a pack of banshees rising from the very depths of horror.

The wicked crew had not taken a half dozen steps into the clearing before the chief responded with a coarse yell, "From the water!" at which point eight ready warriors emerged from their tents at the same moment the first of the spears fell harmlessly at the perimeter of the camp, having been sent too early in the excitement of the charge. One of the men rounded the stakes of his tent just as another hand-missile fell from the sky. He raised his left arm in reflexive defense perfectly deflecting the spear with his arm shield. Two other men dodged spears as they ran into the clearing behind their dwellings; one spear became lodged in the poles of another tent, and one drove harmlessly into an empty tent.

With the first onslaught so easily taken, the men were emboldened as they formed a line at the perimeter. Each man wore a leather breastplate, helmet, and arm shield, and carried a short iron sword. The blades had been beaten into the shape of a large dagger and both edges were ground to as fine an edge as their tools could produce. A skillful blow by a strong arm could nearly sever an enemy limb; indeed, many of these very swords could lay claim to countless slain in one blow. For these were no ordinary swordsmen; these men had been chosen by the king himself to receive special training and the finest swords so that he might call upon them as he needed. They were in fact, part of the training group for his personal guard, the reserves to be called upon when an enemy force attacked. The king had wisely chosen several clans to reinforce his position if the goats from Armoun should ever be foolish enough to mount a full fledged attack on Kamaresan territory. Trade in all but the smallest metal weapons was strictly prohibited, thus giving the King's elite swordsman a distinct advantage.

Had this morning's roving band of goat-soldiers known any of this, they would have left the meadow in peace, glad for their lives. As it was, just when the special equipment of their foe was becoming apparent to the first wave, the other half of their number roared out of the forest and raced pell mell down the slope toward the camp. Another shout from the chief and ten more well-equipped warriors stepped into view facing the second charge. Their surprise was evident in the sudden slowing of their charge, for instead of racing unopposed into the camp, they now had to consider raising their clubs against ten razor-sharp swords. The hesitation was all the swordsmen needed. As one man they bolted across the few meters of grass left between them and their attackers. One or two of the hairy creatures actually turned and ran back toward the trees. Those who stood matched blows as best they could, blocking swinging swords with their clubs. Some were able to hold their ground for two or three blows, but the swordsmen could change the angle of their attack more quickly than the clubs could be brought in defense, so it was only a few agonizing minutes until the charge had been repelled and those who remained standing were running for their lives from the pursuing swordsmen.

At a call from the chief, the pursuit was ended and the men returned to the camp. Only two of the men were seriously injured, while over half of their attackers now lay dead in the clearing. One of the goat warriors had struck a glancing blow to the head of one man, causing him to bleed profusely, although his skull appeared unaffected. Another had sustained a broken forearm while blocking a roundhouse club swing. Two women were busy setting the bone and fashioning a crude splint with an assembly of twigs and leather thongs. The other injuries were limited to a few scrapes and bruises and one abrasion from a near miss with a flint knife. As the chief surveyed the aftermath, he decided it was a victory they could be proud of; one in fact the king would be gratified to learn of. His troops were learning their lessons well.

During the battle, the women had remained huddled together in one of the larger tents, several spears pointed at the closed door-flap in case an attacker stumbled into their hiding place. After the skirmish ended, the women had been quick to emerge from the tent carrying water and poultices used to stem bleeding. They were all pleased to find their healing services were not much needed. A warrior named Thorel had survived the battle unscathed, a fact which greatly relieved a certain new mother. As the women finished tending the minor injuries, the chief walked among his men, congratulating them for a well-fought battle. When he approached Thorel, he took a moment longer, speaking privately with him, giving him special attention.

As soon as the chief left him, Thorel joined the small crowd that was forming around his beloved. In the commotion which occurred immediately after she had returned to camp, none of the details of her delivery had been shared. As he pressed near to her, he looked into her eyes for a sign.

"It is a lovely girl child," Marah said smiling faintly.

His look of anticipation fell momentarily, then he imitated her half smile as he said, "And she is well?"

"Yes, and our Father has called her Morning Sky because her eyes are the deep blue of the sky at dawn." They looked together at the little blue pools in the tiny face, then at each other. Changing from the painful subject she continued, "Mother tells me the seer spoke strange prophecies last night."

"Did she tell you one of them was about you?"

"It is not clear to me that this child is the one," she said, instinctively holding the baby closer.

"The seer said, 'The next child born would be the savior of this people.'"

"But Thorel, this is a girl," she reasoned. "What could she do? He must have meant the next man-child."

"I think everyone understands this to be the child. You heard the greetings as you came to camp this morning?"

"I heard strange salutations, yes, but my heart was in such fear at that moment that I didn't stop to think what it might mean."

"I have an idea that things may be changing soon," he spoke more quickly and softly, as if in secret. "The chief has sent me to the king to report this attack and our skillful victory. He is sure the king will call his guard together to respond to these attacks. We may soon be moving south even to attack Armoun and finish these goat-beasts." This last was spat out with great disgust.

"But I don't see how this involves my little one..."

"Oh, I think it is clear," he interrupted. "You came from delivering this one to warn us of the attack. We were saved from a great slaughter, I think."

"Surely the prophecy meant more than that," she argued. "Besides, it was me who warned you, not her."

"Well, yes, but if this attack is the one the king uses as the final insult and mounts a successful attack on Armoun..." he trailed off, realizing his theory lacked something.

"It is no use our trying to imagine what the seer meant," Marah concluded. "If he wants us to know more, he will have to tell us. For now, you need to go see the king. I hope it doesn't mean a battle, but I fear you may be right. Going on a siege, and me with a new baby...." Although she was too young to have seen a major war, she knew what it would be like from the stories her mother had told her. Things didn't change that much for the women. They still had to mind the camp, feed the men, and in war, mend the wounded and mourn the dead.

He reached out and moved the covering slightly away from the baby's face. "Morning Sky," he intoned, "what are you going to bring us?"

CHAPTER SEVENTEEN

Pressed by a fear of something greater than darkness, the small group hurried farther into the night than customary on the day they fled Armoun. Thus it was late on the second day that they were sighted by Nuwach's servant who had been posted on the hill behind the compound. In fact, he had been packing up his kit when one last look revealed small band of travelers heading toward the pass. The sun having sunk low in the sky behind them, they were impossible to identify from the distance of his post. There seemed to be at least six people, rather than the four he was expecting, although expectation was too optimistic a word to describe the faint hope he harbored. To his way of thinking, his was a futile task, likely to be rewarded only by discouraging reports day after day. But the master had insisted that someone keep watch every moment of daylight so that good news might be learned that much sooner.

Ben'Sedek waited until the light had grown so dim that he lost sight of the travelers in the gloom, still not having made positive identification. They were still moving toward him when he lost sight of them, so it was probable they were intent on making the compound that night, despite the gathering darkness. The man assumed that the only reason anyone would do such a thing was if they knew the end of their journey waited just beyond the pass; to walk into a situation so promising for bandits suggested they knew they could safely pass through in the dark. With these thoughts in mind, he hurried as fast as the darkness on the east face of the hill allowed to prepare his master for possible visitors, praying for his master's sake that the number in the group meant all the missing had been recovered.

When he unfolded his tale to Nuwach, the old man sprang into action. "Prepare some food, woman; they will doubtless be famished from their journey." Having said this he fairly ran to the shed and emerged with three torches he kept in readiness for the rare nighttime emergencies occasioned by his livestock. Lighting them in the fire in the house, he handed one of the sputtering brands to Ben'Sedek and kept the other two in hand as he rushed out the door and ordered his servant to follow. With speed uncommon for his age, he reached the gate, threw it open and rushed down the road toward the pass, the torches leaving clouds of black in his wake.

The travelers on the other side of the pass were greeted by a strange sight indeed. They first noticed the rock walls begin to glow orange, then yellow and all at once, three balls of fire emerged eerily from the opening. It was El Channah who intuitively described what they were witnessing. "Look, they are coming to meet us."

They were close enough to make out two figures rushing toward them in the glow of the torches. Although they were too far distant to identify, they had no reason to suspect this was anything but a welcoming party. Without a word being spoken, the tired band stepped up their weary pace to close the gap as quickly as their exhaustion would allow.

After a few moments, a voice was heard calling across the distance, "Who comes there? Identify yourselves."

With all the strength he could muster, Sha'ym cried, "Father?"

In a much stronger voice, El Channah replied, "It is El Channah; I have all your children safe."

At this, two of the torches fell to the ground while the third bobbed on for a few steps, then retreated only to also be thrown to the ground. With the light now on the ground, it was impossible for the travelers to see that Nuwach had fallen to the earth, partly from exhaustion, but more from relief at the news he had been yearning for these last long days. Ben'Sedek returned to him and gently helped him to sit up.

"Go on if you can," the old one ordered. "Take the light to them; I will wait here." These words were gasped out in heaving breaths as the man struggled to regain his composure. When the servant hesitated he said again, "Go!"

Shoving one of the torches into the soft earth near where Nuwach had fallen, the servant grabbed the other two and continued down the road at a near run. In a few moments he closed the gap between them, panting from the effort. Since he had a torch in each hand, it was an awkward greeting he offered, but truly heartfelt. "The god of Araq be praised! He has brought you home safe."

When El Channah freed his hands of the torches, he continued the motion he had begun, clasping his hands before his chest and bowing as if saluting royalty. El Channah passed one of the torches to Ramah and with the group now illuminated, a cry went out from the distant Nuwach and he again fell to the earth, this time in a posture of a prayer of gratitude. Seeing him, Sha'ym broke from the group and ran to his father, finding strength from some unknown reserve. Chamah was torn by his love for his father and a healthy sense of guilt at what had brought him to this position and he stayed with the others.

"Come; you are almost home," Ben'Sedek said. "The mistress is preparing food for you."

The thought of food energized their steps since they had eaten only two loaves and some fruit shared between them: all they could hastily gather in their flight from the city. Had not El Channah magically coaxed some water from an underground spring, they would have been far worse off than they were even now.

When they reached Nuwach and Sha'ym, the two were still locked in an embrace where Nuwach sat, his sobbing voice saying over and over again, "My son, my son."

When he noticed the light from their torches through his tears, he struggled to his feet and repeated the ceremony with Chamah, sending relief through the boy so that he too began sobbing, "I'm sorry, Father; I'm sorry."

Stepping back slightly from the boy he next spotted Sharaq and began sobbing all over again as he embraced her. She too began weeping, letting go the floodgates of fear and tension that had dammed up her tears for the last many days. Then she suddenly gasped, as if she recognized something amiss, "My father? Is he all right?"

"Oh yes, dear girl," the old man said, catching somewhat more normal breath by now. "He has not slept for four days. He finally fell asleep tonight from sheer exhaustion. When I heard of travelers approaching, I didn't have the heart to wake him, knowing not if it was you. In truth," he added, "I am not sure I could wake him.

"But come, you can wake him with the softest voice, I am sure, as long as he doesn't imagine he is dreaming."

"Come," he waved to all of them and started toward the pass.

Suddenly realizing he had not greeted all of them, he paused and looked at Ramah saying, "I assume you are a friend of El Channah's; pardon my ill manners. I meant you no slight, you see..."

El Channah interrupted by saying, "This is Ramah, a true friend indeed. Without him, your second son would not be secure this night, as he is."

With this information, Nuwach stopped again and took the man's arm firmly and placed his hand on his shoulder. "Welcome, Ramah; you are welcome in my home. And I owe you a debt I will never be able to repay."

"There are no debts between friends," Ramah gracefully replied.

The old man sighed deeply and shook his head, "No, that is correct, friend; no debts, but my sincerest gratitude will ever be yours." Then, almost as an afterthought he turned to El Channah, "And you, my friend; I have forgotten to thank you as well. Surely I am becoming a doddering old man who can't even remember his manners. What can I say to you?"

"You need not say anything else to me. All thanks and praise belongs to the god who has brought your family back to you," was his humble reply.

"Yes, yes, you are right, of course. All praise to him who made the Araq and the sky. Thanks be to him alone."

Realizing they were again stopped he said, "Come. I am still forgetting my duties as a host. Food and drink awaits." When they began moving again, he asked, "And who is this lovely young girl; I feel as if I have seen her before."

It was Chamah who answered this. "This is Delyah, the daughter of Delzar who visited us from the city.

"Of course," he exclaimed, looking again at her. "It's the eyes; she has her fathers eyes. Where is your father, child?"

At this the girl started to cry loudly and again Sharaq put an arm around her to comfort her as they walked. Each one by turns explained parts of the rescue while they continued on the road. Eventually they reached the sad conclusion that Delzar had not made it out, and they feared the worst.

Just before the alarms had sounded in the city, a meeting was taking place in the depths of the temple. All of the officers and most of the rest of the garrison at Armoun had gathered at Fauxxin's command. Meetings such as this were rare, since fellowship and comradery were little appreciated. In addition, gatherings tended to emphasize the differences in rank, and these creatures despised any reminder of the hierarchy. It was the nature of the beasts to disdain authority.

This naturally made the Rhuyh Klaxxin the favorite method of advancement. It involved a delicate orchestration of the usurpation of authority and the accomplishment of some great evil which would be viewed favorably by the higher powers. In essence it meant doing an end run around one's immediate superior to impress those further up the chain of command. Done well, one might hope to replace one's leader. Done exceptionally well, one could even leapfrog above one's leader. Done badly, one could expect a fate worse than death. It was precisely these high stakes that constantly drew members of the dark host to attempt the Rhuyh Klaxxin. They loved the thrill.

On this afternoon, in that packed chamber, three of Fauxxin's lieutenant's had come to the meeting prepared to mount a challenge. Usually a single peon would attempt a coup on his own, but an officer of Fauxxin's standing would have been hard to undo by a single stroke. So, these three had plotted with their counterparts in Ningirsu's ranks to overthrow their leader, taking Armoun with him.

So it was that when the alarms sounded the attack while they were gathered in the lower chamber, the three looked briefly at one another, pleased with the good fortune of the timing. Here they were, all three in the presence of the despised leader at the moment their Rhuyh Klaxxin commenced.

The alarms, more sensed than felt at such depth, stopped Fauxxin in mid-sentence. After a nod of agreement among the three, they all flung themselves at the dark beast before them shouting, "Rhuyh Klaxxin! Death to the weakling, Fauxxin!"

Although Fauxxin was much larger than any one of the three, because they caught him completely off guard, the rebels were able to seriously wound him before he gathered himself in defense. The crowded condition of the chamber made their attack somewhat awkward, or they might have finished him off with their initial lunge. As it was, one of them attached himself to Fauxxin's right wing below the claw; the second clamped his jaws on a leg, and the third was left fluttering about the other wing.

Bearing his massive rod of darkness in his left hand, Fauxxin was able to strike a stunning blow upon the one free attacker. He then brought his left wing claw sharply onto the back of the rebel on his leg, trying to tear him away. At the same time, he swung his rod against the beast on his right wing. The blow was enough to knock him loose, but the attacker on his left recovered and lighted on Fauxxin's back.

With his wings both momentarily free, he dug both claws into the unfortunate on his leg and wrenched him off, nearly tearing him limb from limb in the process. He now had one on his back, and another facing him about three meters away. When the one facing him moved to attack again, Fauxxin crouched as if to meet him at ground level, then to everyone's amazement he dematerialized, leaving the two lieutenants flying at one another. Just as they came to a clumsy stop almost on top of one another, the room was filled with a great roar followed by a rushing sound as if a mighty wind were filling the chamber. Before their gaping eyes, the crowd saw the two rebels swept suddenly aside and crash into the far wall. Then Fauxxin reappeared, following the stroke of his rod and finished one of them off with his jaws while he parted the other in two with his wing-claws.

The giant immediately turned and faced the awestruck group remaining in the chamber. He roared, "Would anyone else care to join this pitiful Rhuyh Klaxxin!"

Fawning, whining obeisance, several responded, "No master."

"You are the great one."

"We always honor you will."

"Remember well what you have seen here today," he warned them. "Not even twelve of you could overtake me," he said, already exaggerating what had taken place. "Anyone who dares to challenge me will meet a similar fate.

"But enough! These traitors have allowed an attack to begin. I see now their treachery is responsible for the missing sentries. No doubt, Ningirsu thinks he will have little resistance in the city today." Pulling himself to his full stature he shouted, "But the vermin god is WRONG! Fauxxin will not be defeated!

"All of you, go immediately to the gates and the walls. We must aid the humans in their defense and repel whatever puny host Ningirsu has brought. Away! Fight for your lives! Go!" he swept them from the room with a roar.

From his position on the east ridge above Armoun, Hamayn, Talizar's second, now in command of the post, saw a large force of human attackers virtually materialize before his eyes. Admittedly, he had his back to their advance, but he was ashamed he had not sensed them coming, so great was their number. Talizar would not have missed their approach, he thought, wishing his master were back at his post. The attackers overwhelmed the small human guard at the pass and poured down onto the unsuspecting city. Hamayn's first thought was to warn Mistrea and the others who had entered the city, but fearing he might reveal their presence before they could complete their rescue, he flew directly to Iadrea's position above the opposite side of the city. By the time he reached them, it was obvious that his news was already known, as they had been looking more or less toward the oncoming attackers when they appeared.

As the attenders watched, a huge mass of darkness flooded down the road and through the pass into the city in concert with the movement of the human troops. After a moment's pause, the resident dark host poured out of the temple to meet the advancing rush in the air. While human soldiers clashed on the ground, the dark forces likewise battled in the sky above.

As many of the Kamaresans had swords, they were able to slash their way past the guards at the still open gate. The few who made it inside engaged the guards who were nearby, but due to the narrowness of the gate, their fellows could only enter two or three abreast, and the Armounians were able to spear or club sufficient numbers to keep the force inside from growing quickly. Because the alarm had been sounded as soon as the defenses at the pass fell, time allowed both soldiers and temple guards to rush to reinforce the gate. Gradually, the Kamaresans within the walls became outnumbered sufficiently to allow the shear volume of war clubs to trump even the power of their swords.

And the real cause of their success was more evident from the attenders' vantage point. Even as the dark host from Armoun battled their airborne foes, they took every opportunity to reach down and smash their terrible rods onto surprised Kamaresans. Fauxxin seemed to be everywhere at once, smashing and clawing dozens of his dark foes into oblivion. Between the human war clubs and the rods of darkness, the attackers were gradually driven back through the gate and outside the walls.

Even though it assured the loss of the troops already outside, once the last of the Kamaresans was out, the captain of the guard ordered the gate closed. With the city once again secure, the invisible guard of Armoun concentrated on their counterparts in the sky, leaving the humans to battle sword against club. Now in the minority, the club wielding defenders quickly fell to the flashing steel of their enemy. At the same time, the dark host sensed victory and redoubled their efforts at repelling their attackers.

With the gate closed, the troops had assembled atop the wall and began throwing spears and large rocks down upon the combatants below. This led the attackers to withdraw back to the foot of the pass, just out of reach of the enemy missiles.

Immediately, a roar went up from the humans on the wall, seeing their efforts succeed so well. Fauxxin also declared victory, although the skirmish was still heated, "Not today, Ningirsu, god of vermin! Not today!" Saying this he crashed down upon several combatants, even wounding some of his own as he clawed and clubbed the lesser demons aside as if they were dirt to be swept out of his city. No one matching Fauxxin's strength had joined the battle, an obvious sign that they did not expect his participation. With this thought he gathered himself up for one last charge and literally bowled the remaining attackers into the ridge with his massive wings.

As Iadrea and the others watched the dark guard from Armoun chase the attackers over the ridge and into the plain beyond, they refocused their attention on their primary concern, Mistrea and Ramah. By this time they had made their way to the wall and were gathering their things to leave.

"Should we descend to protect them?" Hamayn asked.

"I don't think we will have to; look, the dark ones are all busy chasing the scalded dogs. The less we are seen to be helping, the less attention they will pay." Glancing again toward the ridge and beyond he continued, "No. They will appear to have made a purely human escape from a troubled city. This is to our advantage as much as their own."

As he finished speaking, a half dozen attenders streaked up from the city, having finished their material work. They stopped as they reached Iadrea.

"Well done, my brothers. You have blended your efforts well with the Father's plan. The chosen ones are nearly all gathered. Watching them will be easier." He looked back toward the small band hurrying down the road away from Armoun. "Protecting them may yet prove to be a great challenge."

When the travelers had finished their meal at Nuwach's compound, the old man gathered them all around the fire. Even though it was very late, the events of the past few days had their heads spinning and no one could consider sleep, even though they were exhausted. Even Imanaq had roused himself from his deep sleep to greet his returning daughter.

"There is something I must tell you all," Nuwach began. "Among all of you, only Imanaq and my wife know anything of my life before I came to this place. There is much to tell and I am ashamed I have waited so long to share it." He paused, blowing out a long breath as if even now he might hesitate to go on.

"Many years ago I lived in Armoun, working as a carpenter. It was barely more than a village then. My brother was the chief at that time." He paused, waiting for the older ones to make the connection. "Yes, the present lugal is my nephew."

This revelation registered as a shock to everyone except the man's wife. He continued, "There was a prophecy spoken by the ancient one, told to me by my father, Lamech. When I was born, I was foretold to be the savior of my people." Again he paused, almost thinking he should not go on, but the wall was broken within him.

"My brother sought to overshadow me by taking every advantage among the people, and becoming chief mostly by force. When our father died, my brother became even more violent, so that I feared for my very life.

"It was then that I left the city and settled here. When his son, my nephew became strong enough in his own right, having learned his ways from his father, he began to defy his father's will at every turn. He led the people farther and farther from the worship of the god of the Araq, from the old ways and into every form of false worship and debauchery. I felt the displeasure of the one true god in my very soul. I knew that he would not let such rebellion go unpunished. I made frequent visits to the city to speak out against my brother and nephew whenever I could; I tried to reconcile them to one another and to god, but more and more, the people turned from our god and sank deeper into the evil ways.

"Finally it became so bad that our god revealed to me the meaning of the ancient prophecy concerning me." He looked around the fire at the rapt faces before continuing. "The Creator god of the Araq had determined to destroy the evil in his world by a great flood of waters. I was commanded to build a large boat which would save me and those who came with me from the rising of the waters which god would bring to cleanse the Araq. This compound where you now sit is the beginning of that boat I began when I first came here."

Each one was stunned by this revelation, looking around, trying to imagine a boat as large as the compound. Gradually, several things dawned on Sha'ym, who spoke next, "This explains the pitch on the outer walls you said was for protection from insects."

"And why we must continually bring more timber from the hills when we already have more than we need," Chamah added.

"And the walls standing on planks," Imanaq reasoned, "these are not only for bracing as you have said, but are the floor of the boat?"

"It is as you have all said. Oh how I wish I had not halted the construction. I feel the time of the cleansing is near. With each new moon, the water in the well rises higher. I fear god may wash us away too, if only to punish me for my disobedience." The old man hung his head in shame.

Everyone was silent for a long time when Nuwach's wife spoke in a forgiving voice, "Perhaps it is not too late to finish what you began so long ago, husband."

"I don't know woman. God chides me every day with a reminder that the water is coming. Gathering clouds darken the sky more with each passing season. I don't know..."

"But Father," Sha'ym said hopefully, "would our god give you this plan for escape and not allow you to complete it?"

"It is good to hear your words of faith, my son. It gives me hope that perhaps there is yet time. Perhaps if we all work together..."

"Of course, Father," Chamah chimed in, more from a sense of self protection than faith. He didn't fully believe the idea that water could flood the desert, but having so recently made a narrow escape from danger, he was anxious to build whatever protection might be possible.

Ramah looked at El Channah as they shared a thought, then he spoke, "I may have some friends who could assist you in this."

Nuwach looked at the new-found friend quizzically. "Why would they want to help?"

"Perhaps they will be as interested in a safe place as you are," came the quick reply.

Nuwach nodded thoughtfully and silence again overtook the small circle. Then the old man spoke again, "Perhaps god will honor late obedience as well as early. What else can we do but try?"

There was nodding all around at this. "We could start tomorrow," Nuwach's wife suggested, "but we will need some rest in any case."

"There is wisdom, woman," Nuwach said, putting his arm around his companion. "Let us to bed; in the morning we will survey what is yet to be done."

CHAPTER EIGHTEEN

After traveling the short distance back to their base camp, Thorel and the other Kamaresan warriors who escaped unharmed were completely exhausted and entirely disheartened. The young warrior surveyed the scene before him as he sat beside his tent. His chief, who had been given charge over the attack force, had chosen this spot, hidden in a small canyon, to prepare for the attack. Their forces had moved in stealthily, clan by clan until there were twenty-five tents in a rough double semi-circle backed against the canyon wall. The spot was located far enough from the road that no one was likely to happen upon it by chance. One small cooking fire was allowed to burn only at night so that the smoke would not alert anyone of their presence.

Once the chosen warriors from each of the four clans had arrived, Thorel sat with the other men as his chief explained the battle plan. The chief was wise in the ways of war and the plan he presented to them sounded foolproof. They were to await the new moon, then approach the city in the last hours before twilight. As soon as the sun had risen high enough behind them to give them an advantage, they were to storm the guards at the pass and pour into the city before the gates could be closed.

"The king and all his seers have agreed the gods fight with us today," the chief had said. "Mighty Sababba joins with Ningirsu to crush the goat-scum."

Thorel looked now at his battered shield, adorned with a simple drawing of an eagle, the mighty Sababba, clutching a sword in one foot and a shield in the other. He wondered if the gods suffered as great a loss as the humans. The plan had worked perfectly at first. Their approach to the pass was a complete surprise. The guards there had just enough time to sound one note of the alarm before the entire force of twenty men was hacked to death by the flashing swords of over one hundred charging Kamaresans. They flooded down the hill and crossed the short distance to the gate just as it began to swing shut. Several of his fellows had thrown themselves against the gates to hold them open for the others who charged in through the narrow opening.

Once inside, the battle took a different turn. While the swordsmen outclassed their club wielding foes, they were unable to get sufficient numbers through the gate to stand against an ever-increasing number of defenders. Then too, Thorel, who had been one of the first to follow his chief through the gate, witnessed a strange thing. Just moments after crashing the gate, he dispatched the man before him and turned to see his chief raise his sword to strike, then suddenly fall backward to the ground as if thrown off his feet by mighty blow. Immediately the Armounians nearby began clubbing him mercilessly, and though he was able to gash open the belly of one of them, they succeeded in smashing his skull.

Thorel himself took a blow to his back as he hesitated in the aftermath of what he had seen. As he fell to his knees, he cursed his momentary lack of vigilance, spinning his body to present his sword to his attacker. To his surprise, the nearest goat soldier was too far away to have struck him. There had been no time to consider this strange effect, as more and more clubs and spears were filling the small open space near the gate. Eventually they had been forced to flee back through the still open gate and up the hill they had so recently charged down shouting victory. A few Armounians were foolish enough to chase down a single swordsman, only to find that one-on-one the odds were wildly against them.

When the last man from the city gave up the chase, the Kamaresans gradually formed together on the road and limped hang-dog back to camp. Little was said as each man nursed his wounds, both physical and emotional. Finally a man not from Thorel's tribe said, "The gods were not strong with us today."

Partly in defense of his chief's assertion to the contrary that morning, Thorel shot back, "How can you say such a thing!"

The man stopped walking and looked straight at Thorel. He was much older than the young warrior and had a tough look about him. "How can I say this?" he said angrily. "You are still a boy. When you have fought as many battles as I have, you might understand." Then softening his tone somewhat he continued, "I watched three of my men fall to the invisible ones. Our swords should have slaughtered them, but we were pummeled back out of the city. Why do you suppose that is?"

"The gods did this?" Thorel asked as he remembered his own weird experience.

"Son," the man spoke more kindly now. "If the gods don't fight with you, you will do well to stay in the camp with the women and the baggage. We brag of our swords — how they flash like the talons of Sababba, no?"

Thorel nodded.

"Well today Dumuzi trampled those talons."

The older man turned and continued the trek to camp, leaving Thorel to consider his words. As a boy he had always thought it would be his skill and strength that would win battles. The stories about the gods were just that: stories to share around the fire. Now as he sat by this fire, a vanquished warrior, his chief dead along with several of his friends, he began to doubt his own abilities and to wonder what other things he had to learn about these gods who had suddenly become so very real indeed.

At the very moment Thorel sat contemplating these things, two of the creatures he thought of as gods were at the point of coming to blows. "You placed too much hope in the traitors, fool!" the larger one shouted. This was the one known as Sababba to Thorel's people, the sky god. He and Ningirsu were in league against Dumuzi and Inanna. He was berating one of Ningirsu's captains whom he blamed for the failed attack on Armoun.

"I should smash you into oblivion for your stupidity."

"And then face me?" a voice said from behind Sababba. He wheeled around to see Ningirsu. The patron god of Kamaresh stood almost as tall as Sababba, and had proven in many battles to have fighting skills beyond his size.

Sababba growled a deep, dissatisfied rumble and responded, "No, but we should not have left the battle to these peons. They have cost me many good soldiers."

"You are forgetting that I lost troops as well," Ningirsu retorted. "And you also forget that this was only one battle, not the whole war. Do you think we would have faced only Fauxxin if we two had joined the battle? Dumuzi would certainly have come to his aid. Are you ready to wager which side Inanna will support?"

Another low rumble of discontent from Sababba.

"Go ahead and grumble; at least you still have wings. Had Inanna joined Dumuzi you would be crawling in some pit right now."

Sababba squirmed slightly.

"Yes, I know: you think that because you are the "Sky god" Inanna favors you. I don't deny that you may be right, but I am not prepared to stake my life on it. Ruling in Kamaresh is better than crawling in a tar pit."

"This was a test, Sababba. We have learned their strengths without revealing ours. Now I will have no trouble convincing the king to mount a full siege since his petty vanity was wounded today. He will feel compelled to restore the honor of his vaunted swordsman. While he prepares his humans for the attack, perhaps we can convince Meslantaea to join our cause. Then I will wager my own life that Inanna will come into the battle on our side, and victory will be assured."

"Your words sound so wise, Ningirsu," the sky god said mockingly, "but I remember thinking the same thing when I let you convince me to lay our hopes on the traitor's plan. You say you learned something today? Well so did I: I now know that if this new plan of yours fails, I will face you in combat, even if it means joining Dumuzi."

"Patience, my comrade," Ningirsu spoke in uncharacteristic tones. "You shall have your mountain kingdom, and I shall own the Tyriean plain. Between us we will rule all these beastly humans and send Dumuzi back to his goat herds."

"Patience is not one of my virtues," Sababba growled. "This had better work." Saying this he flew into the sky, circling under one of the larger clouds he was learning to form to escape the accursed rays of the sun.

When day broke at Nuwach's compound, there was a feeling that the events of the previous day might have been a dream. Their dramatic escape from Armoun and the revelations of Nuwach upon their reunion had a distinct air of unreality in the morning sun. As each of them was attempting to make his or her own sense of the situation, another weight was laid upon them.

"Nuwach, come quickly!" the woman called to her husband as he labored at the morning chores.

"What is it woman," Nuwach said as he rushed back into the house. "I was almost finished when you..."

"It is Imanaq;" she interrupted, "I can't wake him."

They both moved quickly to the sleeping mat where the old man had spent most of the last several days. "I feared he was not well," Nuwach said as he stooped near his dear friend's head.

"Imanaq, old friend," he said as he gently shook the man. "Imanaq," he repeated.

Sharaq, who could not help noticing what was happening stepped closer to the two near her father. Nuwach's wife instinctively cradled her with one arm while saying, "Your father has not been well since you were taken. He pined dreadfully for fear you were dead. Then, last night, to see you safe and well...." She was unsure how to finish the thought.

Her husband rose from Imanaq's side and finished for her: "He is dead, my child."

The girl turned sobbing into the older woman's breast as Delyah came over and embraced them both, sharing as she did her deep grief. As the three weeping women clung to one another, Nuwach placed a hand tenderly on Sharaq's shoulder and raised his eyes and an inaudible voice in prayer to the unseen God of the Araq.

This scene greeted the other men as they returned to the house after completing the morning chores. Sha'ym and Chamah did not know what to make of it, but El Channah and Ramah stepped discreetly aside, knowing precisely what had taken place. Nuwach motioned to his sons when he noticed them. As they approached the tearful group, Nuwach spoke.

"Sharaq, my daughter," he began with obvious compassion. "I know you will have a season of weeping for your father; this is good and comfort will come in time. But know this:" he turned slightly to look down at the peaceful form laying on the mat. "Your father has gone before you to be with the ancient ones. In fact, even now I suspect he is breaking bread with your mother and enjoying a cool breeze in that better place."

At the mention of her mother, the young woman lifted her head slightly and looked into the eyes of wisdom before her. "Do you really think this is so?" she asked plaintively.

"I am sure of it, child," he answered without hesitation. "He waited for your safe return, then went to be with her." With his hand still resting on her shoulder, he reached out his other to place it on Sha'ym's. He continued, "It has already been arranged for you to marry my son so you know I have begun thinking of you as my daughter. One day, we will all gather with your mother and father and have a huge wedding feast like nothing you could have imagined."

Sharaq sobbed reflexively as she peered deeply into the old man's comforting gaze. She saw peace there; she remembered similar words spoken to her as a child when her mother died so many years ago. She remembered that then, as now, she had taken comfort in the thought that she would meet her mother again. She struggled with the thought now, wondering if only children could believe such things. But in the old man's peaceful eyes she could see that there are some things we always believe as a child, no matter how many years we have lived.

Then she looked at Sha'ym; here was her life now. Only last night this had seemed like such a wonderful prospect, if entirely unknown. When her eyes met his, she saw for a moment the same uncertain yet hopeful longing in them, and she stepped into his arms and began crying all over again.

After they had finished a simple breakfast of bread and fruit, eaten mostly in reverent silence, El Channah spoke. "Ramah and I will beg your leave now, Father," he looked respectfully to Nuwach. "Perhaps we can enlist some of our friends to help in your building project."

"I can not tell you how much I have appreciated your help already. I had hoped..." he paused, at a loss for words. "When the boys were older..." he began again, but still could not make words of his jumbled thoughts. The enormity of the task daunted him as much now as it had at the first.

Knowing the old man's heart, El Channah rescued him, "You take up the work where you left it; we will return with help to finish." He rose to take the old man's hand. Facing each other, right hands clasped around the other's forearm, left hands on the other's shoulder, they looked into each other's eyes. "May our God protect you until we meet again," the tall man said.

"And may He watch over you as you travel," was the return. "I fear there may be more dangers on the road then ever, if the cities are making war against each other."

"Fear not," came El Channah's strong reply. "Our God can take care of us all as we seek to do His will." With this he and Ramah stepped into the morning sun, called to their trusted four-legged friend, Jireh, who had been lying near the door, and made their way out the gate.

When they had disappeared from sight, Nuwach turned to his sons and spoke to Chamah with a slight twinkle in his eye, "So, my son, do you still love that axe you once prized so highly?"

Chamah looked at his father sheepishly at first, then seeing the look on his face responded, "Yes, Father; how may I help?"

"There are many logs in need of splitting and shaping. Unless El Channah returns with an army of helpers, we are going to have to do it ourselves."

"I will do my best, Father," the boy responded, beginning to catch some of the excitement, without realizing the immensity of the task.

"Sha'ym," Nuwach looked to his oldest son, "if our friend does not return soon, I fear we may have to make another trip to the forest for more logs. The meager pile we have will not last long once we begin construction."

Sha'ym thought it odd at first, to call the huge pile of logs they had amassed over the years meager. Neither he nor his younger brother could envision the great quantities of wood that would be required to complete the Heavenly Father's plan. Perhaps if Nuwach had revealed the design in its entirety, they would have themselves joined the scoffers, for nothing of its size had been constructed by any man entirely of wood. The temples and city palaces were larger, to be sure, but they were made of mud and stone. This building would have to float. The grandest merchant vessel on the Western Sea would appear tiny next to the boat Nuwach was building.

The compound Nuwach had constructed with hired help years ago measured just over two hundred meters in length and thirty-five meters in width. The walls themselves rose nearly fourteen meters above the planks which formed the bottom of the structure. The planks had been pegged to the bottom framing after pouring pitch onto the ground beneath them. More pitch was spread over the planks and dirt spread on that to provide a surface on which to walk.

Braces still held the walls erect between the various two-story outbuildings which had been constructed adjacent to the outer perimeter in each corner and directly opposite one another at points along the wall. The plan was to construct a framework to connect these mid-wall buildings across the compound and eventually to build a second and a third floor, or deck throughout the entire structure. Lengthwise down the center ran what would be called a street, if this were indeed a walled village, as it appeared. In reality, this central passage was to be the access to the compartments on either side, and the space for ramps to the upper levels.

There was only one entrance, which now served as the gate to the compound, near the center of the east wall. The opening was four meters square and was closed by two doors which swung inward. When completed, the doors were to be reinforced by a one-piece ramp, hinged at the floor, which would be hauled shut with ropes and sealed with pitch after everyone was safe inside.

Mistrea and his two fellows had dematerialized immediately after passing out of sight of their human charges. From their vantage point high above the compound, the man and his sons and servants did look very much like men going to work in a small village. The task seemed easier to contemplate from there as well, not only because it looked smaller, but because they knew the super-human resources which could be brought to the aid of the human workers. Although humans were generally left more or less on their own in their physical labors, the council had already discussed plans to speed the work at Nuwach's compound. Even though Iadrea himself did not know the exact time of the coming flood, he could tell by the course of events that it would not be much longer.

"Mistrea," Chantar, who had been known as Ramah spoke, "I will keep watch here; you and Multar should report to Iadrea."

"Very well. I will tell him things are going well here, and begin the deployment of the zensak along the animal trails."

"May the Light be with you, my friends," Chantar said as the two attenders raised their arms and streaked away on the wings of Mentridar.

Later that afternoon three men and a donkey appeared at Nuwach's gate. "Hail Nuwach!" one of them shouted. "Peace be upon you and all whom you protect."

From across the compound Nuwach called, "Who is there, and what do you seek?"

"We are friends of El Channah whom we met on the road this very morning. He tells us you may require assistance in a building project."

Nuwach hurried to the gate and raised the bar. Once the men appeared in the open gate he continued, "Any friend of El Channah is truly welcome here. He has lately brought both joy and peace to this old man's heart."

"We do not doubt he has, good sir, for he has many times proved a blessing as we labored together as well," the man replied. "I am Arvad; I take great pleasure in coaxing planks from gopher wood logs. These are my friends Beerah and Keziz. We have recently left another building project to seek work some distance from the tribal wars which once again plague the city."

Nuwach greeted each one in turn and said, "I have heard of the war myself, and it is just that from which El Channah has brought me my joy."

"Yes," Arad said, "He told us he ran into your sons in the city and was able to deliver them from some trouble."

"In his humility he may not have told you he saved their very lives and brought them safely home. He has earned a place of highest honor in my home.

"But come," he interrupted himself. "Let us water your beast and find you some refreshment."

"Your hospitality is appreciated, but in fact, we need only a drink of water ourselves and then we will join you in your work. "Look," Arad opened a bag slung over the donkey. "We even have iron tools."

Nuwach stopped to admire the metal axes, mauls and hammers the open bag revealed. "These are beautiful instruments; anyone who works with such tools is obviously a true craftsman. I must tell you now, I am not a man of means. My wealth is in my family and the land you see around you. That is," he stumbled slightly for the words, "I can not pay you as you must be accustomed."

"Be at peace, Nuwach," Arad responded. "A loaf and some wine; the God of the Araq has blessed you with these, no?"

At the mention of his God, Nuwach's spirit soared. Except for El Channah, no one outside of his family had mentioned Him in years. "Wine!" he said, almost cheerily. "I can offer you the sweetest wine the Araq can produce. And my wife is gifted at preparing simple food that pleases both mouth and stomach." At this he patted his midsection, which while not fat, proved his point in not a subtle way.

The next morning, two more men appeared at Nuwach's gate, ostensibly fleeing the turmoil at Armoun, and having run into El Channah on the road. That afternoon, three more, and so on until by week's end there were no less than twenty skilled craftsman laboring on Nuwach's project. When El Channah himself returned with Ramah and two others, the full complement reached twenty-four. "My friend," Nuwach addressed El Channah on the evening he returned. "I am without words to thank you for all that you have done."

The tall one extended his hand palm down and shook his head slowly, but before he could say anything, the old man continued, "It is amazing enough that you found this great number of craftsman and more so that they are willing to join us in this, but wonder of wonders," here Nuwach's hands were raised beside his shoulders in true puzzlement, "they all serve the true God!"

"Not so amazing, really, my friend," El Channah finally inserted. "Some professions are more heavily populated with His servants than others." A knowing look at Ramah and Arad who were closest to him brought smiles, then laughter.

"Just so," Arad chortled, "our profession boasts many followers of the true God." At this all the craftsmen around the fire began to laugh even more heartily, so much so that Nuwach and his people themselves began to chuckle self-consciously, not seeing the humor in the observation, but being caught up in the infectious laughter of those around them.

There was no laughter in the court of the king of Kamaresh as he and his tribal chieftains gathered that same night. It had been nearly two weeks since the defeat of their test force. Thorel was honored to be selected as a representative for his clan in place of his fallen chief. This meant he sat with the chieftains as they discussed the next move in their overall plan to take Armoun. Since this was his first war council he was surprised learn that the battle in which he fought was not expected to be successful.

King Ningu-Simga spoke deliberately as he paced around the fire which burned in the center of the circled leaders. "We can be proud of men who taught humility to the goat soldiers. Their blood is to Ningirsu a sweet offering." Nods and mumbled agreement came unanimously from the men in the circle. "We mourn them, but it is a great victory when we lose only one for each five of the enemy, is it not?" He raised his voice slightly at this last. The men caught the intonation and many spoke words of praise for their dead in a concert of assent.

"And I am proud of you, Javan, my son," the king continued. "You fought valiantly and brought honor to our family." Again the men around the fire voiced their assent, praising Prince Javan's valor.

When the chorus subsided the king continued, "Ningirsu fights with us, and yet..." he turned to face the seers and priests who were gathered in one quadrant of the circle, "... and yet Dumuzi was stronger than we were led to believe, was he not?"

The shamans squirmed somewhat under the glare of the king. They had in fact assured him that Dumuzi would not enter the battle, and they still maintained that he had not. Even so, they were at a loss to explain why Ningirsu had not succeeded in keeping the minions of the goat god from clubbing many of their soldiers into the ground.

"May the king live forever," one of the seers began. "We know that the great god Ningirsu is still entreating Sababba to join us. Perhaps our efforts to show ourselves strong for our gods will persuade the Sky king to make his alliance with us."

"Iron and men trained to use it I can count. These gods of yours who may or may not join us...." The king stopped. He realized that the gods were a force that must be considered. He dared not openly challenge their place in all the doings of men. Yet in his heart, he believed only in one thing: if he could arm enough men with iron weapons, Armoun would be his.

"By all means, we must know when Sababba will join us," he continued, still looking at the shamans. "Seek out this information for me; it will be of great comfort when we attack. But know this," he returned to pacing around the fire and looking into the eyes of the soldiers he could count, "We will attack!"

The circle erupted with raucous war whoops and cries which continued for several minutes. The king urged them on, knowing the value of this behavior, warming the blood, steeling the spirit. He clapped his son's back and the two looked approvingly around the fire.

"I have no doubt that in Armoun they are celebrating another victory," the king continued. "This is just what we wanted." Thorel could not conceal the look of surprise on his face, and to his dismay, the king's glance happened to fall upon that look. "Young Thorel," the king singled him out, "do not think I am making light of the sacrifice your family has made. Your Father's death will be avenged many times over when we complete our plans."

In the grip of the his sovereign's stare, Thorel's look changed to one of confusion. "You did not sit in council when we planned this war. You must understand: the Armounians expect us to attack from time to time to test their strength. Each time we have failed, we have given them many moons of peace before trying again. Today, they are sure we not coming back. By next moon, they will barely remember we were there, and in two moons they will relax in the thought that we are defeated. That is when we will attack in full force such as we have never done."

King Ningu-Simca now resumed his magisterial pacing around the circle, drawing maps in the air as he spoke, "We will divide our men into two forces; the smaller one will attack again as we did this time, only with greater force and more speed. With the gods help," he nodded towards his seers, "they will gain a stronghold inside the city gates this time. The other force, the largest we have yet sent in battle, will approach from the Tyriean plain and storm the south gate after the battle is engaged on the north."

"Madai," the king addressed one of the chieftains directly, "I know you have expressed your doubts about this plan...."

"No, my king..." Madai began.

"Silence," the king cut him off short. "Do not deny what I know to be true. I would rather hear your dissent openly and know I am getting true counsel than to have you spread the poison of doubt among your clan." The king had stopped walking directly in front of Madai and now stood waiting for him to speak.

Getting slowly to his feet, the chief began tentatively, "May the king live forever, I only said to my men that we have tried this before and we...." he paused to think of a word other than "failed," but in the silence the king rescued him.

"You are correct, Madai," the king placed a hand on the chief's shoulder. "But this time there are two important differences: we have forged a thousand more swords since then, and the tribes of the Tokarmaanu will reinforce the northern attack force."

The news of help from Tokar took all but Prince Javan by surprise. The king explained, "You know we have been trading with the Tokar people for many years now. They hold Sababba in high esteem, just as many of you do, and they hate the goat-scum as well. By agreeing to arm them with iron weapons, I have secured their pledge to help us wipe Dumuzi's smell from the Tyriean plain."

Emboldened by Madai's example, another chieftain spoke up, "But what is to stop them from turning their new swords against us, my king?"

"Good," the king turned to face the new challenge, "now you are thinking. And so have I thought of this. We will only arm a small part of their army, and they will not be as well trained as our best swordsmen. If they attempt to double cross us, we should have no trouble cutting them down.

"But I don't think they will. Tokarmaanu is not interested in the plain. When we control the land from Kamaresh to Armoun and then to the Western Sea, we will share a border with them as far as Tyriea. They would much rather have us on their border as friendly trading partners than the goat-herders. Besides this, remember that they once worshiped Inanna, and many long to see her cast off her ill-found husband, Dumuzi."

The questioner nodded his satisfaction at the king's answer.

It was Madai who spoke up next, "My king, I am pleased that Tokar will join our fight, but unless you foresee a long siege, we must gain an element of surprise that we have not had in the past."

"You are very perceptive, Madai," the king answered. "Javan, my son, explain to Madai how this will be accomplished."

"The northern forces will be divided into two groups. One will head east from Kamaresh before all the others to join with Tokar's force and give them their swords and a few days of training. The other part will gather little by little in the canyon just as our recent battle plan required. The two will join at the ridge above Armoun from the east and the west when the moon is new. With a combined strength of over five hundred swordsmen, they should have no trouble accomplishing what our one hundred nearly did two days ago."

Javan looked around the circle as the men nodded in agreement, then continued, "The rest of the army will be divided into three groups. The first will be made up of those of you who live to the east and south of Kamaresh. I will gather you as we move southward to the southern trade route, then head east and enter the Tyriean plain from the southern end. The second group will be made up of those of you who dwell south and west of the city. You will move south until you meet the trade road at what is called Nuwach's vineyard. You will wait there for the eastern tribes to join you." Javan looked around to see if the men seemed to be following his description of the movements. Their rapt attention convinced him they were.

"Finally, the last group, led by my Father, will move to the pass at the foot of Mt. Tabor, where we have launched our previous attacks. But they will wait on the west side of Tabor until the battle is joined by both the northern and southern armies. Then they will move in either to reinforce the southern troops or to join them in their victory celebration." With this last he smiled and looked confidently at his father.

"May it be just as you have said, my son," the king regained the crowd's attention. "I would like to have the pleasure of wetting my sword with some goat blood, but if you have already secured the city, I will not be too disappointed."

The rest of the long night was spent discussing smaller details of the campaign. Thorel was surprised to learn that his clan would not be in the northern force again, but would travel with Javan. As it was explained to him, the king's elite guard would have a contingent in each of the groups, first to train the rest of the soldiers in the finer points of sword battle, and then to be the backbone of the attack force at each point.

In the weeks that followed, each of the clan leaders was to return home and prepare by packing as much food as they could gather and breaking their camps when the appointed time to travel arrived. Thorel pictured the beautiful meadow where he lived. The thought of leaving it was somewhat painful, but the lure of adventure and conquest drowned those thoughts quickly. Then too, with the chief gone, he would probably be free to take Marah for his mate. Again the domestic thoughts of helping to raise Morning Sky and provide for a family entered his mind briefly, but the trained warrior in him cleared his mind for what was ahead.

Even the women had an important role in warfare. They helped carry the supplies, cooked the meals and tended the wounded or buried the dead. And sadly, when their men were not successful, they were either killed as their camps were overrun, or taken as slaves by the conquerors. In victory or defeat, war was as hard on the women as it was on the men. The difference was that the men thrived on the glory of war, despising the cost, while the women often despised the glory and more dearly counted the cost.

CHAPTER NINETEEN

As Mistrea and Multar began to deploy zensak along the animal trails, it became obvious that something was happening among the various species. The farther the two ranged from Nuwach's project, the more frequently they saw gatherings of animals moving together. This was not unusual for herds of antelope or prides of lions, but even solitary creatures from lizards to leopards were moving together. It was as if Nuwach had some type of animal magnet and creatures of every description were being drawn toward it. First one, then two, then four the animals gradually came together as they grazed or foraged or hunted. Seen individually they appeared to be carrying on their normal habits, but taken all together it became a concert of movement flowing toward a single center.

"Master," Multar asked at one point, "why do we need to place zensak over the animal trails? I thought it was only useful against detection by the dark ones."

"And so it is," Mistrea replied. "We do not want the enemy to detect the herding until the last possible moment. Remember that many of these creatures are favorite playthings of the dark ones. Take Dumuzi for example: long ago, before he rose to his high position, he was assigned to a tribe of goat herders. As he consolidated his power among his minions, he became known as the goat-king. Even though he now holds a position far higher than that, he still retains the title, and those still tending goats feel an allegiance to him.

"If the movement of the goats or lions or any species became suspicious, the more powerful dark ones associated with them would be informed. The zensak keeps the lesser powers just confused enough to allow us to keep herding them without interference. I must say though that sooner or later an alarm will be raised, probably because of the turf battles that will inevitably break out between species as they come closer together."

"I see," Multar nodded as they continued their work.

"But that is not the only reason for the zensak," Mistrea continued. "The zensak also has a calming effect on the creatures as well. We hope it will tend to draw them into its peaceful ways and help us to guide them toward our goal. It may also delay some of the squabbling between the animals themselves."

Mistrea suddenly stopped talking and became dead still. Multar took the cue and tried to determine what had caught his master's attention. Reaching out with his senses he could tell something was different, but could not identify it. In a moment Mistrea spoke, "There is a large group of humans coming this way."

Multar strained to catch the distinct impression of the humans. "Yes, he thought, "I feel it too."

The two attenders rose into the sky to get a look at what was coming. At two hundred meters in the air they could see a large area of the forest, but the trees were too dense to locate the people. After scanning the area for enemy activity, Mistrea signaled Multar to move with him toward the approaching group. They slid cautiously among the trees at ground level until they reached a position abreast the moving people. What they discovered was nearly one hundred Kamaresans moving southward on the trail they had been covering. The humans appeared to have all their worldly goods with them: tents, tools and cooking gear. It looked like a large village on the move.

"This is curious," Mistrea observed. "If this were only a clan I wouldn't think it odd, but such a large group..." He stopped to consider for a moment. "Perhaps we should tell Iadrea; he knows more about the habits of these people than I. It could be nothing, but I don't want to take the chance.

"Keep watch here while I find Iadrea. There will doubtless be dark ones with these humans, so keep yourself hidden. I will return quickly." With that he raised his wings and shot straight upward before Multar could express his doubts at being left alone in this situation.

It was only a moment after Mistrea had left when his prediction proved true: Multar saw two dark forms hovering above the line of marching humans. Although they were not large, even the smaller of the two was at least a head taller than Multar. It suddenly occurred to him that he was uncloaked. While they had been working with the zensak, neither had bothered to take on any protection since they were virtually bathed in it as they worked. Now, however, Multar was beginning to feel the presence of the dark ones, and he felt frighteningly naked and exposed.

At the moment he began to slide backward, away from the trail, a pair of yellow eyes suddenly looked his way, searching the forest for something felt, but not seen. Multar tried to melt into the ground, hoping to mask his essence from the prying enemy. The young attender had moved through solid objects at speed before, but moving slowly was a new experience. His body felt massive and sluggish as he tried to drift backwards through the soil. He watched as the two dark ones conferred for a moment, then to his horror, the smaller one began to move in his general direction.

The frightened attender considered trying to contact Mistrea by thought, but immediately realized he was too far distant for his meager powers. Besides, thought communication would be like sending a beacon to the searching enemy. His only hope was to extract himself from the restricting soil and take wing back to the zensak in hopes of using it for cover. Against all natural instinct he began to rise out of the ground so that he could lift his wings even as the scout moved nearer to his position. When his arms and shoulders were free, he slowly raised his wings in preparation for flight. This was just enough activity to allow the enemy to zero in on his location. As Multar struggled to extract his lower extremities from the ground, the dark one spotted him and began rushing in his direction.

Multar signaled the cxings to take flight before he had completely separated from the soil. The acceleration rate of his upper body outpaced that of his still-earthbound parts so that he stretched out many times his normal height. While this gave Multar a strange tingling feeling, it also gave the rushing enemy the impression that the small attender was much larger than he actually was. This led him to halt his attack briefly, until he realized his foe's size was an illusion. This momentary halt was just enough to save Multar. When the dark one realized he had been fooled, he charged on, swinging his club just soon enough to catch Multar's foot as it left the ground.

Multar felt a sharp pain in his foot and had trouble directing his flight as the lower portion of his body corkscrewed wildly from the force of the blow. The dark one shot up after him, but couldn't lay a club on him due to his erratic flight. Once Multar regained full control of his trajectory, he bee-lined for the zensak with the enemy close on his trail. When evenly matched for size, attenders can easily outpace the enemy's slower more awkward flight mechanism. In this case, the enemy's extra size made up for any deficiency in his capabilities and he was gaining on his retreating foe.

Just as the dark one was about to strike another blow, they both entered the mass of zensak. It was as if the pursuer had suddenly consumed gallons of strong drink, for he could still sense what was going on around him, but it became very difficult to decide what to do about it. Thus with club raised to strike he slowly coasted to a stop in a complete daze. Multar turned with drawn sword, prepared to dispatch his pursuer, but paused when he saw the confused look and lowering club. Strangely he felt a moment of compassion for this hideous creature who had seconds before been intent on killing him. It seemed unfair to take advantage of his debilitated state this way.

During this pause for thought, they both drifted out of the zensak and the dark one regained his composure. Quickly he raised his club and began a roundhouse swing at the little attender. Multar instinctively drew back from the blow which took him into the zensak again. At this point he saw the other dark one approaching, having realized his companion was in pursuit of a prize.

"Stand back, you worthless bumbler," the larger one shouted as he dove at Multar, "I'll finish him."

Not wanting to be deprived of his trophy, the smaller one raised his club again and lunged at Multar. This put him directly in the path of his charging partner. "NO! He's mine," he screamed as he again entered the zensak and forgot why his club was raised. He was bowled into the ground by the club and body of the larger one who couldn't stop or change course soon enough, he too being dulled slightly by the zensak. When they both pulled themselves out of the ground and faced their prey, the larger one realized what was happening and backed out of the poisonous mist.

Multar, still uncertain of his moral position, watched as the larger one cleared his head and then turned to charge tooth and claw towards him. He barely had time to brace himself for the crushing blow, for surely the dark one's momentum would carry him on in spite of the zensak. But the blow never came as a sudden flash of light tore through the attacker from shoulder to hip cleaving the enemy's body in two. The pieces crashed into the ground on either side of Multar as the form of his master appeared in place of the charging enemy.

Meanwhile the smaller dark one had recovered and had flown backward to some height above and behind Mistrea.

"Master, behind you..." Multar shouted as the dark one attempted to imitate what his partner had done, charging full tilt at the attenders. Mistrea instantly turned and moved aside, giving the dark one a clear shot at Multar. The dark form smashed directly into the small attender and they both fell to the ground. At first their was no movement at all, then Multar gasped, "Get this thing off me; Oh this smells bad!"

Mistrea easily rolled the stinking corpse off his young friend and they both watched as it gradually melted into the soil, leaving only Multar's sword sticking up where it had impaled the attacker on impact.

"You did well to avoid these two monsters, my friend," Mistrea said in honest compliment.

"It wasn't my skill that saved me, Master, but sheer luck," the young one replied.

"There is no such thing as luck, Multar," the teacher counseled. "Luck is a word used by unbelievers to describe the providential care afforded by the Father. Those who seek to deny His presence must invent means by which to explain their good fortune; the longer I live, the easier it is to believe there is an unseen hand guiding events than to imagine luck or chance directs their course."

"Well then, I am just glad His hand guided you back here when it did, or I would be in very bad shape right now."

"That's the attitude; and so your light remains to serve the Father yet one more day," Mistrea agreed. "And I owe you an apology for taking off on our little reconnaissance without cloaking. And, the news from Iadrea means we must be even more careful in the coming days.

"He has had reports of other groups of humans from Kamaresh moving south. It seems they plan to mount a massive attack on Armoun from the south." One party is already camped at the pass near the compound of Nuwach. Our orders are to finish here as quickly as possible and return to Nuwach's.

It was after sunset the following day when Mistrea and Multar glided back into the area above the compound. It was obvious that their companions had been busy while they were gone. What had been a mostly open compound was now a fully enclosed structure with only a few sections of the roof yet unfinished. It resembled some of the log lodges to be found in Kamaresh, except that it was larger than any that had ever been built. Approaching it at ground level, one in fact had the impression that it was more a small city than a large building.

The other thing that was remarkable from the attenders' perspective in the sky was the sizeable encampment sitting across the road from the structure. Several cooking fires burned throughout the camp, lighting the front of the tents that circled around them. Mistrea estimated that this group was even larger than the one they had met on the trail earlier.

"It appears the Kamaresans have no quarrel with Nuwach," Mistrea shared his thought with Multar.

"Yes, but see how the dark ones line the road opposite the compound," Multar observed.

"They are taking great interest in the work. I suppose it was inevitable that they would discover it sooner or later," Mistrea answered.

"Why are there not more defenders around the wall?" Multar wondered.

"Don't forget the work crew we provided," Mistrea explained. "They will be of service if a battle breaks out. But there are others here as well." The large attender swept his gaze around the horizon. "Reach out; tell me what you sense." The young one strained to feel what he could in the immediate area. Gradually he began to realize that there were many dozens of attenders along the ridge, behind the compound and some distance outside of the Kamaresan camp as well. He discovered that the area was in fact surrounded by a host much larger than the few dark ones sitting by the road.

Mistrea let it sink in and then said, "We are still being as covert as possible in our protection; no need to start an all out war before it is necessary.'

"There will be war, won't there, Master?"

"It is very likely, I am afraid. Once the dark powers realize what is happening, they will do whatever they can to disrupt the Father's plan.

About this same time a high-level conference was taking place deep below the temple in Armoun. The great Dumuzi himself towered over Fauxxin's left side while Sababba rose to nearly the same height on his right. Fauxxin's six captains stood huddled some distance from the three leaders, unsure of what the meeting might hold. Distrust was the normal mind set for these creatures, so the presence of their supreme leader and a non-aligned stranger of massive strength was unsettling, to say the least.

It was Dumuzi who spoke first, "So the air monster would challenge me again?" he said, his burning yellow eyes piercing through Sababba.

Wincing slightly at the appellation, the sky god thought for a moment. While he was proud of his domination of the sky, his peers never missed an opportunity to remind him that he ruled no land, no mountains, no seas, or, as they held, no substance. His alliance with Ningirsu had in fact been intended to remedy this by eventually taking Meslantaea's mountain kingdom for himself. He knew that Dumuzi probably understood this, but for effect was charging the sky god with an attack on him.

"But no, great one," he began, feigning respect, "I have no designs on your kingdom; you are too powerful for me to challenge."

"You lie, but you do it very well," Dumuzi responded. "I respect that in you and I suspect that is how you gained the trust of the puny Ningirsu. Now however, it is time for you to prove your loyalty through action, or I will personally carry your smoking corpse to Inanna as an offering." He paused momentarily trying to read Sababba's thoughts. Sensing a still willful spirit, he continued, "Or do you wish to make an open challenge?"

Although the Rhuyh Klaxxin was the preferred method of coup among lesser demons, often the higher placed demis would mount an attack directly on their target or place an ultimatum before them requiring battle. These direct challenges often took the form of duels between the two, with their supporters observing at a distance. The onlookers were kept from interfering not so much by their respect for the rules of combat as by their uncertainty of who would prevail. Not wishing to be found on the losing side, they would wait until a clear victory was won by one of the combatants, then pile on the loser in a frenzy of tooth and claw, or slink away to avoid notice by the winner.

Sababba doubted he could take Dumuzi in mortal combat, and his effort to link with Ningirsu against him had so far proved ineffective, so he took the only option he saw. "I do not lie when I say you are the great one," he fawned, "and I will be pleased to do whatever you ask to prove my loyalty to you." If he couldn't get land by alliance with Ningirsu, he reasoned, perhaps he could win some by joining Dumuzi against him.

The goat king let out a great stinking breath while boring his gaze into his former challenger. "You are treacherous, Sababba," he began. "I admire this in you just as Inanna respects me for it. I know that you would gladly feast on my flesh if the Nin-gu-worm were the more powerful. But you are wise to see that he is not. You will prove your wisdom by inciting the Tokar humans to betray their alliance with the vermin from Kamaresh. You already have the worship of many of the smaller tribes; it should be no problem to gain the ascendancy after a crushing defeat of the king who calls himself Ningu-Simga."

"I am your trustworthy servant, great one; it shall be as you have said."

"You are indeed my servant," Dumuzi sneered back, purposely leaving off the adjective. "This much is true."

Having one issue settled, the hulking goat-king turned his stare toward the host of the meeting. "Now Fauxxin, I hear you are having trouble on your southern border as well. Are you unable to keep any of your borders secure?"

The tone in the snarling rebuke made Fauxxin shrink to insignificance between the two monsters on either side. By extension, the six captains began to fear that it may not go well for any of them if Dumuzi was unhappy.

"Not so, great and honorable master," Fauxxin whined. "Meslantaea spars with us but weakly among the hills. I assure you the border is secure."

Unknown to Fauxxin, Dumuzi had a source inside Ningirsu's leadership. The impending attack on Armoun was not going to surprise him at all. In fact, Inanna had given his blessing to Dumuzi's plan to let the factions engage so that they might crush Ningirsu. "You are a blind fool and I should sweep you into the pit right now." The city god and his officers began to quake visibly. "But I need your troops ready for the larger battle and I can't afford to have them fighting among themselves for your position. "Prove yourself in the coming battle and I may let you live."

Hugely relieved, Fauxxin let out a stream of praises for the ultimate wisdom of his leader, the captains joining in as they saw a chance to impress the one who might tap them as the next city god if Fauxxin fell.

"Stifle that weak attempt to garner my favor. I need to see your ability in action. Your humans need to be prepared for an attack from the south." Fauxxin allowed a small look of surprise to cross his face when Dumuzi continued, "Yes, stupid one, there is an army massing at your southern border. Send some human scouts immediately." He stuck out his left wing claw and placed it under a now quivering chin. Lifting Fauxxin slightly off the ground he finished by saying, "Fail me again and you will be on Inanna's altar."

Thorel and his wife, Marah, now pregnant with their own child, had grown close to Yepheth as he had been put in charge of seeing to the needs of the encamped Kamaresans. As the family sought water from Nuwach's wells and bartered for milk, cheese and wine, the boy had been taken by the charms of the blonde haired toddler who never left her mother's side. Seeing his enchantment with the golden haired child, Yepheth's mother had sewn a small doll made of scraps of lamb skin. The boy was as delighted to offer the gift as the young girl was to have it. It went everywhere with her.

One day when Marah was at the well near the compound gate, Nuwach, having risen from his work with an adz to stretch his back, spotted his youngest son playing with the toddler. As his wife approached him with a cup of water he said, "Look how joyfully our son plays with this child."

"Isn't it a wonder," she replied, handing him the cup. As he drank she continued, "I'm not sure if it's her strange golden hair, or her musical little laugh, but everyone seems to be smitten with her, don't you think?"

"I have noticed that her clan holds her in high regard, due to her hair, I assume," Nuwach answered.

"Yepheth told me her people think it is a sign from their gods. Her mother told him that a seer spoke a strange prophecy over her when she was born. Isn't it ironic that you, my husband of the prophecy, and this little one should be together at such a time as this?"

"Do not place too much importance on the words of the strange god's prophet, wife. They sometimes seem to know the future, but I will trust only the one god who I believe creates the future."

As she took the water cup from him with one hand, she touched his arm with her other and said, "It is just as you say, husband." Then as she began to walk back toward the house she turned and said, "I will still think it ironic, with your permission."

Looking at her winking smile, he nodded his head briefly, then shook it gently as he bent to pick up the adz and return to work.

The Lugal of Armoun stood near the well at the center of town with water flowing over his sandaled feet. The high priest, Gishnan, stood opposite him with dry feet. "Where is your boasting now?" the city ruler accused. "You have always claimed to control the supply of water by your incantations; why can't you stop it?"

The priest looked helplessly at the water flowing over the top of the well and down the street, eventually making its way out under the south gate of the city. "The ancient ones speak of a stream which flowed through this valley, coming from a spring near here. Perhaps the gods wish to bless us with a river once again."

"Perhaps!" the lugal exploded. "You are the spokesman for these gods; 'Perhaps' does not imply a close knowledge of their activities." Squinting into the sun he drilled his stare into the priest, "Perhaps I should seek my information from another source."

Momentarily Gishnan considered taking a stand against the lugal whom he secretly hated for his constant denigration of the priestly role in their society. But on further thought he realized that his temple guard was no match for the superior number of the lugal's troops, even after their decimation in the Kamaresan attack. Swallowing his indignation he attempted to change the subject. "Have you heard from the scouting party yet?"

It had been at Gishnan's insistence that scouts had been sent into the plain to search for enemy action. The gods had revealed to him an attack from the south was forthcoming. If the scouts reported any such thing, his power might be made more secure by the evident foresight.

"No, not yet," the lugal replied. "Since your information was none too specific," he said in a mocking tone, "they are taking great care not to be ambushed. It will be several days before I expect to hear.

"In the meantime, this water is flooding several houses and shops. The owners want to know what I am going to do about it. Since you have always claimed to control it, I am sending them to you with their complaints," he said as he held out his hand, palm up, as if offering the gauntlet back.

"What am I supposed to do for them?" Gishnan retorted without thinking first.

"I will leave that up to you and your gods," he said as he turned and sloshed onto higher ground, heading back toward his home.

Far down stream on the plain, the water alternately soaked into the dry ground, then bubbled further along, only to again be consumed by the thirsty soil. As the incessant flow continued, it formed an ever wider and deeper stream, finding the course it once tracked on its way to the sea. Delzar and his hand-picked scouts followed the stream for the first day of their reconnaissance. The water was tracing what had formerly been known as the Armoun road, but would apparently have to be renamed as a river. Early on the second day, the scouts found the stream taking a westerly bend, so they filled their goat skin water bottles one last time, hoping it would last until they reached Nuwach's wells.

Their progress was slowed by their scouting method. One soldier would press ahead under cover, checking for signs of the enemy they were told to locate. After a short distance, the point man would signal to the rest to catch up, then the process would be repeated, always keeping to cover as much as possible in the mostly barren plain. At night, Delzar took the men to a hill or the highest outcropping available so that they could survey as much terrain as possible for campfires.

Delzar was very good at what he was doing, but he had a recurring sense of unease about the mission. Both the lugal and the priest had unwavering confidence in him. After he had been found unconscious in the temple corridor next to the lugal's dead son, everyone naturally assumed that Lamaq's death had come at the hands of the intruders, against whom Delzar had obviously fought valiantly. He had quite naturally not corrected their assumptions.

When asked to undertake this mission, he saw it as a way to leave the city with no intention to return. He was given leave to choose his own men, so he was surrounded by those he thought he could trust, but he had not yet revealed to them his ultimate intentions. His missing daughter was never more than a thought away, his hope being that whoever it was he met that strange day had taken his precious one to safety. He couldn't bear the thought that the Kamaresan attackers had somehow taken her, but if it was so, and if they were the enemy he was sent to scout, it all still played into his hand. He was determined his daughter would not meet the same fate as his wife. Not if he could help it.

On the night that Delzar made camp under a waning moon and less than a day from the pass to Nuwach's, the Kamaresans received the word they had been waiting for. The hastily trained Tokaran army was in position and the attack was planned for the next new moon. The months of preparation and weeks of waiting were soon to be over. A war council was called immediately. Thorel was chosen to lead a small party onto the plain at first light to scout the route the army would take into Armoun.

Thus it was at mid-morning the next day that Delzar's point scout signaled an enemy presence. According to their plan, Delzar and his remaining men split, sending four to the west and five, including Delzar, to the higher ground east of their scout. Delzar's plan was brilliant. The point man would signal them as to the exact route the approaching troops were following. His men would then adjust their positions to form a two sided ambush if that was the chosen course.

If the enemy force was deemed too large to attack, both the eastern and western squad would send a runner back to Armoun to warn them. By sending two messages on two different routes, the chances were doubled that the word would reach Armoun. In addition, if one contingent were discovered and attacked or captured, the others might have a chance to escape unnoticed.

As it worked out, Delzar didn't need his point man's direction, for as he climbed higher into the hills with his squad, they began to see the Kamaresans for themselves. They were apparently intent on following the base of the hills, rather than dropping onto the plain where the travel would be easier. Delzar could see the wisdom in this approach, as it gave them the benefit of height to increase their sight distance. He used this same benefit now to ascertain everything he could about them from his higher elevation, so that he could determine how to treat them.

First he noted that they had one pack animal which was apparently well laden. He assumed this meant they were not far from their base. Secondly he counted twelve men walking more or less in line, and although they appeared to be vigilant, they did not seem to be overly concerned about being detected. This implied that they were either terribly arrogant about their own strength, or that they had little expectation that they would encounter the enemy any time soon. Finally he realized that they were what his people referred to as the pale ones; tribes from the far north with fairer skin and lighter brown hair than any of the people of the plain or even the Kamaresans.

It was this last detail that prompted Delzar to let the band pass by. In a rare moment of unguarded exposure, Gishnan had told him that the Tokarans were planning to double cross the Kamaresans. It was thought this would make it easy to convince the recruits from the northern tribes to side with Armoun since Tokarans also worshiped Sababba. Everyone assumed their allegiance to the same god would prove a stronger bond than the mere geographical ties with Kamaresh. When they were enlisted to fight, it was always more for their own individual glory or that of their clan that any political allegiance. What Gishnan didn't know, or perhaps was blind to, was their genetic hatred of the goat people, as they called him and his. Given time, this would prove to be a serious oversight.

But on this day, Delzar looked upon the small troop as potential allies for two reasons. Not only would he go along with Gishnan's appraisal, he had a secret motive not to make enemies out of those who might hold his daughter's life in their hands. He was certain where his allegiance lay; if it coincided with Gishnan's, so be it. Cupping his hands around his mouth he made two sharp calls, imitating a crow quite successfully. This was the agreed signal to let the men pass.

From the west came three sharp calls in return. Delzar responded with two more as the planned confirmation. Thorel and his men were far enough away that they barely took notice of the bird calls. From their distant vantage point, the sound was convincing enough to be real crows. So they moved between the two squads of enemy soldiers without incident.

Once Thorel's group was several hundred meters past their position, Delzar again made one call, paused, and made two more. Again, three calls from down the hill indicated that the order to reunite had been received. By the time they were back together, the sun had passed its zenith. The men were only a little surprised when Delzar said they would not be sending a runner to Armoun. His excuse was that it was late in the day, and that he was convinced that the main body lay within reach of the next day's light. When they knew more, he assured them, they could take the information back to the city.

"I am going to scout back along their trail as far as I can in the remaining light," he told them. "If I don't return by mid morning, go quickly back to the city and tell them what you have learned." He didn't bother to say that he knew precisely how far it was to Nuwach's from where they were, and that he would be there shortly after nightfall. Nor did he share his thoughts that he would not be seeing them again, for whatever lay ahead, he knew he would never be returning to Armoun.

CHAPTER TWENTY

Deep beneath the surface of the Araq changes were taking place, virtually unnoticed by anyone on the surface. These changes had been occurring almost since the Father of Lights formed the planet from a ball of molten rock. As the young planet spun wildly through space, the gravitational forces of the nearest star and the centrifugal forces resulting from its spinning created layers within the ball of liquid minerals. Soon the frigid temperatures of space began to cool the surface and the minerals began to solidify, forming a crust on the still molten ball. Surging and roiling beneath the fragile crust, the hot minerals often fractured the fragile surface. Eventually the cooling sunk deep enough into the planet to more or less trap the remaining molten material deep inside.

A by-product of the heating and cooling and mixing of the materials was a number of gasses, primarily oxygen, hydrogen and nitrogen. Great volumes of these gasses escaped from the infernal mixture, but were held close to the planet by its own gravity. As the whole system became cooler, some of the gasses condensed, forming water as a secondary by-product. Some of the water gathered in the low spots on the surface; some was trapped below the crust, either in mixture with porous rock or in large subterranean seas. Some of the water remained above the planet in the form of vapor; this created the perfect blanket, insulating the planet from the harshest radiation of the nearby star, and also distributing the heat evenly around the surface.

The water near the surface and the water in the air made it possible for the lushest of botanical gardens to be planted by the Creator. This in turn created the perfect support for the animal life that completed the plan. By the time Nuwach's earliest ancestors were placed on the planet, a more ideal setting could not have been imagined. But this perfection did not last long. The ancient ones told of a rebellion, a considered disobedience among the creatures which caused the Creator to withdraw his stabilizing force from the planet. This set in motion the decay that was now, in Nuwach's time, about to wreak such havoc as the planet had never experienced.

The cooling which continued after the crust was formed also involved continued contraction. This shrinking left gaps in some places between the crust and the material beneath. Some of these gaps were filled with water or escaping gasses from the still molten rock deeper beneath. In a few spots, fractures in the crust were so severe that it was only a matter of time before large plates simply fell into the void which had opened under them. Where there was water beneath the collapsing plates, there would inevitably be an exchange of dry land for sea. With the same inevitability, the shifting of pressure as plates fell would cause others to move as well, creating a deadly wave of movement and squeezing oceans of water from below to above the surface.

As if this would not be devastating enough, the introduction of heated gasses into the atmosphere in huge quantities would cause the temperature to rise, with an accompanying upward surge of the moisture laden air. Once the surface air mixed with the cooler air in the upper atmosphere, the water would condense and fall back to the surface as rain — the first rain ever to fall, as the perfect balance had previously kept large changes in temperature from forming precipitation. As the last few animals were gathering near Nuwach's floating zoo, all of these water sources were poised and ready to wash the surface of the Araq in one giant cleansing flood.

And so it happened that as two great armies sat poised for battle on the surface of the planet, and two other armies battled in the sky above, a vanquishing force of "Nature" was about to reset the scoreboard to love-love and start the match over again.

The tension in the air around Nuwach's compound was palpable. On every level things were tilted so far from stasis that the inevitability of cataclysm was like a ringing in the ears that one hears behind every other sound, a scent that lays behind the senses like spices in cooking or ozone after rain. To the Kamaresans it was the coming battle; to Nuwach's family it was the coming flood; to the animals it was not something conscious, but more like the instinctual urge of birds to migrate. To the unseen forces above it all, it was a growing sense that the biggest conflict since the Rebellion was going to break out at any moment.

Iadrea mentioned this to his lieutenants one evening as the moon rose, a shrinking sliver of light in the east. "I know the time must be near," speaking to no one in particular.

"Virtually all the species of animals are gathered; they won't be able to stay in this area for long." It was Chantar who commented.

Suddenly Iadrea stiffened. His essence faded slightly, then reconfirmed as his senses reached out for meaning. "Something is happening." He paused, faded slightly again, then continued, "A betrayal... slaughter."

The words were barely out of his mind when Hamayn flew into the circle. "Master," he addressed Iadrea.

"What has happened?"

"Just before the moon rose tonight the forces of Tokar united with those of Armoun and attacked the Kamaresans in their tents. Many were killed before they could even reach for their weapons. The battle still goes on, but the outcome is certain. The Kamaresans never had a chance."

"And what of our enemy?" Iadrea asked.

"Sababba has joined with Dumuzi. They have joined to battle with Ningirsu."

"What do you know of Meslantaea?" Iadrea probed.

"I am not certain, but I think he may be watching."

"Doubtless you are right. He will wait until he is certain who will win," Iadrea agreed.

"Master," Hamayn continued, "there is another matter."

"Go on."

"Jephunnah interceded on behalf of two of the Kamaresans. They were fleeing, pursued by a single Tokaran." He paused momentarily. "Sir I am afraid he deliberately slowed the Tokaran so that the others escaped. I tried to stop him, but…"

"Do not worry, Hamayn; this too will fold into the Father's plan. I know you have been doing your best to train the young one not to interfere. It is hard to stay aloof, is it not?"

"I wanted to do something myself," the attender responded.

"Such a feeling is normal; if you ever cease to feel it I will be concerned," Iadrea said warmly. "Do not worry about Jephunnah's rash act. There is no place we can stumble into that the Father can not reach in to steady us. Return to your post and let me know if Meslantaea makes any moves."

As the attender disappeared Mistrea asked, "What do you think it means for our task here."

"I am afraid, my friend, it means that things will become much more heated here very soon," the general answered.

At this moment a single attender flew in from his post at the pass. "Master, a lone traveler is approaching the compound."

"A human?" Iadrea asked with surprise.

"Yes."

"Because of our orders to remain discreet, I did not get close enough to see who it was, but I sensed no ill from him. I am not sure, but I think he is..." the attender paused while searching for the right word. "I think he is worried, sir."

"Thank you for the report; you may return to your post," the general said, and turning to Chantar he continued, "Go mingle with those near the gate and see who he is."

The large attender nodded and slipped out of the circle. On the surface he appeared as Ramah and began talking with his fellow-workers.

When Delzar came cautiously through the pass, he was amazed at what he saw. Although the moon offered little light, the glow from the numerous campfires confirmed what he deducted from the scouting party. He expected an army, but the size of this force startled him. His surprise multiplied when he saw Nuwach's gate open and dozens of people in scattered groups talking and laughing near the opening.

As he began to pass the edge of the camp, a few people stopped to look at him, but no one challenged him. A strange sense of peace overtook him as he walked on until he was surprised to hear his name.

"Delzar? Is that you?"

A large man strode toward him and repeated, "Delzar, welcome."

"Ramah?" he asked in surprise once he was close enough to make out his features.

"Praise be, it is you. We thought you were dead," Ramah said, speaking only as Ramah, for Chantar had known of Delzar's recovery for some time.

"What brings you here? And at such an hour?" Ramah asked.

"My daughter... what happened to my daughter?"

"We were able to save her and her friends," Ramah reported. "They are all safe here with Nuwach; come, I will take you to them."

As the two men walked toward the compound, the attender directed his thoughts to his leader, far above them, "It is Delzar, master; I am taking him to be reunited with his daughter."

"Very well," came Iadrea's silent reply. "Find out what you can about the plans of the others who came from the city with him."

"Did you travel all the way from Armoun alone?" Ramah asked with feigned ignorance.

"Oh, no; there is much to tell. Please, after I set my eyes on my daughter once again, we can gather the important ones and I will tell you all the news; please," the father begged.

"Of course; this way."

Ramah led him through the gate and down a corridor which was only recently the path to Nuwach's house. Now Delzar was amazed to find himself in what appeared to be a huge stable. There were stalls on both the right and left, some large, some smaller. The air was ripe with the scent of freshly split and planed wood. When they came to the wide central corridor, Nuwach's former house sat on the corner, now the first of three floors, with a stairway leading to the next level along the outside of the house. Looking down the central corridor, Delzar could see that half its width was a ramp which led to the level above. Both sides of this corridor were also lined with various size stalls.

"Come," Ramah said stepping to the stairway, "I suspect your daughter will be on the upper floor."

Only Delzar's strong desire to see his daughter kept him from asking the obvious questions. His curiosity could wait.

He followed Ramah up the steep stairs. As their heads rose above the planks forming the second floor, Delzar could see much the same arrangement as the lower level. When they reached the top of the stairs, they turned back toward the center and the next set of steps leading to the upper floor. Glancing down the central corridor before mounting the stairs, Delzar could see men working on one of the stalls. Ramah called to them, "Is the family in their quarters?"

One of the men stopped his work on a door and answered, "The women should be there; the men are probably still working on the cages near the end of the sh- barn."

Delzar could not detect the instantaneous thought messages that occurred between the beginning of the word "sh —" and its completion as "barn." Ramah had corrected his fellow-worker in mid speech for the benefit of this uninitiated listener. Ramah felt no desire to further complicate the poor man's understanding with the knowledge that they were in fact building a ship.

Oblivious to what he had almost learned, Delzar followed Ramah up the last flight of stairs. Before he had climbed half way up he could see pale moonlight filtering through an opening the height of his forearm just below the roof. As he continued upward, he discovered this opening ran all the way around the structure so that the walls, in effect, stopped just before meeting the rafters. The overhanging roof sat suspended on the beams or pillars which formed the skeleton on which the outer planks had been pegged. This construction allowed light and air to enter the otherwise enclosed structure. Indeed, the pungent smell of cypress was being replaced by the sweet smell of the plain at night as the breeze wafted through the opening.

Once fully on the third level, Delzar could see a door opening off the landing onto which he had been led. The smell of fire now mixed with the other scents making for a rich aroma, and explaining the dancing light he saw coming from the doorway.

Stopping in the opening Ramah announced their presence, "Grace to all within. I have a visitor to see Delyah of Armoun."

A grey haired woman squinted through the smoke-laced air at the man in her doorway. She sat on a stool near a large flat stone upon which a small fire blazed. She had some sort of handwork in her lap and was taking a moment for her eyes to refocus from the close work to the man across the room. The firelight was just sufficient for recognition of her visitor. "Ramah," she said. "Grace to you as well; come in and bring your visitor too."

The two men stepped into a room that was roughly ten meters square and similar in appearance to the house the family used to occupy on the ground floor. The three inner walls were just taller than a man's head, allowing the air to move freely over them while effectively separating them from the rest of the structure. The fourth wall, which was the outer wall of the compound, had one small window at eye level. Opposite the window, along the inner wall to the right of the door, four cubicles or stalls had been created by extending three short walls into the room and hanging curtains across the openings. From the sleeping mats spotted on the floor, Delzar intuited their purpose.

Near the wall opposite the door, a long table was flanked by two benches of equal length. Two wooden bowls sat near the center of the table and a plate with the remains of a loaf of bread rested toward the end. Delzar realized he was smelling the yeasty odor of bread rising and found the source when he looked to two large cloth draped bowls sitting near the fire. Beyond them at the edge of the stone floor piece was a clay dome with an opening in one side and another in the top. Black soot around both openings revealed that the small coal oven had been in steady use.

Seeing Ramah's eyes light on the rising dough, the old woman said, "I am sorry that I can offer you little to eat. With so many mouths to feed, I can barely keep up." Glancing behind herself at the table she continued, "There is but one pitiful heel of bread left, to which you are surely welcome. I can offer you water or wine if you need something to drink." She got up and moved toward two earthenware pitchers which sat in the corner near the table.

Delzar interrupted her saying, "The hospitality from your heart is duly recognized, Mother," addressing her according to the custom of his people. It was an insult not to offer food and drink to guests and equally an affront not to accept. "But truly, the longing of my heart so far outpaces my stomach that I can wait until morning for you to fulfill you duty."

This unusual speech from the stranger stopped her and she turned to face him. Standing as he was now, in the full glare of the little fire, she looked at him closely for the first time and wavered slightly, reaching into the air about her as if grasping for something to steady herself.

Ramah stepped forward with his hand extended and she took it gladly. Then with a gasp she said, "Ramah, you have brought us one from the dead?"

"Pardon me, Mother, for my lack of manners. I should have prepared you for this. Delzar was not killed as we thought, but only severely wounded. Our God has brought him back to life so that he might see his daughter once again."

"Delzar?" she looked intently at him. "Of course! Even as you spoke I thought your voice seemed familiar somehow."

The dark bearded one bowed his head slightly before speaking, "Pardon my impatience, Mother, but where is Delyah?"

"Delyah!" the woman exclaimed, only then realizing the shock the young girl had coming. "She will be so glad to see you." He brow furrowing slightly she continued, "She still has a dark place in her heart where she grieves for you. It is so good that you have come before..." She paused, not sure how to go on.

"Before anything else could interfere," Ramah completed her sentence, nodding largely at Delzar.

"Yes," she agreed. "Sharaq, my son's wife, whom you helped save," she looked at him with deeper gratitude remembering how important he was to her family, "Sharaq has been a real comfort to your daughter, since they both lost their parents..." again she stopped, this time to correct herself. "Or thought they had both lost their parents...

"But forgive me," she caught herself, "the children are carrying feed into the granaries. I am surprised you didn't see them on your way up. They left only moments before you arrived."

She had barely finished speaking when the sound of young laughter lilted up the stairs. Then a voice hauntingly familiar to Delzar squealed, "Stop it, you! If you keep throwing it at me there'll be nothing left to store away."

A herd of sandaled feet stomped up the stairs onto the floor below and raced across the landing to the next set of steps. Delzar moved to the doorway and stopped on the landing just as a dark eyed young girl nearly exploded up the stairway. When she saw him she screamed in fright, spilled her armful of hay at his feet and covered her mouth with both hands.

Unable to see what was before her, four racing youths bumped to a stop behind her, each in turn a step below the person above. "Delyah," a deep male voice said from the stairway, "what is the holdup?"

Chamah, immediately behind the girl, thinking this was part of the game, shoved close enough behind her to look over her shoulder. As she stumbled forward from his impact, the boy also dropped his sheaf upon seeing the apparition on the landing.

"Let's go," the deep voice said impatiently. "I don't want to be all night at this."

"Are you... real?" Chamah asked on behalf of the still speechless girl in front of him.

"Yes, quite real, my son," the apparition said smiling.

By this time the boy's mother and Ramah had come onto the landing behind Delzar.

"Mother, it's Delyah's father," the boy said stupidly.

"Yes, my son," she replied. "The great God of the Araq has granted him life after all."

"Father?" said the girl finding her voice.

"Yes, daughter," he said, stepping towards her.

She recoiled slightly, pressing against the boy behind her, not yet believing her senses.

"Delzar, you're alive," Sha'ym exclaimed from his position down the stairway as the man on the landing moved into view.

Ignoring the young man, Delzar looked straight into his daughter's eyes and said, "I am alive." Saying this he held out his arms to her. Finally daring to believe she stumbled across the pile of hay she had dropped between them and fell into his waiting embrace.

Chamah and Yepheth stepped onto the landing, but there was still no space for Sharaq and Sha'ym in the crowded hallway. "Come. Come inside everyone," the old woman said. "No, Sha'ym," she corrected herself, "Go find your father and bring him too."

Soon all but Ramah were seated around the big table as the pitchers of wine and water were passed. Everyone was talking at once when Sha'ym and his father burst through the doorway.

"Delzar," Nuwach exclaimed. "Somehow I knew our God had not let you die. It is fitting that you should be here."

Nuwach walked to the table as Delzar stood to receive his customary greeting. After they had clasped arms, Nuwach repeated, "I just knew it."

"I am coming to have something like faith in your God," Delzar said. "Ever since my visit here I have cared less and less for the gods of the city."

"Then you are wise indeed," the old man said. "There are many good reasons for you to be here at such a time as this."

Delzar thought he read something deep in what the old man was saying, but had no way of knowing how deep it truly was.

"When Ramah brought me here..." he looked toward the door, but the humble attender had already discreetly extracted himself from the family scene.

The air which fell down the pass onto the plain at Armoun was thick with the smell of blood that night. Hamayn's estimate of the outcome of the midnight ambush had proved accurate. Before the moon was two hands above the horizon, The Armounians and their Tokaran allies had slaughtered every man they could find or chase down. The old women and children were likewise put to the sword or club; only the young women of child bearing age were spared. Many of these too would die as they struggled against the will of the attackers. Those few who submitted would enter a life of slavery or perhaps become wives of the conquerors.

In the air above a parallel rout was taking place. Dumuzi and Sababba led their combined forces against the smaller army of Ningirsu in a lopsided running battle. Wave after wave of demon hordes blasted down against the invaders from Kamaresh. Many of the duelers in the sky found themselves tumbling into the human fray that went on beneath them. Often the dark ones would take a swipe at their human opponents in an instant when they dared take their attention off their true foes. Consequently, there were not a few humans who found themselves driven to the ground by blows from unseen weapons of incredible power.

Both Dumuzi and Sababba searched for their arch enemy, but Ningirsu kept himself far to the rear, eventually running like a scalded dog when he realized he was defeated. Near the end, Sababba took leave to find the coward, but his search was unsuccessful. One by one, Ningirsu's troops either fell to the rod's of their foes, or slipped into the night after the manner of their leader.

Hamayn and two other attenders watched from some distance to the south. Their hearts went out to the humans who were being slaughtered, but there was nothing they could do, first because they were too few, but also because they had no protection orders for any of them. It was an attender's nature to be compassionate, but they also knew too well that war and death were integral parts of the fractious story they were witnessing.

Suddenly they noticed two lone men from the Kamaresan force escaping to the south. One of the Tokarans was following hard after them. In a flash, one of Hamayn's helpers shot down to intercede.

"Jephunnah!" Hamayn screamed.

Before the thought of his name was completely formed in his master's mind, Jephunnah had dropped to the earth in front of the pursuing Tokaran and materialized enough to trip him. The startled warrior tumbled to the ground with a crash, cursing his awkwardness. In the moment he looked back stupefied at what had tripped him, his quarry moved far enough ahead of him so that when he returned his attention, they were gone. As the man sat panting on the ground, it occurred to him that there had been a flash of light just before he fell.

Nor was he the only one who noticed the flash. It was at this point that Hamayn had taken wing to Iadrea to make his report. Had he stayed at his post an instant longer, he might have noticed that someone else had seen the rash young attender's streak of thought. Dumuzi's gaze had been in their direction at the moment Jephunnah flashed to the ground. The huge dark one drifted closer to that area, but not so close as to draw the remaining attender's attention to his movement.

Dumuzi was painfully aware that his mortal enemy had spies watching nearly everything that went on in his kingdom. He marveled that one of them deemed something so important that thought speed was necessary, knowing that his act would be broadcast to all. He called Fauxxin.

"Something is going on to the south," he said when the peon arrived. "Send two scouts to check it out, but warn them to be careful; there are light beasts in the area."

Fauxxin was somewhat incredulous. He thought to himself, "A glorious battle is raging; we are routing the enemy and his eminence wants to know what's going on in the woods."

Suddenly, Fauxxin felt a huge claw under his chin, lifting him to his master's level, forcing his gaze directly into Dumuzi's blazing yellow eyes. "You stinking piece of filth; you think you know what is important; you think this battle is the only concern."

Fauxxin tried to wriggle off the point of the claw. In response Dumuzi swung his other wing behind the smaller one's neck and poked its claw into the flesh. "There is a much larger, more important war we constantly fight against our true enemy; an enemy you seem to let wander in and out of your little city at his will. Perhaps you have grown fond of the light. Perhaps I will stake you in the sun tomorrow. Would you like that?"

"No, Master; you are right, of course, Great One; I will go myself, your Darkness..."

"Silence!" Dumuzi roared out loud. "You will not go yourself; you will send two scouts as I commanded. Do you think I want someone of your bloated size and meager intellect trampling all over the woods?"

"No, your Eminence; you are right again, of course, your Greatness; I am much too, ah, large to be in the woods…"

At this point, disgusted, Dumuzi spun the hapless peon like a child's top with his two claws tearing at the flesh of the smaller demon's neck, then with a well-placed kick sent him sailing awkwardly back toward the fray below them. Fauxxin almost got clubbed by a sizeable warrior from the enemy forces before he got control of his flight and tried to regain his destroyed dignity. "Tell your scouts to report directly to me," came Dumuzi's last thought as Fauxxin flew off to find his lucky candidates.

Late the next day, two exhausted warriors dragged themselves into the camp at Mount Tabor. The perimeter watchmen quickly escorted them to the king.

"What news," he asked of the two, then to another, "Bring water."

"Father, the northern — force — is lost," one gasped.

"The Tokar-scum betrayed us," the other spit out.

"I was afraid of this," Madai said from behind the king.

"Silence," the king shouted. "This is a great loss, to be sure. The northern tribes and the Tokarans would have been good allies, but our troops are still intact. Doubtless there are less of the goat-scum than before. This is to our advantage. We will still continue with the plan."

"But my Lord," Madai protested, "there will be no distraction to the north. They will be able to focus their defense against our attack. We have tried the southern siege before…"

"Madai, I have made up my mind. There will never be a better chance in our lifetime. I will not waste all the preparations we have made because one part of the plan has gone badly." Turning to face his commander directly he continued, "If you are squeamish, I will gladly relieve you of your command."

"That will not be necessary. You know my allegiance is always with you, my Lord. I was simply offering a voice of…"

"…a voice of reason? Is that what you meant to say, Madai? Maybe you are right. Maybe this seems unreasonable to you, or to others." He stopped to look around the fire at his other commanders. No one flinched.

"Many of the great battles that have been won by our people in the past seemed unreasonable. But we stand here today on the graves of those who died to deliver us to this place. Shall we not honor them with our own blood if necessary? Shall we not take this last opportunity to wipe the goat-scum from the face of the Araq?"

With one exception, the men around him cheered and shouted epithets against the forces of the goat king. When the king's eyes met Madai's he nodded submissively. The king had once again worked his spoken magic on his followers.

Meslantaea was hovering close to the campfire where this conference was taking place. With Ningirsu's absence, and only a few of Sababba's northerners in this band, Meslantaea held sway over the remaining dark forces. "So, the attack continues," he mused to the dark shadow beside him. "With Ningu-scum on the run, this may be the time for us to take our rightful place on Dumuzi's hallowed Tyriean plain. What do you think?"

The dark shape uttered a guttural sound and nodded a grotesquely shaped head, red eyes bobbing slowly up and down with the motion.

"The king will be want to warn his son; follow the king's messengers; make sure they make it to the son's camp."

The darkness floated without a sound down and to the south to wait for the two men who would soon be heading that way.

Two days after Delzar's arrival at Nuwach's, the bustle of activity continued. By daylight, it became apparent that there was still much to be done. Primarily, the roof over the final floor, or deck, was unfinished. A few meters remained uncovered near the south end. Workmen were busy climbing up and down scaffolds made of saplings and small branches, pitching the entire outer surface according to Nuwach's instructions. Then there were innumerable chores yet to be done on the inside. Not the least of these was bringing on food for the animals and, of course, the humans who would be on board.

Delzar joined in with the rest of them, setting his hands to whatever presented itself. So relieved was he to be with his daughter again, so happy to be out from under the pressure of the city, that he felt happy for the first time since he lost his wife. In fact, the very happiness he felt seemed to be endemic to the whole area. The warriors from Kamaresh and the Northerners even pitched in. They kept their swords on their belts as they worked, and constantly listened for a warning cry from the watchers in the pass, but they worked alongside the unusual crew that had assembled at Nuwach's compound from near and far.

Stranger still, Delzar began to see more animals than he had known existed. The air seemed to be filled with all kinds of birds. Smaller creatures such as lizards and field mice and squirrels were constantly being discovered scurrying in and out of the compound, or the ark, as many were beginning to call it: the tebah-Nuwach -- Noah's Ark. Delzar had asked the meaning of the word, as he was unfamiliar with it. Someone told him it meant "a place of safe-keeping." He had taken this at face value and adopted it himself, for certainly, this was no longer a compound, and it was too large to be thought of as merely a barn. "Ark" sounded just strange enough to fit the strange structure and company of which he was glad to be a part.

On the morning of his second day at work on the ark, there was a general stir among the Kamaresans. Delzar knew only a few of the people from the war camp, so he asked the man walking with him to the tar pits with empty buckets if he understood what the commotion was about. "It has something to do with their war plans," the man answered. "More than that I cannot tell. They are concerned about something gone awry."

After returning from the pits with full buckets of pitch, Delzar walked across the road to the encampment where a group of Kamaresan men were having an excited discussion about something. Not wishing to intrude, he stayed some distance from the group, close enough to hear, "failed plan," "Goat-scum," "Tokaran warriors." Nothing made sense to him at first. Then Thorel, a young warrior he had met with Nuwach's family noticed him standing nearby and said to the group, "Here is one who might be able to tell us more," as he pointed to Delzar.

All eyes immediately turned in his direction. He was thrown into quandary because he did not know his customary duty in this situation. He had told Nuwach and his sons what he had heard from Gishnan as it explained why he was willing to let the Northerner scout patrol pass and approach what should have been regarded as an enemy camp alone and in an unguarded manner. Apparently someone from Nuwach's family had told Thorel about this. But now, facing these warriors who should have been his enemies, he was not certain of his path.

"Delzar, tell us what you heard in Armoun," Thorel pleaded.

Reasoning that Nuwach or one of his sons had already revealed most of what he had said, he could imagine no prohibition against sharing with these men who had become his co-workers rather than his enemies. "I don't really have much information," he began. The men crowded around him as he retold what he knew of Gishnan's cryptic comments and his orders as head of the scouting party.

"You see," Thorel said as Delzar finished, "they are expecting us to attack from the south."

Javan, the king's son, spoke next, "You left before the attack on our troops, is that right?"

"Yes," Delzar answered, "I arrived here on the night of the attack."

Javan thought for a moment then began again, "So they planned the attack at the north pass before they sent the spies south, but they gave the spies no specific instructions." Again he paused to think. "They must suspect we are here, and wish to know our strength, but why would they proceed with the attack without hearing from the spies?"

It was Thorel who answered, "Because they knew from the Tokarans of our plan to attack on the new moon. They had to attack us after we had gathered, but before the new moon."

"Yes, that much is true," Delzar agreed, "but there is more to it than that." The men looked more intently at him now. "The lugal was ranting about some ancient prophecy made by his father or too his father, I didn't understand which. But I did clearly hear him say that Nuwach had stolen his right to something. He seemed to blame his son, Lamaq's death on Nuwach." Delzar paused to try to reconstruct exactly what had been said. "There is some animus between those two which I don't understand, but I know it has something to do with sending me here."

"So will they mount an attack on us, or wait for us to come to them?" Javan posed the question. Answering for himself he said, "I think they will mount an attack, thinking to surprise us. If it goes badly for them, they imagine they can run into the walls of their city for protection. But it is we who will surprise them."

"Endar," he turned to one of his men, "Go with all speed to my father and tell him all we have heard tonight. Tell him we will begin the march as he ordered. Suggest to him that he wait, on my request, until we approach to see if they are coming onto the plain. If they do, my Father must wait until they pass his position. Then we will have them between us and we can crush them like grapes."

The man nodded once and moved off in response to his prince's command.

CHAPTER TWENTY-ONE

The men of Armoun celebrated their victory throughout the day and into the next night after the battle. The lugal gave orders that they should rest and prepare to march at sunrise the following day. Thus it was on the same day that two armies began to march toward one another, each hoping to surprise the other.

There was no such illusion in the sky however. The en-lil carried the news of Sababba's betrayal in one direction, and the ire of Meslantaea in the other. Dumuzi was not threatened by the tree god's anger. Although the tree sprites outnumbered Dumuzi's and Sababba's forces combined, they were mostly small, insignificant demons. They might peck and poke at their larger foes, but one swipe of their terrible rods would send a dozen tree sprites into oblivion.

Higher in the space above the planet, another grander plot was developing. The one called Inanna saw a chance for his own advancement. Second only to the Prince of Darkness himself, Inanna seethed with a jealous lust for the highest position. With Ningirsu on the run, there might be a chance to use Meslantaea as a wedge to pry Dumuzi out of his place, landing all of the inhabited territories under his control. From that platform, he reasoned that he could challenge the Prince's right to rule.

On the night of the new moon, there was celebration and revelry such had not been seen since the Rebellion. The attenders watched from a distance as dark demons danced and whirled and flew in makeshift formations, often crashing into one another and tumbling into heaps of cackling laughter. Those who had grown fond of human sexual pleasures found women who were willing or simply unfortunate and had their way with them. Some went into the stables and barns to have their pleasure there.

There was a heightened state of alert around Nuwach's. Most of the debauchery was taking place far to their north, but no one wanted to take any chances. The zensak was stretched out over the entire Kamaresan camp and into the pass. This would keep smaller demons from causing trouble. If any larger ones appeared, the attenders would deal with them as necessary.

Near midnight Meslantaea was reported drifting toward their position. Iadrea moved into the sky just north of the camp and waited. The women and children left behind in the Kamaresan camp would be easy targets for even minor demis. Soon the giant attender could sense the approach of a terrible darkness. Meslantaea and his ugly henchman floated slowly into sight, but stopped short of making a challenge. The two generals stared at one another through the empty night sky. Iadrea stood facing north with his sword drawn, making a clear statement of his intentions. Come any closer, and we will fight.

After what seemed an eternity, Meslantaea looked over the area, doubtless taking note of the many warriors, human and otherwise, sensing the zensak covering, knowing something very important was at stake, and then turned slowly back to where he had come from. Iadrea felt a sense of relief; he had fought this one before and knew they were well matched. He would fight him again when necessary, but he was glad it would not be necessary just yet.

Soon after the sun rose the next day, the forward scouts of the two human armies reported contact. The Armounians were somewhat surprised to find their enemy so far into the plain, but they were so stoked with valor from their recent victory that they barely gave it a second thought as they prepared for battle. The front ranks were all armed with swords now. Many had long carried the iron weapons, but the majority were newly equipped, following the slaughter of the northerners. The Tokaran swordsmen had been assigned the rear guard position in case the Kamaresans made a flanking move in an attempt to cut off their retreat into the safety of the city. This would prove to be a wise move.

Nor was the sky battle without strategic planning. Meslantaea had gathered his sprites along the hillside from the pass at Nuwach's to Tabor. There were so many of them that the trees teemed with them like cxings over zensak. They were minuscule compared to the giants gathering over the plain, but their sheer number made them a force to be reckoned with. Meslantaea was unsure whether Ningirsu would return to his forsaken human worshipers, perhaps bringing an army composed of the cowards who had fled the northern battle. He didn't really care, for he trusted in his secret ally, lurking still on the dark side of the moon.

Dumuzi and Sababba foresaw a straightforward conquest. Even if Ningirsu did show up at the last minute with a rag tag army, they reasoned that they had beaten him once; another licking would be no real contest. Once they had swept the plain clean of the no account tree sprites, they expected Meslantaea to follow Ningirsu's lead and disappear.

The Kamaresans had deployed two thirds of their men in the open plain, giving many of them orders to remain hidden as much as possible. They hoped this would mislead their enemy as to their true strength. The other third of their force was secluded behind the rocks and trees on the hillside. Not only would their number be uncounted, but they could sweep down upon the Armounians after they had mounted a frontal attack, effectively forcing them into a two-front battle.

As the armies approached each other on the ground, Meslantaea called his sprites into formation above the Kamaresans. In answer they began swarming beneath him like thousands of bees. One of Fauxxin's soldiers thought to earn some early glory and charged alone into the swarm. Although a few of the demis were struck down by the swing of his rod, it was only moments before he himself fell to the ground, the victim of a thousand blows by a hundred angry sprites. His fate disconcerted some of fellows who had thought themselves impervious to the little demons.

Finally it was the Kamaresans who called the charge. Swords, spears and clubs raised they ran full speed toward the opposing ranks. Just before they met, the spear throwers sailed their missiles over the heads of their compatriots into the front ranks of the enemy. Most of the Armounians were able to dodge the spears, but a few of the points found their mark in human flesh. More to the point, the flight of the spears was timed so that it threw the front ranks into disarray just as the Kamaresan swords fell upon them. Many who deftly turned from a flying spear were unable to recover quickly enough to avoid the flashing blade of a sword.

So the battle began. From high above the plain, Iadrea, Mistrea, Multar and many of the attenders watched as the human combatants pulsed and throbbed at each other. The battle line gradually spread out over a wider area in the natural movement of such a struggle. Soon the Kamaresans could be seen falling back slightly, causing the Armounians to collapse in on them somewhat. Then there was a blast from a horn and one hundred fresh Kamaresans poured down from the hills onto the left flank of the Armounians.

Even with this advantage, the Kamaresan army was gradually being forced back toward the pass. Then, just before the sun had reached its peak, a second army drove into the rear of the Armounians. A roar went up from Javan's forces as they saw his father, the king lead the charge. At first it seemed as if the two Kamaresan forces might crush both fronts into the middle, but slowly the Armounians regained their ground and began swelling out against the Kamaresans.

What the attenders saw explained why the Kamaresan pincer didn't work. At the moment the rear guard was attacked, Ningirsu came charging from the hills, directly into Sababba. There had been little activity among the dark ones since the ill-fated charge against the tree sprites. Now, this new attack drew everyone's attention. There were a few soldiers with Ningirsu who joined him in the attack, but the real surprise was yet to come.

Just when the attention was focused in the rear, Meslantaea was joined by none other than Inanna himself. Meslantaea then dove on Dumuzi who saw him coming just in time to avoid a direct hit on his head. What he least expected came next as Inanna's huge rod sliced through the air and caught the goat king squarely in the mid section and sent him sprawling halfway across the plain.

Multar was shocked at the massive size of Inanna and asked, "Is that the Prince of Darkness?"

"No," Iadrea answered. "But there is none larger nor more powerful except the dark lord himself. That is Inanna, his second in command. He seldom shows himself in battle since he has everything to lose and little to gain. Something strange is happening here."

The attenders watched amazed as Inanna's giant weapon, nearly the size of a mature cedar, swung in expertly guided arcs, bowling over one demon after another. Wounded, but still able to fight, Dumuzi rejoined the battle by flying straight at Inanna from behind. Before his blow landed, his target turned as if eyes in his back warned of the charge. The two met rod to rod and Dumuzi nearly lost his grip on his weapon. Recovering, he swung again at the feet of is prey, but Inanna deftly rose above the swing and again sent Dumuzi sprawling with a blow to his mid-section.

Meanwhile tree sprites were finishing off the wounded who had fallen under Inanna's rod. In the distance, Meslantaea and Sababba were likewise engaged in a one-on-one duel. Crashing rods, growls of pain and angry screams filled the sky as the demon forces clashed above the human fray. Just when it seemed the Kamaresans were gaining control of the earth-bound battle, a huge black cloud, spinning like a tornado crashed into the northern front. Kamaresan warriors were lifted and flung like a child's dolls in every direction. With their foes decimated on the north, the Armounians refocused their efforts toward the south, and began pushing the Kamaresans back toward the pass.

"What is that?" Multar gasped as he saw the whirling darkness work its terror on the human warriors.

"That is the Prince of Darkness himself," Iadrea responded. Then sending a thought to all his troops he said, "Form a battle line on me at once."

Immediately, the sky was filled with a phalanx of attenders, swords drawn, facing the demon hordes battling to their north. The entrance into the fight by the dark lord himself caused most of the demons to pause momentarily, so there was a sudden lull. In the north, the spinning cloud materialized into the biggest, ugliest creature any of the attenders had ever seen.

"Prepare for an attack," Iadrea signaled, knowing that their arch enemy had not appeared merely to throw the human battle his way.

As the Kamaresans saw their advantage fade, they began to retreat to the pass for a last stand in better position. At the same time, the dark forces above them inexplicably united and began to form a battle line against the massed attenders. Their former rivalries disappeared as the irresistible power of their leader molded them into a force to do his bidding.

Suddenly, like a tidal wave pushed by unseen force from beneath, a black swarm rose and crashed into the front line of the attenders. Swords met rods and wing claws with a flurry of light and motion. Dismembered dark ones fell with terrible screams. Here and there and outmatched attender dropped from the line like a dim falling star. Again and again like storm tossed waves against a rocky cliff, the dark force hurtled into the flashing swords. Iadrea hovered in the rear, guiding his troops by thought and sheer will.

"Chantar; Mistrea," Iadrea barked. "Take a squad to Nuwach's and guard against an end run.

Immediately the two sailed back toward the ark, Multar and twenty-some of the others who had been helping as humans followed on their thought commands. Once they formed an armed perimeter around the chosen ones, it became obvious that the human battle was not going well for the Kamaresans. By now they were backed into the hills at the pass. Skirmishes were taking place along the ridge on both sides of the pass. The front was gradually getting narrower as some fell to the Armounians and some fled through the pas to make preparations for a last stand.

Delzar had taken up his sword against his former citymates. He and Thorel were fighting side by side near the entrance to the pass as the line folded into the opening. Realizing that they were now defending their wives and children against the screaming goat warriors, the men seemed to gain strength. This, and their optimum defensive position at the pass gave them hope they might live to see another sunrise.

With the dark unseen forces occupied in their own struggle, the ground war reached a stalemate at the pass. But the relentless surging of the black waves against the light was moving the skyward front closer to the ground battle and the precious chosen ones beyond.

The attenders hovering above the ark watched in horror as their comrades drifted ever closer to them. Soon, the battle was raging almost directly above the ridge. Mistrea began to feel the surges of evil impulse that drove the dark hordes against them. Eventually, the blackness was beating down upon the humans in the pass, and they began to lose their advantage.

Iadrea directed several of his warriors down into the human fray to stave off the attackers, but even this proved to be too little to stop the Armounians from gaining entrance through the pass. The battle was now raging on the edge of the camp. Women and children ran screaming into the far reaches of the tent village as some of the goat warriors began slashing through the animal skin huts. Thorel and Delzar flanked by two super-human combatants still fought valiantly against the pressing throng.

Suddenly Mistrea noticed that Nuwach and his sons were watching horrified from the door of the ark. "Chantar, look," he directed his companion. "We have to get them inside."

Instantly, Ramah, El Channah and his dog, Jireh, came charging around the corner of the ark, rushing toward the family. The humans were watching a clot of warriors battling almost directly across the road. The two attenders began to urge the men to get the family back into the ark and to close the door. Suddenly, interrupting them, Sha'ym shouted, "God help us! He's going to kill the child."

Turning to the scene across the road, they could see a woman in tears, red-faced and wailing as she watched Thorel, her husband, valiantly trading blows with two sword wielding Armounians. His superior skill was keeping them at bay, but nearby, Delzar and the two attenders in human form were being pressed ever closer to the women by a crowd of men with clubs and swords. Despite the attenders' efforts, limited as they were to their chosen level of human capability, one of the attackers broke through with a swipe at Delzar which left a gaping slice in his right forearm. Dropping his sword in a groan of pain, Delzar ducked a swing of the war club to his right as the sword bearing man rushed past him and headed for the screaming woman and her child.

El Channah bolted across the road, followed closely by Multar, but had to go around the swinging swords of Thorel and his two attackers. Delzar pulled his dagger from his belt and dashed after the man who wounded him, leaping on him just as he swung his sword at the child. Delzar's blade opened the man's throat, but their combined momentum threw them into the frightened mother and child. El Channah arrived just in time to sweep the child out of the way.

When Delzar rolled the Armounian off the woman, her face was frozen in a horrific scream, and sword handle protruding from her chest. Just then, another scream broke the air, this one lower, guttural, coming from Thorel as he stole a quick glance at what had happened.

Ignoring the danger, Sha'ym and Yepheth raced across the road following El Channah. Now, one of the Armounians broke off attacking Thorel and charged the defenseless young men. El Channah all but threw the child into Delzar's arms and jumped to their defense. Thorel had been an even match for the two of his attackers; one alone stood no chance against El Channah's expert sword. One block and one thrust dispatched the goat soldier.

Thorel was equally successful at defeating the one remaining contender and ran to scoop up his wife. This left only El Channah and two attenders to stave off the rushing mass of clubs and swords.

Ramah was about to tell Nuwach to gather his family inside when Delyah, who had been watching from the door of the ark, rushed out crying, "Father!" Ramah fairly tackled her to keep her from getting into harm's way. "Father!" she screamed again.

"Stay inside child," Ramah insisted. "We will see to your father. Then to Nuwach, "Get them all inside," motioning with his drawn sword at the boys across the road. "Then bar the doors." Then he rushed to the aid of his peers.

Sha'ym and Yepheth were huddled in front of Delzar who still sat where he had fallen, and Thorel who knelt weeping with his slain wife in his arms. Delzar was holding the child cradled with his left arm, his left hand gripping his right wrist in a vain effort to staunch the flood of bright red blood. "Take her," he rasped. "Take her to safety."

"Yes; take her," Thorel pleaded, tears running down his face.

As Delzar released his grip on the child, freeing his hand from his wrist, blood spurted onto the ground. At once the boys heard the voice of their father shouting above the sound of the battle, "Sha'ym; Yepheth. Get over here now."

They looked once again at Delzar. "Go," he said with pleading in his eyes. "Take care of my Delyah. Tell your brother…"

Sha'ym took the child in his arms as Delzar slumped backward onto the ground. "Come on," he said. "We have to get inside."

The attenders were holding the attackers at bay, leaving a path for the boys to cross to the ark. Ramah glanced back at them and shouted, "Get in the ark!"

As they stood up to run to safety, they watched a club come down on Ramah's shoulder, his momentary distraction to urge the two to safety costing him painfully. He dropped to his knees from the force of the blow, and would have had his throat cut by the dagger which followed the club, but suddenly a red dog leaped into the air and clamped his teeth on the forearm of the attacker. Dog and man tumbled to the ground. The man tried to swing his club at the dog, but Ramah regained his feet and plunged his sword into the man's neck, pinning him to the dust.

The two young men and the child took this all in as they dashed back across the road and into the ark. Once they were safely inside, Nuwach reluctantly closed the heavy doors and dropped the bar to lock them shut. It tore at his hear to leave his valiant protectors outside with no safe retreat, but he was doing as they had ordered. He, and they, would have to trust their lives to God alone.

Above this scene, Iadrea watched with increasing dismay as black hordes were pushing his army slowly back toward the ark. The dark prince had uncanny power to meld his army together, almost as if it became one giant black beast lashing again and again at the hated light soldiers. Iadrea feared that even if he called all his warriors from the ground into the sky battle, it wouldn't be sufficient force to stop the incessant black waves. As soon as he saw the doors of the ark close, Iadrea signaled to his commanders on the ground, Chantar, Mistrea, and the others, "Star of Twelve."

Mistrea told Multar to change back into sky body with him. "You wanted to see what else the Star can do," he said when they met in the air near the rear flank of the army of light. "Stay here and watch."

Mistrea then flew to his position above and behind the mass of attenders still fending off the flailing black beast. Almost immediately the form of a three dimensional twelve-pointed star began to materialize. Next a ray of light exploding with every wave length in the spectrum struck out from the center of the star and swept across the first line of attacking demons. They evaporated like the fog that disappears when the morning sun strikes a shrouded valley. When the beam completed one sweep, it started back across the remaining dark troopers. They vanished.

Before a third sweep could be executed, the beast began to break up into individual demons cowering in retreat toward their master, or if they dared, out into the night. "Cowards!" the head of the beast roared. "Attack!"

None charged.

Then the beam began to swing directly toward the dark prince himself. Demons scattered from the path of the deadly ray. "Cowards! Scum! Fight you worthless…" But his words were drowned out by the increasing cacophony of a million demons fleeing, screaming in terror.

Just as the beam was about to land full on the Prince of Darkness, he took a mighty swing with his rod as he darted aside. Multar couldn't be sure if he heard a sound to accompany the visual effect of the ultimate dark weapon meeting the best light had to offer. It seemed as though there was an extremely low frequency blast, like a clap of thunder too low to hear, but visceral something that pulsed physically through the air, shaking even the hills as it echoed off them. As for the beam, it seemed to shimmer slightly, waver only minutely, then dissolve the awful rod where it met the light.

In an instant, the sky went soundless. The demons and their master had all fled. The beam retracted into the star, and the star dissipated, becoming again twelve separate beings of light. On the ground below, things were also quiet. Once the ark was secured, the attenders had disengaged from the fight. The few Kamaresans who remained alive fled. The ground was strewn with corpses, though, mercifully, most of the women and children had been able to escape behind the defense of the attenders. The Armounians, drained of the adrenalin of battle, were succumbing to the calming effects of the zensak. Being unable to see no need to lay siege to Nuwach's compound, they gradually wandered back through the pass and onto the edge of the plain to make camp for the night.

As if called by some unheard voice, animals began to crowd into the open space around the ark. "We still have one more task," Iadrea said pointing to the animals. "Chantar; is the ark complete?"

"Loading the rest of the animals and a little more food is all that remains to be done," the attender answered.

"Then let every one who had a human role materialize and get to work. I sense that the time for the cleansing I near."

In the minutes before Delyah had seen her father come into view, she and Sharaq were standing just inside the door of the ark, deep enough to be in the shadow, but shallow enough to see some of the camp which lay across the road. In front of them, in the door opening itself were Nuwach and his sons Sha'ym and Yepheth. Behind the two girls, deeper in shadow, stood Chamah and his mother. When El Channah and Ramah appeared coming around the north corner of the ark, Nuwach and the boys stepped a few paces toward them. Delyah then took their place nearer the opening. The scene from her new vantage point caused her to catch her breath. Leaning out of the doorway to peer past the men who had taken a few steps along the wall, she could see the leading edge of the attackers in the outskirts of the Kamaresan camp. Four or five Armounians were being held at bay by two defenders. The afternoon sun was on the backs of the attackers as they madly swung their clubs and swords. The sharp pinging when swords met and the dull thud when club or shield struck iron became frighteningly clear, as did the shrieks and grunts of men pouring all their strength into their efforts.

As the combatants pressed deeper into the camp, the sun lighted the bearded face of one of the defenders. Delyah gasped. Sharaq, having followed Delyah into the opening, placed a hand on her shoulder from behind. "What is it?" she asked, leaning forward to look over the younger girl's shoulder.

Delyah felt a pang in her rib cage, as if something sharp or hot had touched her between her breasts. "Father!" she cried.

The two watched terrified as Delzar, flanked by Thorel and two men who had been helping with the ark, fought against the relentless attackers. Delzar raised a shielded left arm to block a flashing sword, then powerfully swung his own weapon in a backhand motion to stop the crashing club of another attacker.

Then Delyah watched in horror as another thrust from the sword on her father's left glanced off his shield and sliced his right forearm from elbow to wrist. The sword fell from his hand. As he instinctively stooped to retrieve his weapon, he narrowly avoided the swinging club of the man on his right. Before the attacker could recoil his spent club swing, Thorel drove his sword under the man's arm between his ribs and deep into his body. His face frozen in wide-eyed disbelief, the goat soldier fell in front of Delzar's squatting form.

In the instant this all happened, the man who had wounded Delzar began racing toward one of the nearer tents in the camp. Beyond the charging attacker Delzar could see a young woman standing beside the tent with a small, golden-haired girl clinging to her hand. At the same moment his daughter saw the frightful scene unfolding. She watched El Channah explode across the road to stop the attacker. She saw her father bolt up from his stooping position, drop his shield, and sprint after the villain pulling his dagger from his belt. As the attacker raised his sword to slice at the child, the mother reflexively stepped forward to protect her. Just as the sword began to fall, Delzar landed on the man's back, drawing the dagger across his throat. Their momentum carried them tumbling into the mother and child.

When Delyah tried to run to her father past the men by the wall, Ramah reached out his powerful arm and scooped her up by her waist. Sharaq had tried to stop her with the hand she had placed on her shoulder, and had thus been pulled a few steps into the open as well. The men were also watching the dreadful scene unfold and Sha'ym and Yepheth burst across the road on El Channah's heels before they could be restrained.

Delyah and Sharaq both stood frozen with fear until the boys hurried back across the road carrying the child. It was at this point when Ramah and El Channah insisted that they retreat inside and bar the doors. Delyah had to be carried sobbing into the ark.

Once in the ark, Yepheth took the toddler from Sha'ym and the older son helped his father with the door. Yepheth pulled his sleeve onto his hand and began wiping tears from the sobbing child's face. "There now," he said softly. "It will be alright. You're safe now – I'll take care of you. Shhh." He shushed gently as he stroked a golden strand of hair from her wet face.

"Her mother was..." he stopped his explanation to his own mother who had come alongside.

He began again, "Her mother couldn't come with her." The terrible sadness in her son's eyes, the blood on the child's rough garment told the woman all she needed to know.

"Come," she said sweetly. "Let's get you cleaned up."

During this exchange Delyah had remained near the door. Now that it was closed she had both hands pressed against it, her forehead resting between them on the cool wood. Sha'ym stood on one side of her, Nuwach on the other. Neither had yet thought of anything to say to comfort the girl. Sharaq stepped behind her and took one hand from the door, turning her gently. She drew her to herself, wrapped her in her arms and let her cry.

For a moment Sharaq felt glad that her father had gone quietly in his sleep. Then she felt guilty for feeling glad. She could hardly imagine what it must be like to watch your father die a violent death. This poor child would now have to mourn her father's death twice."

"He saved the child," Sha'ym said.

"Yes he did," Sharaq agreed. "He saved the little girl's life."

Delyah sobbed noisily through her nose as she lifted her head off Sharaq's breast. She looked dimly down the corridor as the little golden-haired girl was being carried up the stairs. "He did, didn't he?" she whispered.

Ramah appeared first on the morning after the battle, knocking at the door, "Nuwach, open up; it is safe now – and you have more guests."

There was a scraping sound on the wood as the bar was lifted, then the door swung open. To Nuwach's surprise, not only Ramah, but several others appeared, some carrying huge armfuls of straw or hay, others with branches unnaturally laden with berries of a size and number unlike any Nuwach had ever seen.

Then there were the animals. Mostly in mating pairs, animals of every sort began wandering toward the ramp and into the ark. In some cases they were led into suitable pens inside; in some cases they walked in on their own and made themselves at home. Birds flew in and out through the space between the walls and roof. All day and through the long night the parade continued so that by morning, the scent of cypress wood in the ark was overcome by the warm, musky odor of animals and all that goes with them.

The sky was strangely heavy the next morning. The sun, usually seen as a bright yellow glow in the sky, was not visible. It was replaced by masses of mean grey clouds sailing shoulder to shoulder overhead in unbroken armadas. Then, about mid-morning, when everyone had stopped to rest, having worked all night, all were jolted into a sudden awareness that the ark had moved slightly.

The ark had not in fact changed its position in the dirt, rather the ground beneath it had moved ever so slightly. The cause of this lay hundreds of kilometers to the north where a large section of the planet's crust had suddenly fallen into an underground sea. This drop caused the surrounding pieces of the crust to shift. This in turn relieved the pressure in another location far to the east where another massive plate sank rapidly into a void beneath it. These movements were just the beginning of the vast changes that were about to take place on the surface of the planet.

Nor was the air above without change, for the escaping gasses heated the atmosphere and began, for the first time, continental movement of air masses. Moist air driven by the heat from the escaping gasses rose into the cooler reaches of the upper atmosphere. When the moisture cooled enough to condense into droplets, the droplets fell until they were caught in an updraft of heated air. As they rose, they collected other droplets until they became too heavy to be carried up, and so they started falling again.

Eventually they became too heavy for the updraft to lift so they fell all the way to the surface of the planet. And so it happened that for the first time in his six hundred years, Nuwach felt a rain drop. He was standing near the ramp, watching some men carry a few more sheaves of hay onto the ark when something wet struck his cheek. He looked up in surprise to be greeted by the sight of other drops falling all around him. Soon they were too numerous to be thought of individually; they were collectively an event, a momentous event not just because there had never before been such a thing, but because of what they were going to accomplish.

"What is this?" Nuwach asked Ramah.

"This is the cleansing, Father Nuwach," he replied. "The time has come."

Nuwach looked at the ground around his feet. No longer dusty, it was soaked with the falling rain. "But I don't know if I am ready," he protested. "I don't think I have enough…"

"It is enough," Ramah interrupted. "Trust the God of the Araq not to begin too soon."

A thought suddenly occurred to the old man. "Sha'ym," he shouted.

The young man appeared at the door of the ark and stopped, stunned by the sight of the rain. "Father?" he said, questioning what he saw more than what he had been summoned for.

"Sha'ym, did you get the vines I asked you to dig?" the man asked, ignoring the obvious curiosity in his son's face.

"Yes, Father, as you asked; but what is this?"

"The cleansing, my son," he replied. "God has begun the cleansing of the Araq."

El Channah walked up to the men as they were talking. He held out his hand palm up so that several rain drops landed on it. He placed his finger in the water collecting in his hand then extended it as if questioning Ramah.

"Yes, my friend," Ramah said. "I was just about to tell Nuwach that it is time to get inside out of the rain."

Nuwach looked again at the ground, now wetter still, then at the well where water had been rising over the bricks for several days. Then he looked again into Ramah's eyes.

"Come," the stranger said, extending an arm toward the open door of the ark.

As they moved up the ramp, Ramah and El Channah stayed back as father and son entered the doorway. "Close the doors," Ramah directed.

"But Ramah," Sha'ym protested, "you and El Channah… the others… if you are outside…" his voice trailed off.

El Channah reached out for Sha'ym's hand in the customary greeting. "In the short time I have known you, I have seen you become a man in many ways. Now in this too, watch your father." He looked into the old man's eyes and he finished, "Just as he trusts our God to care for Him, so you must know that he will also take care of us."

Sha'ym pulled himself toward the big man and threw his arms around him. "Thank you, El Channah, for everything."

"You are welcome to it all as a service to our God," he replied.

Ramah took Nuwach's arm in greeting and said, "Be well, Father Nuwach; go with God."

The old man looked in the stranger's eyes with a gratitude that no words could express. Looking at El Channah he said, "Thank you both; thank you all."

"Thank our God," the tall man said.

The two strangers stepped back out of the doorway into the rain. It wetted their faces and glistened of their muscled arms. Each of them raised his right hand in salute as the father and son closed the doors of the ark.

After raising the ramp against the doors and pegging it in place, the remaining attenders slathered pitch into the gaps as rain fell harder and harder. The water in the well began to gush over the bricks and was soon mixing with the rain as it lapped against the side of the ark. Oblivious to the rain, Chantar, Mistrea and Multar hovered just above the scene.

"After the cleansing, will there be harmony like on Mentridar?" Multar asked.

"I do not know," his master responded. "What do you think, Chantar?"

"I wish it could be so," he said, "but I think there may be much more to do before that can happen. The dark ones are quiet for now, but they are not gone. I fear they will continue to stir up disharmony until they are finally defeated."

"I hope we can be there to see that," Multar said.

"So do I, my friend," Mistrea said, "So do I."

Printed in the United States
201697BV00002B/142-180/P